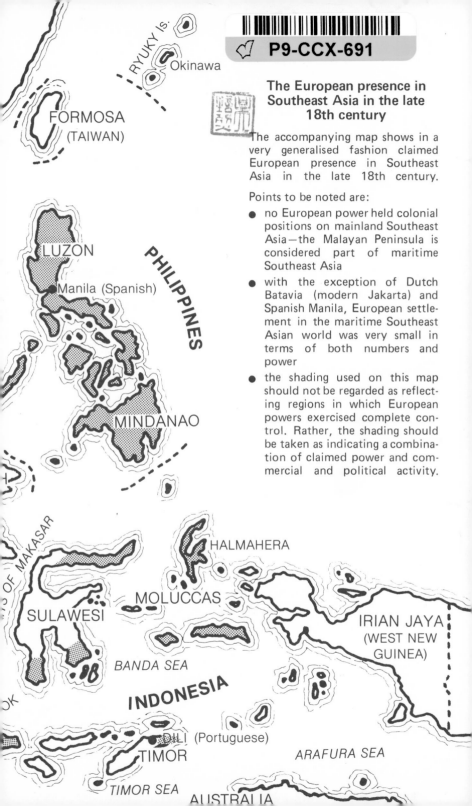

The European presence in Southeast Asia in the late 18th century

The accompanying map shows in a very generalised fashion claimed European presence in Southeast Asia in the late 18th century.

Points to be noted are:

- no European power held colonial positions on mainland Southeast Asia—the Malayan Peninsula is considered part of maritime Southeast Asia

- with the exception of Dutch Batavia (modern Jakarta) and Spanish Manila, European settlement in the maritime Southeast Asian world was very small in terms of both numbers and power

- the shading used on this map should not be regarded as reflecting regions in which European powers exercised complete control. Rather, the shading should be taken as indicating a combination of claimed power and commercial and political activity.

RYUKYU IS.

Okinawa

FORMOSA (TAIWAN)

LUZON

Manila (Spanish)

PHILIPPINES

MINDANAO

STS OF MAKASAR

HALMAHERA

MOLUCCAS

SULAWESI

IRIAN JAYA (WEST NEW GUINEA)

BANDA SEA

INDONESIA

DILI (Portuguese)

TIMOR

ARAFURA SEA

TIMOR SEA

AUSTRALIA

SOUTHEAST ASIA

Also by Milton Osborne

BOOKS

The French Presence in Cochinchina and Cambodia: Rule and Response (1859–1905), 1969

Region of Revolt: Focus on Southeast Asia, 1970, Revised and expanded edition 1971

Politics and Power in Cambodia: The Sihanouk Years, 1973

River Road to China: The Mekong River Expedition, 1866–1873, 1975

Before Kampuchea: Preludes to Tragedy, 1979

RESEARCH MONOGRAPHS

Singapore and Malaysia, 1964

Strategic Hamlets in South Viet-Nam: A Survey and a Comparison, 1965

SOUTHEAST ASIA

An Illustrated Introductory History

MILTON OSBORNE

ALLEN & UNWIN

First edition 1979, 2nd Imp. 1980
Second edition 1983 2nd Imp. 1984
Third edition 1985, 3rd Imp. 1987
Fourth edition 1988
Fifth edition 1990
Second impression 1991

Allen & Unwin Pty Ltd
8 Napier Street, North Sydney, NSW 2059, Australia

National Library of Australia
Cataloguing-in-Publication entry:

Osborne, Milton 1936–
    Southeast Asia, an illustrated introductory history.
    5th ed.
    Includes index.
    ISBN 0 04 442215 6.

    1. Asia, Southeastern — History. I. Title.

959

Printed in Singapore by Chong Moh Offset Printing

Contents

Illustrations

Maps

Graphs

Introduction

In this new edition of *Southeast Asia: An Illustrated Introductory History*, I have, as before, reviewed statistical information and revised the list of Suggested Readings in the light of new publications. Additionally, I have included a new chapter that provides a brief overview of Southeast Asian art and a survey of fictional writing that takes Southeast Asia as its setting. As previously, I have been concerned to retain the book's *introductory* character. Illustrations and maps not otherwise acknowledged are the author's own material.*

I remain grateful for the comments on earlier editions given me by David Chandler, John Legge and Merle Ricklefs, and I again record my debt to the late Professor D.G.E. Hall and Professor O.W. Wolters for the inspiration they gave me when I studied under them. In this new edition I add further thanks to Pamela Gutman for her comments on the section dealing with Southeast Asian art and to Bill O'Malley for his suggestion of novels for inclusion in my review of fictional writing.

Milton Osborne
Canberra, 1989

---

* The picture on page 46 is from J.Y. Schley engraver, Vue de Batavia, engraving, *In* J.P. de Bois, *Vies des Gouverneurs Généraux, avec l'Albrégé de l'Historie des établissements Hollandais aux Indes, Orientales*, 1763, National Library of Australia.
The picture on page 50 is from W. Bell, J. Stadler engraver, A village house in Sumatra, engraving, *In a history of Sumatra*, p 86, London Marsden 1811, National Library of Australia

1

What is Southeast Asia?

THERE is no better place to start than with a discussion of size and scale. For a newcomer to Southeast Asian history the past is more confusing than the jumbled present. Yet even when considering the present an outsider has the greatest difficulty in visualising just how large an area Southeast Asia occupies in geographical terms, and how substantial is the size of its population. The fact that Indonesia's population is more than one hundred and eighty million may be well known. But how often is this fact recognised as meaning that Indonesia has the *fifth* largest population in the world? Only China, India, the Soviet Union, and the United States outstrip Indonesia in terms of population. And how many casual observers think of a now united Vietnam of over sixty million persons as having a substantially larger population than such countries as Spain (thirty-nine million), Egypt (fifty-one million), Poland (thirty-seven million), or Canada (twenty-five million)? Yet Vietnam is only one of four Southeast Asian states, in addition to Indonesia, whose populations are each in excess of thirty million. Figures can only be approximate where population is concerned, but of the world's population in the late 1980s Southeast Asia accounted for no less than 8 percent. The significance of this percentage is made clear when the population of China is expressed as a percentage of the world's total. China, the world's most populous country, accounts for between 20 and 25 per cent of the total. Against this yardstick alone, therefore, the population of the Southeast Asian region is substantial indeed.

Size by itself does not mean power, and this is as true for contemporary Southeast Asia as it was for other countries and regions in the past. Whatever the power that an individual Southeast Asian state can exert within its own borders, or outside them, none of the

1

countries in the region has yet developed the global power that was once exerted by some European powers, such as Britain in its imperial heyday, or by the superpowers of the last quarter of the twentieth century. Here, right away, is a major question for historians of Southeast Asia to answer: Why has the Southeast Asian region, despite its size, played so small a part in the shifts of global power over the past two thousand years?

The answer, or more correctly answers, to this question will need to take account of many factors, not all of them agreed among those who make it their business to study the Southeast Asian region. To a great extent, moreover, the answers will point to the need to think about Southeast Asia in terms that will often seem surprising for those whose cultural background has been strongly influenced by Europe. Here is where scale as well as size deserves attention.

When dealing with the unknown or little-known there is a strong tendency to think of cities, countries, or groups of people as being in some way smaller in size and importance than is the case for better-known areas and peoples. In the same fashion there is a familiar readiness to discount the achievements of unfamiliar civilisations by comparison with the presumed importance of our own society and cultural traditions. This may be less of a feature of life today than it was a hundred years ago when the exploring European and his successors, the administrators, missionaries, planters and men of commerce had not the slightest doubt about their own superiority. Nonetheless, the problem remains today as Southeast Asia is still an unfamiliar area to most who live outside its boundaries.

Because we know that London and Paris are major cities today, and that these are the modern successors of settlements dating back to Roman times, our tendency is to think of their always having been large and important. *Londinium* was important in Roman times, possibly more so than the settlement of *Lutetia*, which was to change its name to Paris in the fourth century. But because of our familiarity with the name London it is hard, perhaps, to visualise just how small this centre was in Roman times and through to the period of the Norman Conquest. When William of Normandy was crowned in Westminster Abbey on Christmas Day 1066 London still did not enjoy the status of being England's royal city. No more than 35,000 persons lived in the ill-kept streets of this medieval city; yet this is scarcely the image London summons up.

At the same time, in the then unknown land of Cambodia—unknown that is to the men and women of Europe—a population of more than a million grouped around and supported a city that could rival and surpass any then existing in Europe for its architectural achievement, its sophisticated water engineering, and its capacity to produce a regular harvest of three rice crops each year. This was the city of Angkor from whose ruins with their accompanying rich stock of inscriptions we have come to know of a civilisation of remarkable achievement and high technological complexity. But whereas the wonders of Europe, of Rome and Venice, of Paris and London, and a dozen other major cities, have preoccupied scholars and interested observers for hundreds of years, the great Cambodian city of Angkor, the centre of a powerful empire for nearly six centuries, only became part of Western consciousness in the nineteenth century, and then only slowly. Hard though it may be to believe nowadays, the first European visitor to Angkor in the mid-nineteenth century, a missionary priest named Father Bouillevaux, was unimpressed by what he saw.

The point may be made over and over again. Athens, Thebes, and Sparta were tiny states, nevertheless they live in the minds of those who study European history for the contributions that they made to the development of European culture, in that term's broadest sense. By contrast, it is still rare outside either specialist circles, or among the ranks of the exceedingly well travelled, to find any awareness of the empire of Pagan, a centre of Burmese power during the eleventh, twelfth, and thirteenth centuries and the site of a temple complex that some believe rivals the buildings of Angkor. Those who are the inheritors of the Western tradition are not immediately receptive to the religious and cultural underpinnings of the societies that built Pagan and Angkor. The same problem of a lack of immediate sympathy is apparent when attention turns to other early empires of Southeast Asia. It is easier to conjure up a picture, accurate or otherwise, of Crusaders travelling to the Holy Land than it is to picture the heroic navigational feats of Malay sailors who voyaged to China and made the Sumatra-based empire of Srivijaya such a powerful force in early Southeast Asian history.

The contrast between our awareness of Europe and unawareness of Southeast Asia should not be stressed beyond reason. There are a great many good reasons why it is easier to understand segments of European history and why real and continuing difficulties stand in the way of acquiring a similar background awareness of the historical process in Southeast Asia. To gain more than a superficial knowledge of early Southeast Asian history requires time, dedi-cation, and a readiness to learn a surprisingly large range of languages. All this is required for the study of problems that may often seem lacking in general interest. Generations of scholars have laboured in some cases to leave little more than fragments for incorporation in the overall fabric of the region's history. For the general student there is, fortunately, some middle ground between a broad lack of knowledge and scholarly devotion to detail that is, however admirable, the preserve of the specialist.

So far in this introductory chapter the term Southeast Asia has been used in a general, undifferentiated fashion. Fifty years ago this would have caused surprise, for only a few persons at that time thought and spoke about 'Southeast Asia'. Some writers used the term 'Further India' to describe sections of Southeast Asia, as if all that was to be found beyond the Bay of Bengal was the Indian subcontinent on a smaller scale. It is only necessary to think of the influence that China has had over the formation of Vietnamese cultural life, or of the extent to which the Philippines has acquired a very special character because of the long-term Spanish influence in those islands, to realise how inappropriate the term 'Further India' is. Another general description that was used before the Second World War was 'Asia of the Monsoons', a term deriving from the monsoon weather pattern that is important in almost all of Southeast Asia. This term, used by geographers most particularly, did not relate merely to the area that modern scholars have termed Southeast Asia, for Ceylon and parts of India, as well as areas of southern China, might equally well be described as monsoon lands.

For the most part, however, neither the foreigners who worked in Southeast Asia before the Second World War, whether as scholars or otherwise, nor the indigenous inhabitants of the countries of Southeast Asia, thought about the region in general terms. The general tendency to do so came with the Second World War when, as a result of military circumstances, the concept of a Southeast Asian region began to take hold. From a strategic military point of view it was apparent that an area existed that was not India, nor China, nor part of the Pacific. Instead, a sense began to grow that Brunei, Burma, Thailand, Laos, Cambodia, Vietnam, Malaysia, Singapore, and Indonesia—to use modern names rather than those different ones which, in some cases, were current in the early 1940s—formed some kind of geographical unit. The omission of the Philippines is deliberate, at this stage, for the question of whether or not the Philippines formed part of Southeast Asia was to remain a matter of scholarly uncertainty as late as the 1960s.

The sense of Southeast Asia being a geographical and cultural unit did not, of course, depend solely upon strategic thinking. Already, in the 1920s and 1930s, anthropologists and historians had begun to take account of the similarities that could be found between one region of what we now call Southeast Asia and another. Similarities in the rituals used by the various royal courts throughout mainland Southeast Asia were recognised as an indication of a common inheritance or tradition. Basic similarities in family structure were found to exist over a wide area. And for all of the evidence that was accumulating of the importance of foreign ideas, and of foreigners, throughout Southeast Asia's long history, historians had begun assembling the evidence that showed a regional pattern of international relations within Southeast Asia from its earliest historical periods. Southeast Asia was not, in other words, merely a region that sustained the impact of its greater neighbours, China and India. Empires within the region waxed and waned and at various times links were established between the mainland and the islands of the Indonesian Archipelago involving both politics and trade.

With the end of the Second World War the tendency to think of Southeast Asia as a whole gained even greater currency as there was a sharp increase in the amount of scholarly attention given to the region. Now, more than ever before, the underlying similarities to be found throughout a wide range of the region were stressed by historians, anthropologists, political scientists, and linguists, to mention only the prominent academic disciplines. To sense why these scholars found their work so exciting, and to emphasise the way in which the picture of Southeast Asia as a unit deserving of study in its own right emerged, it is useful to review briefly some of the features of the region that are now taken for granted but which only gained general recognition in the post-war period.

Probably most important was the recognition that the countries of Southeast Asia were neither 'little Indias' nor 'little Chinas'. The impact of those two great countries on the Southeast Asian region cannot be dismissed, though the degree and character of their influence is still debated, but the essential right of Southeast Asian countries to be considered culturally independent units was generally established. To put the matter in another fashion, if the tendency in the past had been to think of Southeast Asia as an area shaped by external cultural values, most particularly those of India and China, scholars now paid just as much attention to the strength and importance of indigenous cultural traditions. Where Indian or Chinese influence did play a major part in the development of Southeast Asian art, or religion, or political theory, stress began to be placed on the extent to which Burmese, Cambodians, Indonesians, and others adapted these foreign ideas to suit their own needs and values. The importance of Indian religious concepts, for instance, must be recognised for a broad area of Southeast Asia. But one of the most essential features of Hinduism, the caste system, was never adopted in the countries outside India. Indian artistic and architectural concepts played an important part in the development of Southeast Asian art. Yet the glories of Pagan, Angkor, and the temple complexes of Java stem from their own individual character, just as the exquisite Buddha images that were created in Thailand are quite different from the images to be found in India. Even in Vietnam, where dependence upon an external, Chinese cultural tradition has clearly been more significant than elsewhere in Southeast Asia, the strength of non-Chinese cultural life, particularly below the level of the court, belies any picture of that country as a mere receiver of ideas, unable to offer traditions of its own.

Southeast Asian and foreign scholars alike came to recognise that Indian and Chinese influence had been overemphasised in the past and that insufficient attention had been paid to fundamental similarities existing in the societies making up the region. While uniformity most certainly is not present throughout the societies of Southeast Asia, certain broad similarities spread across a wide area are striking. The importance of the nuclear or individual family in much of Southeast Asia, as opposed to the importance placed on the extended family in India, was one of these broad similarities found over much of the region. So, too, the generally important place allotted women in the peasant society of traditional Southeast Asia reflected both a widespread value and a contrast with both Indian and Chinese societies.

Another factor leading to interest in the Southeast Asian region as a whole was the recognition of how much linguistic unity there was from area to area, cutting right across the boundaries set, in many cases, by colonial powers. There are still ill-informed people who have not shed the illusions fostered by the former colonial powers which sought to emphasise disunity rather than to recognise broad similarities. So, at the level of a single country, there are some who still speak and write as if the Vietnamese of northern Vietnam speak a different language than the Vietnamese of the southern regions of that country. The reality is that Vietnam, like almost any other country, has dialectical variations from region to region. But, if linguistic unity is taken as a significant factor indicating basic broader social unities, then Vietnam despite its political history is unified indeed. The difference between the Vietnamese spoken in the north of that country and the Vietnamese to be heard in the south is certainly no greater than the difference between 'educated southern English' and broad Scots. And the difference is a great deal less than that to be found between the dialects of northern and southern Italy.

When looking at areas larger than a single country such as Vietnam, the presence of broad linguistic unity is more striking.

Some of this unity is apparent only to the most skilled scholars. This is the case with the quite recent suggestion that modern Vietnamese and Khmer (or Cambodian) have a common, if very distant, linguistic ancestor. For the non-specialist this is difficult to comprehend, in part because of the fact that of these languages Vietnamese is tonal, while Khmer is non-tonal. But a non-specialist can respond to the striking fact that the Tai language, admittedly with considerable dialectical variations, is spoken not only in Thailand, but in parts of southern China, in Vietnam, in the Shan states of Burma, in Laos, in both western and northeastern Cambodia, and, though this is less and less the case today, in the extreme north of peninsular Malaysia. Here is a situation full of interest and im-

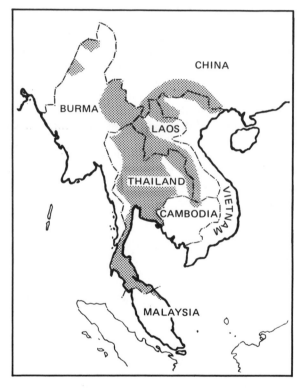

Map 1   Mainland Southeast Asia: Distribution of Tai Speaking Peoples
The Tai language is not only the principal language of the population of Thailand. It is, in addition, spoken widely by the Shans of Burma, by the lowland population of Laos, and in the northern parts of Vietnam, Cambodia and Malaysia. Tai speakers are also to be found in the extreme south of China.

portance. That the Tai language has such a broad distribution alerts us to the often artificial character of the border lines drawn on maps, for if a common language were taken as a basis for establishing a state then to divide the lowland areas of Laos from Thailand seems hard to justify. At the same time, an awareness of the presence of Tai-speaking persons over such a wide area of Southeast Asia brings a recognition of the extent to which many of the states of modern Southeast Asia are troubled by disunity resulting from the presence within their frontiers of minority groups. Their interests, including their linguistic interest, are not shared by the majority or dominant and governing group. Many Tai-speaking Shans in Burma, to take only one example, continue in modern times as in the past to resist control by the Burmans who are their long-time rivals, speaking a different language.

Another most important instance of linguistic unity is the broad spread of the Indonesian/Malay language. Here again the dialectical differences from region to region are considerable but variants of this basic language are spoken throughout modern Brunei, Indonesia and Malaysia, and in the southern Philippines, as well as along the southern coastal regions of Thailand, Cambodia, and Vietnam where there are long-established Indonesian/Malay-speaking settlements.

Yet just as the national motto of Indonesia is 'Unity in Diversity', the similarities and unities that have just been described should not blind a student of Southeast Asia to the profound differences that do exist from place to place and between one ethnic group and another. Indeed, a study of the history of Southeast Asia raises some of the most difficult issues of judgement in this regard. What should be emphasised for a region or for a period, the unities or the differences? And to what extent should we concentrate on the continuities that so often seem a feature of Southeast Asian history rather than paying attention to the discontinuities, to the breaks with the past and the changes that disturb any suggestion that we are dealing with an area in which traditional patterns are still dominant and little affected by the modern world?

There can be no certain and agreed answer to any of these questions, for what is involved is judgement, whether individual or collective, and judgement will always be open to argument. Judgement will also always be subject to fashion and there is no doubt that historical and anthropological fashions, to mention only two scholarly disciplines, are as changeable, if not quite as frequently, as fashions in clothes. Yet there might be some sort of general agreement about the following propositions. The study of Southeast Asia over the past thirty years has contributed greatly to the acceptance that this is a region deserving attention as a whole and as an entity separate from the cultures of South Asia and China. To think of Southeast Asia in this framework is very much a product of the post-Second World War years and contrasts considerably with the way that scholars approached the region in earlier periods. Now that the unities and similarities have been generally recognised, however, it remains important to give due attention to the differences that do set geographical region apart from geographical region, ethnic group apart from ethnic group, and which, for a traveller, so often make the physical transition from one area of Southeast Asia to another an easily and sharply perceived experience.

The sheer size of the geographical region making up Southeast Asia, stretching over more than thirty-five degrees of latitude and nearly fifty degrees of longitude, prepares us for its immensely varied geographical character. If population has traditionally been concentrated in lowland settlements, along the seacoasts and by rivers and lakes, this only tells part of the story of geography and settlement patterns. The demands of high-density settlement in northern Vietnam, for instance, have led to a very different approach to agriculture along the Red River from that followed by the much less concentrated Vietnamese population in the Mekong River delta. Yet even along the lower Mekong River a traveller, only a few years ago, could see dramatic evidence of the difference that existed between the physical landscape of Cambodia and southern Vietnam, as the result of differing population pressures in those neighbouring regions and of differing values about the aims to be pursued by an agricultural population. To drive from Phnom Penh to the city that was then called Saigon (Ho Chi Minh City) was to pass, sharply, from one landscape to another. On the Cambodian side of the frontier there was untilled land, while the land that was under cultivation was cropped once a year. Scattered clumps of sugar palms gave a sense of scale to the landscape and emphasised that all other vegetation had not been sacrificed to the growing of rice. Once over the frontier, however, the scene changed immediately. Even to a casual observer it was apparent that a very different pattern of agriculture was followed, one that seemingly left no land untilled and grew its two rice crops each year on land from which the sugar palms had been removed so that the landscape stretching away to the horizon was unmarked by any vertical features.

The contrasts between the physical appearance of the Mekong delta region of Cambodia and Vietnam are essentially those resulting from differing approaches to agriculture. Even more striking are the contrasts that stem directly from basic geography, from the difference between hill and valley and between those areas favoured by climate and those where rainfall is uncertain and infrequent. Almost all of Southeast Asia lies in the tropical zone, yet this does not mean that tropical abundance is universal. For those hill peoples who live in areas of the upland regions of Thailand, Burma, and Laos the pattern of life dictated by their physical environment has little reminiscent of the tropical lushness that, on occasion, may be typical of existence in more favoured regions.

The whole concept of Southeast Asia as an area of lushness, growth, and fecundity needs qualification. It can be all of these things, but only if such factors as population pressure do not intrude and when the land is fertile and cultivable. Nothing is more deceptive than the endless green of ripening crops on the island of Java where an ever-increasing population, probably nearly 100 million in the early 1980s, is jammed into an area little different from England, where a population half the size benefits from the economic diversification of a developed society. Equally deceptive are the rolling hills covered with rain forest of peninsular Malaysia. Seen from an aircraft the forests of West Malaysia run away to the horizon, unbroken by roads or settlement. There is timber wealth here, but little promise of easy agricultural expansion for a growing population.

From the dry zone of Burma to the snow-covered mountains of Irian Jaya (West New Guinea), and from the rolling pastoral grasslands of northwestern Vietnam to the steep terraced rice lands of the Philippine Islands, Southeast Asia is a conglomerate of geographical and agricultural contrasts.

Southeast Asia is an area of many other contrasts. One of the most obvious for a modern traveller in the region is that between city and country. The growth of Southeast Asia's cities has been one of the most striking features of developments in the twentieth century, particularly since the Second World War. A few examples make clear how dramatic the changes have been. Bangkok in the late 1980s has a population of more than 7 million inhabitants. Just over a century ago the *total* population of Thailand was only 6 million persons. As recently as 1960 the estimated population of Bangkok was less than 1½ million inhabitants. The example of Bangkok has its parallels elsewhere in the rapid growth in the size of Jakarta, of Singapore, of Phnom Penh before the exodus of population in 1975, of Saigon, and of many provincial urban centres.

These fast-growing Asian cities are magnets for the rural inhabitants who flock out of the country, where they often see little hope of change and virtually no prospect of prosperity. For them the urban centres, however miserable conditions may be, appear to

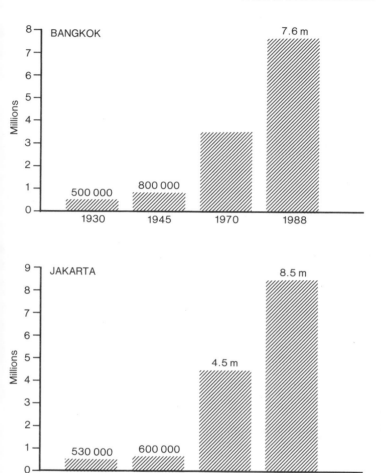

Graph 1 Rapid Urban Growth in Southeast Asia
A Tale of Two Cities: Bangkok and Jakarta
Rapid urban growth has been a striking feature of Southeast Asia's modern
history, particularly since the Second World War. Developments in
Bangkok and Jakarta exemplify this situation. At the end of the Second
World War both these cities had populations of less than a million. Twenty-
five years later, Bangkok's population had quadrupled and Jakarta's had
grown by more than six times its 1945 figure.

The continuing growth of Southeast Asia's primate cities places
tremendous strains on governments faced with the need to provide services
for their populations and to find work for those seeking employment.

offer some hope of personal advancement. Such hopes often cruelly evaporate in the face of unemployment, over-crowding, and an inadequate system of city services. Yet nothing could better illustrate the contrast between city and country in modern Southeast Asia than the continuing migration of rural inhabitants into the urban areas. For this migration is, in considerable part, a reaction against the life offered in the countryside with its limited horizons, its frequent drudgery and, in the eyes of many younger men and women, the limitation of tradition-bound existence. The disadvantages of life far from the cities has, for the rural and provincial population of Southeast Asia, been made all the clearer by the communications revolution that has placed a transistor in almost every household's dwelling, and by the greater availability of transport that has made visits from one area of a country to another so much more readily possible.

Richness and poverty, development and a lack of development, these and many other social contrasts stand out more clearly in Southeast Asia than in those areas of the world that benefited from the great industrial changes of the nineteenth century. If Southeast Asia is also an area that has been marked by a notable degree of political instability, this is scarcely to be wondered at in terms of the broad range of unresolved problems—in almost every aspect of life—that have confronted those who govern, and those who wish to govern, since the countries of the region attained independence after the Second World War. The one exception to this observation, Thailand, was never under European colonial rule. In terms of the problems Thailand has faced and faces, however, its historical experience has many parallels with the former colonial territories.

Here, to return for a moment to similarities present among the countries of Southeast Asia, is another important reason for thinking about the region as a whole rather than solely in terms of individual countries. With the exception of Thailand that has just been noted, all of the other countries of Southeast Asia sustained varying periods of colonial rule. What were the similarities and differences to be found in this common experience? Did it matter whether the alien colonial power was Britain, or France, or Holland, or the United States? And why did some colonial regimes leave peacefully while others fought bitter wars to try and remain?

To refer to the colonial period in Southeast Asia is to raise another much-debated historical problem: how much attention should be given to the colonial element in Southeast Asian history? The answer will vary from person to person and from period to period. The realisation that too often in the past Southeast Asians were excluded from their own history by the non-Southeast Asians who wrote about the region has had a healthy effect so that most historians are aware of the importance of essentially Southeast Asian developments and the role played by Southeast Asians in them even if they continue to see some value in discussing the part played by Europeans and others who came to seek power and fortune in the area.

What will be examined in this book, then, is an immensely varied region marked by some notable unities and containing great diversity. An attempt will be made to discover the factors that have been important in determining why Southeast Asia has its present character and why it is that such sharply differing political developments have occurred in countries that at first glance seem to possess similar historical backgrounds. The region that is the setting for the events and developments we consider will sometimes stagger us by the richness of its diversity. To take one further example underlining this point, the Southeast Asian area continues to be most diverse in its religious character. Islam is strong in the maritime regions and Theravada Buddhism is the national religion of Thailand, as it was in Cambodia until recently. Some sections of the area are strongly Christian, most notably the Philippines, but in other areas a basic animism is the most fundamental of the population's religious beliefs. Even having mentioned these religions is to give a most incomplete catalogue. There are followers of Hinduism, not only the descendants of Indian immigrants but the indigenous populations of Bali and Lombok in Indonesia. Communism is the secular religion of Vietnam, but it is not hard to sense the continuing presence of some Confucian values in Vietnamese society.

For all the diversity we encounter we will still find that there are important common themes in the historical experience of the countries making up the region. Most particularly as we approach the modern period of Southeast Asian history we will find that the problems faced by peoples seeking independence and then of governments seeking to operate within independent states often possess great similarities, even if the attempted solutions to these problems are greatly different in their character.

With its rich past and sometimes turbulent present Southeast Asia is a region full of interest for a casual observer as well as to those who have made its study their lifetime task. An awareness of Southeast Asia's history will not provide any certain guide to future developments in the region, for that can never be history's task. But a review of the area's history will illuminate the present, making clear why the politics of one country are so different from those of another, or why the region as a whole has, in so many ways and over such a long period, been subject to strong external influence.

1   The Sultan Mosque, Singapore
Islam is one of the major religions in Southeast Asia, and the dominant
religion in Brunei, Indonesia and Malaysia. Increasingly, the architectural
forms used for Islamic mosques in Southeast Asia show clear borrowings
from the Middle East, as in this photograph of the Sultan Mosque in
Singapore.

Above all, an awareness of Southeast Asia's history provides an insight into the life and beliefs of a large and fascinating segment of the world's population, which in cultural achievement, quite apart from contemporary political interest, deserves a much greater degree of attention than it has yet received. In an era which has seen the tragic results of a lack of knowledge of the political and cultural background to developments in more than one Southeast Asian country, there is an even greater incentive to learn something of the broad lines of historical development that have made Southeast Asia what it is today.

2
The 'Classical' Background to Modern Southeast Asian History

ONE of the most obvious problems encountered by Southeast Asian historians is that of vocabulary. How should an historian describe, using words or phrases that have been developed for a Western context, a very different historical experience? There is no easy solution to this problem and scholars continue to debate the proper way to describe particular periods in Southeast Asian history and, just as importantly, what these periods are. So, while such terms as 'classical' or 'medieval' have generally acceptable meanings for those whose preoccupation is European history, there is no such agreement among Southeast Asian historians.

One solution is to use words without particular cultural or historical value; to write and speak of 'early' Southeast Asian history, or of the 'traditional' Southeast Asian world. Yet even here there are problems, for different historians will assign different dates to these periods. Because of these difficulties the term 'classical' applied to Southeast Asian history must be recognised as a less than fully satisfactory description. Its value stems from the suggestion it carries with it of there having been a period in Southeast Asian history that was marked by a series of major achievements in art and architecture and in the development of the state, as in Greek and Roman history, before there was a period of general decline, by the end of the fifteenth century. This decline was then followed by the emergence of newly powerful kingdoms. But if we use the term 'classical' we should recognise it for what it is: a useful but highly qualified historical metaphor.

As a metaphor suggesting the greatness of Greece and Rome the idea of there having once been a classical Southeast Asia is indeed helpful since it alerts a newcomer to the weight of Southeast Asia's cultural traditions that might not always be obvious when considering more recent historical periods. This was very much a problem during the nineteenth century. The first Westerners,

16

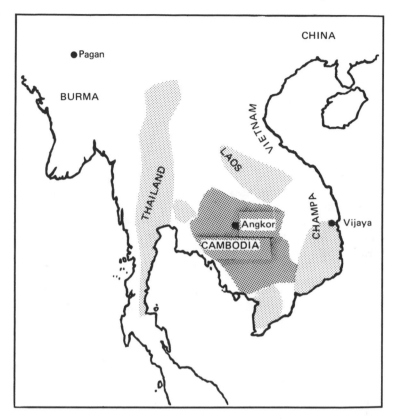

Map 2   The Angkorian Empire at the height of its Power in the 12th century

The Angkorian empire reached the height of its power in the twelfth century during the reigns of Suryararman II (1113-1150) and Jayavarman VII (1181-circa 1219). During these reigns Cambodia was in control of the modern territory of Cambodia, much of southern Vietnam and southern Laos, and had vassal states in central Thailand and in the Kra Isthmus to the south. The exercise of central power over these far-flung territories was not uniform and the more distant a region was, the less direct the involvement of the Angkorian ruler.

Frenchmen as it happened, to visit the court of the King of Cambodia in the late 1850s and early 1860s found it small and lacking in artistic distinction. They took a similar view of the Cambodian ruler of the day, King Norodom, and they could not believe that he, and those whom he ruled, were the descendants of the population that had once lived beside the mighty temples of

Angkor. Partly because they could not believe this was so—though it was indeed the case—these same Frenchmen had the greatest difficulty in understanding that King Norodom saw himself as the defender of his country's traditions and as a descendant, in terms of kingly majesty, of Angkorian kings whose names might be forgotten but whose glory was seen as essentially Cambodian.

Here is one immediately important instance of the significance attaching to the classical period. Southeast Asian individuals and Southeast Asian governments have not forgotten the past glories of their countries, though the manner in which these glories are remembered may be very different to the Western concept of history. Burmans remember the glory of the temples of Pagan built in the eleventh and twelfth centuries, and Indonesians have continued to see significance in the empires claimed for Javanese rulers of earlier historical periods. Sharp argument might sometimes be joined over the extent to which the memories that are preserved are accurate. And it would be misleading to suggest that there are not considerable variations from person to person, social grouping to social grouping, and country to country in the nature and importance that is attached to the so-called classical past. It would be a very rash person indeed, however, who was ready to discount this importance altogether.

There are further reasons for giving some attention to the classical period in Southeast Asia since the rise and fall of the kingdoms tells us much of the factors that were to shape the more familiar course of the modern historical period. If, for the moment, we consider mainland Southeast Asia, then it becomes necessary to ask why it should be that the mightiest of the classical mainland states, Angkorian Cambodia, should ultimately have been one of history's failures, despite the technological achievements and the architectural glories that were such a feature of its years of greatness? Why, to continue asking questions with a rather negative character, did the maritime empire of Srivijaya come to lose its dominant position controlling the great east-west trade between India and China during the thirteenth and fourteenth centuries, after enjoying notable commercial success during preceding centuries? Or why, to move to a more positive vein, was Java to remain the geographical location for successive states that aspired not only to rule over that island but also to a seldom achieved suzerainty over other islands in the Indonesian Archipelago?

It may not be possible to give completely satisfactory answers to all these questions, particularly not in a chapter that is meant to provide background to a later period. But it will be possible to sketch with broad strokes some of the important characteristics of classical Southeast Asia, to give some account of the factors that led to the rise and fall of states and empires, and the nature of their achievements in fields as diverse as architecture and navigation. To do this it is necessary to try and provide a brief picture of the pattern of states that had emerged in Southeast Asia by the ninth century AD. There is much of Southeast Asia at that time that we simply cannot describe either in terms of the location of states or in terms of populations living away from the centres of kingly power. Most of the Philippines remains outside our knowledge at that period, as do other sections of the Southeast Asian maritime world. But once our gaze shifts to the west of the Indonesian Archipelago

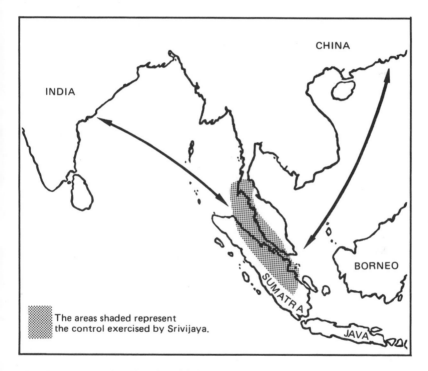

Map 3   The Trading Empire of Srivijaya
Scholars argue over the exact location of Srivijaya, the great trading empire that dominated maritime trade through Southeast Asia and between India and China during the seventh to thirteenth centuries. Srivijaya probably had a number of capitals, with the most important in southern Sumatra. As indicated in this map, Srivijaya maintained its power by controlling the ports and waters of the Malacca Straits. The shaded areas represent the control exercised by Srivijaya.

the forms are easier to discern. Recognisable kingdoms or states had already emerged in Java by the ninth century and these states had demonstrated considerable artistic capacity in the temples and shrines they erected and in the forms they chose to decorate them. Moving further west and north to the island of Sumatra, we know of the existence of a trading empire, Srivijaya, that had risen to power in the sixth and seventh centuries and, despite setbacks along the way, continued to dominate trade between the West (India) and the East (China), as well as more local trade in the Archipelago itself. While the existence of Srivijaya seems certain, however, no physical trace of its capital remains and scholarly argument continues as to where the actual location of that city, or series of cities, might have been. If we risk a broad summary of the situation in the maritime Southeast Asian world in the ninth century, it might be in the following terms. Whatever the petty states that existed elsewhere, the truly significant centres of power that had emerged were linked with coastal Sumatra and inland Java. These centres of power were to remain important in the following centuries, until the end of the classical period.

The situation on the mainland is rather clearer, if still full of difficulties and a rich subject for controversy. During the ninth century there was still no independent Vietnamese state since Imperial China occupied the Red River delta region and administered it as one of the most remote Chinese provinces. Stretched along the modern Vietnamese coast was the state of Champa, populated by the Chams, a people linguistically linked with the inhabitants of Indonesia. To the west was the growing state of Cambodia, which was just beginning its rise to greatness and dominance over much of mainland Southeast Asia. Although we know today that greatness lay ahead for Cambodia, this was far from clearly the case in the ninth century. The first Cambodian kings to rule in the Angkor region had already begun to develop techniques for mastering the environment that were, eventually, to provide the economic base for military expansion and a programme of great temple-building. In the ninth century, however, they were only a little more clearly masters of their quite limited world than were the petty rulers scattered through the lowland regions of modern Thailand and along the great river valleys of modern Burma.

Wherever recognisable states existed in this uncertainly defined Southeast Asian region of the ninth century the rulers and their courts were followers of imported religions, of Hinduism and Buddhism. These Indian religions were one of the most important features of a development that took place in the Southeast Asian region over many centuries, beginning early in the Christian era. The development has been given the name 'Indianisation', though once again there is continuing disagreement among scholars as to just what the term means. Broad agreement does exist, however, about certain features of the Indianisation process, and it is these features that are now described.

Beginning in the second and third centuries AD there was a slow expansion of Indian cultural contacts with the Southeast Asian region. It was an uneven process, with some areas receiving Indian influence much later than others, and with the degree of cultural impact varying from century to century. In the case of the Vietnamese, who were in this early period living under Chinese rule, the process of Indianisation never took place. For different reasons— distant geographical location—the Philippines, too, did not participate in this process. Indianisation did *not* mean there was a mass migration of Indian populations into Southeast Asia. Rather, a relatively limited number of traders and priest-scholars brought Indian culture in its various forms to Southeast Asia where much, but not all, of this culture was absorbed by the local population and joined to their existing cultural patterns.

Several cautionary remarks are immediately necessary. Because Indian culture 'came' to Southeast Asia, one must not think of Southeast Asians as lacking a culture of their own. Indeed, the most generally accepted view is that Indian culture made such an impact on Southeast Asia because it fitted easily with existing cultural patterns and religious beliefs present among populations that had already moved a considerable distance along the path of civilisation. Just because this was the case, the process of Indianisation should not be seen as simply involving a Southeast Asian acceptance of Indian cultural values. Indian culture was absorbed in much of Southeast Asia, and Indian religions, art forms, and theories of government came to be of the greatest importance. But these various cultural gifts from India became Southeast Asian and in doing so changed their character. In some cases, moreover, quite fundamental features of Indian culture and society were not adopted. The caste system of India did not, for instance, accompany the practice of Hinduism in Southeast Asia, however much early Southeast Asian kings might have felt that they were modelling themselves on Indian rulers and making use of caste terminology to describe themselves and their court. Southeast Asian art drew upon Indian artistic models, but then developed its own forms. Indian languages were used in government and religion. Yet while the inscriptions written in Sanskrit remain one of our most important sources for early Southeast Asian history, the use of this language ultimately lapsed as Southeast Asians came to use Indian scripts to render their own languages.

Southeast Asians, to summarise the point, borrowed but they also adapted. In some very important cases they did not need to borrow at all. The techniques of wet rice cultivation seem to have been indigenous to Southeast Asia and not a technological import from another area. In addition, if there was borrowing and adaptation that justifies the term Indianisation, one must realise that our view of this process tends to be shaped by the evidence with which historians must work. We know infinitely more about the world of kings, courts, and priests than we do about the world of the peasantry. The anonymous worker in the rice fields was probably little affected by Indianisation. The complex features of Hinduism and Mahayana Buddhism—the form of Buddhism that first had an impact in Southeast Asia—were the concerns of his masters as he retained his fear and respect for the spirits that he believed were associated with both the animate and inanimate beings and objects that surrounded him.

How might we explain the attraction that Indian ideas had for rulers and men of religion? A partial answer would seem to be that Indian culture provided an organised and developed pattern of doctrine and knowledge for Southeast Asians who were ready to grasp at new ideas promising greater religious and secular power. The legends that tell of the arrival in Southeast Asia of Brahmin priests from India often have a highly practical twist to them. The Brahmins of the legends bring wisdom and advice to Southeast Asian rulers, instructing them in statecraft as well as in religion. For Brahmins were scholars as well as priests. They could advise on the proper ways to conduct relations with a ruler's neighbouring states. They were astronomers as well as astrologers, and architects who shaped their temples not only in accordance with the demands of building technology but also in terms of religious symbolism and astronomical observation. Men such as these were invaluable advisers and it is not surprising that the Cambodian national birth legend, to take only one example, sees the legendary marriage of a Brahmin with a local princess as the beginning of Cambodia's rise to greatness that culminated in the Angkorian period.

In the Indianised Southeast Asia of the ninth century, two states existed that have probably attracted more historical attention than any others. These states, the inland state based at Angkor in Cambodia and the maritime state of Srivijaya with a centre somewhere in Sumatra, are seen as typifying the two very different kinds

2 Angkor Wat
Of all the monuments that have survived from the classical period of
Southeast Asia, those of the Angkor complex in northern Cambodia are
among the grandest. Built between the tenth and fourteenth centuries, the
temples are scattered over an area of some two hundred square miles. The
most notable, and probably the largest religious monument ever built, is
Angkor Wat, shown here from its western approach. Built by King
Suryavarman II, it was completed in the remarkably short period of about
thirty-five years. Angkor Wat measures 669 by 726 feet at its base, and the
central tower rises to 220 feet. *Photograph by Oliver Howes*

of states that can be identified in the early or classical period. They
were also, in contrast to a number of other examples, states that
preserved their existence over a long historical period. As such, an
examination of their history can suggest some of the reasons that led
to the success and development of kingdoms and empires in the
early history of Southeast Asia, and finally some of the factors that
brought decay and collapse.

Angkor rose to a dominating position in much of mainland
Southeast Asia as a result of a notable ·combination of human
genius, religious belief, and geographical location. In order to
survive and then to develop more than a bare subsistence civilisation
in Cambodia it was and is necessary to master the problem of water,

or rather the lack of it. Despite the torrential rains of Cambodia's wet season, the land dries rapidly once the rains cease and nearly six months of rainless weather follows. Settlement is possible along the banks of the rivers, but the further one moves away from these sources of water the more acute the problem becomes. The Cambodian answer, increasingly refined over the centuries, was to develop reservoirs that could trap rain during the wet season for use during the subsequent dry period.

So skilful were the Cambodians, or Khmers to use the other word that describes the inhabitants of Cambodia, in their hydraulic engineering that they turned the once unproductive region around Angkor into a stupendously successful rice-growing area where three crops a year were grown to support a population in excess of one million. This was the agricultural economic base that permitted the Angkorian state to maintain a population able to build the great temples that remain as a reminder of Khmer achievements in the past. Angkorian Cambodia's wealth was in people and in water. Without the right combination of these two assets there could not have been an Angkor Wat, the most famous of the great temples and the largest single religious building in the world. Wealth, it is true, came into the city in the form of captured booty and prisoners of war who were put to work as slaves. But in the broadest sense Angkorian Cambodia was not a state that depended on trade for its existence. The temples built by Angkor's rulers, and on occasion by their great officials, enshrined the religious ideals of the state. The wealth needed to build and maintain them and to feed and clothe the priestly communities associated with them came from the productive rice fields that spread about the temples.

While, until very recently, it was possible to visit the Angkor region the size of the Cambodian achievement during the years between the ninth and the fifteenth centuries was vividly apparent. Temples great and small spread over hundreds of square miles. Scholars are still discovering new and important facts about the society that could bring these magnificent buildings into being. One of the latest discoveries to fascinate historians is the possibility that the great temple of Angkor Wat was built in such a way as to aid astronomical observations. The investigations that have led to this suggestion have shown that the architects and builders who worked on the temple were able to achieve building feats of a quite remarkable character. Accuracy in construction was so great that variations from a theoretically exact line in the height or direction of walls built over great distances was less than 0.1 per cent.

This evidence of technological capacity linked with the knowledge we have of the skilful control of water underlines the existence

3 Apsara at Banteay Srei
One of the most beautiful of the temples at Angkor, and one of the
smallest, is Banteay Srei, founded in 967. It was built by a priest, not by a
king, and is renowned for the beauty of its sculpture and carving. Shown
here is an *apsara*, a heavenly being that enhanced the world of the Hindu
gods worshipped by the Cambodians of Angkorian times. *Photograph by
Oliver Howes*

during Angkorian times of a highly developed society. Its achievements in aesthetic terms matched its capacities in technology. The statues, the carvings in both high and low relief, the architectural forms that were increasingly refined over the centuries of the Angkorian empire's existence, all give eloquent testimony to the richness of Cambodian culture during the classical period of Southeast Asian history. There is other evidence to emphasise the richness of the culture. Even though his visit came at a time when the Khmers of Angkor were losing their grip on the empire they had built up over four centuries, the Chinese envoy, Chou Ta-kuan, who saw Angkor in 1296, was convinced that the city was the richest in Southeast Asia. Despite his Chinese reserve towards the culture and customs of a non-Chinese society, Chou Ta-kuan was clearly impressed by the wealth of the Angkorian ruler and by the dimensions of the city in which he lived.

Yet if Angkor could impress even a sceptical Chinese civil servant, its economic foundations were highly fragile. Cambodian power had extended from its base in Angkor to incorporate within its empire large sections of modern Thailand, Laos, and Vietnam. This was not a trading empire, though some exchange of goods took place. The really important unifying feature for the Angkorian empire was something quite different from commerce. It was the acceptance by many lesser rulers and governors that the king at Angkor was their supreme lord, their suzerein to use a European term once again. When some of these lesser rulers no longer accepted this situation and chose to fight for their independence from the Angkorian ruler they did more than shatter a political relationship. In addition they threatened and eventually damaged the remarkable irrigation system upon which Angkor's very existence depended. The final abandonment of Angkor some time in the fifteenth century was an event of the deepest importance for mainland Southeast Asia, though quite unknown in Europe. A great empire had come to an end and with its end other states began their rise to greatness. The Thais were the people who brought Angkor down and their history from that time onwards was marked by a slow but sure progress towards the achievement of control over the territories that comprise modern Thailand.

The state of Vietnam, which had gained independence from China in 939 AD, did not contribute directly to Angkor's fall. Nevertheless, in the longer-term historical perspective we can see that the collapse of Cambodian power was vital for Vietnam's subsequent expansion into areas of modern southern Vietnam that once had been part of the Angkorian empire. In the west of mainland Southeast Asia, events in Cambodia had had little direct importance for the early Burmese state. A great Burmese city had been built at Pagan between the eleventh and thirteenth centuries, only to be sacked in 1287 by the invading Mongols who at that time ruled China. While these events and efforts made by later Burmese leaders to found a stable state had no direct links with the decline of Cambodia, once again the end of Pagan forms part of a broader pattern in which we can by the fifteenth century discern the emergence of a new pattern of states and power in the mainland region.

To think in terms of a changing pattern rather than in terms of decline and fall is much more rewarding. Angkor collapsed, in large part, because its economic structure could not be maintained under the pressure exerted by the newly powerful Thais. But Angkorian culture did not disappear. The successful Thais absorbed much from those who had once been their rulers. Thai architecture, the written form of the Thai language, concepts of administration, even dance forms owe much to Khmer inspiration. Moreover, if Angkor and Pagan fell, new states arose and other existing states increased their power so that an approach that concentrates on the decline of the most successful of the states in the early or classical period is historically one-sided.

So far, the concern of much of this chapter has been with the mainland and more particularly with the Angkorian empire. As important in its own fashion but cast in a very different mould was the sea-borne empire of Srivijaya. Just as Angkor enshrined the achievements of a land-based, non-trading Southeast Asian state during the classical period, so did Srivijaya represent the greatest achievement among maritime trading powers during this early phase of the Southeast Asian region's history.

Srivijaya's rise to power depended upon trade and upon China's sponsorship. Put in a rather simplified form, the international trade pattern that was of greatest importance in the early period of Southeast Asian history was the east-west trade between China and the region including India but stretching further west to Persia and beyond. Precious Western goods, including forest products believed to have medicinal qualities, were exchanged in China for silks and porcelain, lacqueurs and other manufactured items. By the seventh century control of much of this trade, at least for the trade passing backwards and forwards between the Indonesian islands, was in the hands of Malays whose chief centre of power was somewhere in southern Sumatra, on the eastern coast of that island.

How this came about is still uncertain, as, too, is the explanation as to how the sailors who manned the ships that carried the trade goods to China came to master the navigational difficulties of a long voyage with few intermediate landfalls. Some aspects of these historical developments are fairly clear, however, and these throw much light on the emergence of a state that was very different in character to the land-based kingdoms of both the mainland and the maritime Southeast Asian world. One of the most clearly important factors in Srivijaya's rise to power was its political relationship with China. In briefly surveying this relationship the whole question of China's role in Southeast Asia is broached so that some general observations are necessary.

Whether strong or weak, the successive rulers of China regarded their country as the central world state – the 'Middle Kingdom' of popular usage. This did not mean that away from China's land borders its emperors thought in terms of the existence of a Chinese empire, certainly not in any very normal use of that term. The Chinese view of the relationship with Southeast Asia was both more subtle and more complex, and for a maritime trading state such as Srivijaya vitally important.

For China, over a long historical period, the area described today as Southeast Asia was the *Nanyang* region, the region of the 'southern seas'. Only Vietnam was ever directly ruled by China and only during one dynasty, the foreign Mongol or Yuan dynasty that ruled China from 1280 to 1368 AD, did Chinese emperors seek to impose their will on Southeast Asian countries other than Vietnam by force. The countries of the southern seas were, in Chinese eyes, lacking in discipline and order, and sadly without the proper Confucian state apparatus that permitted the Chinese state and Chinese culture to survive and progress despite foreign threat and internal political upheaval.

Such a region, in the Chinese view, could only function in a satisfactory fashion if the various Southeast Asian states were in a proper tributary relationship with China. Here is yet another instance in which the limits of vocabulary impede easy under-standing. To be a tributary state of China did not mean that an individual Southeast Asian kingdom was ruled by the Chinese as part of some ill-defined Chinese empire. Rather, the tributary relationship was one that involved a considerable degree of give and take. The fact of being a tributary certainly involved agreement not to act contrary to Chinese interests, but the relationship also implied that China would protect its tributary's interests against those who might challenge them. Most importantly for a trading state such as Srivijaya, the recognition that went with being granted tributary status was linked to the right to trade with China. Once China had granted this status to Srivijaya, the maritime trading states that were its rivals were at a severe disadvantage.

With Chinese recognition given to it, Srivijaya's own capacities brought it to the forefront of Southeast Asian maritime power. Much of what is written about Srivijaya can only be supposition, but it is supposition based on evidence that leaves little doubt as to how this maritime state developed. Strategically placed on the Malacca Straits, Srivijaya came to exert control over all significant trade on the seas in the western section of the Indonesian Archipelago, and between that region of the Archipelago and southern China. Although it does seem correct to think in terms of there having been a Srivijayan capital, this had at least two different locations, and possibly more, over the long centuries of Srivijaya's existence. The capital, additionally, may have been only slightly more important than the other port cities and trading settlements that went to make up this trading empire. For any state or settlement that tried to challenge the Srivijayan monopoly we may suppose that retribution was swift. But equally we may suppose that whatever power existed at the centre of Srivijaya, this was tempered by a readiness to allow the component parts of the empire a very considerable measure of political freedom, provided always that the basic trading arrangements were not infringed.

Srivijaya, like Angkor, was adapted to its environment. For the Khmer state at Angkor hydraulic engineering brought a barely fertile region into a high state of productivity. For the Indonesian-Malay state of Srivijaya the open frontier of the sea made up for the lack of a readily cultivatable hinterland along the swampy south-eastern coast of Sumatra and what is today the western coast of peninsular Malaysia. The very sharpness of the contrast between these two states of the classical period is what makes them such good examples of the two broadly differing patterns of historical development that were followed by Southeast Asian states as late as the nineteenth century. It was only in the nineteenth century that major changes came to most of the land-based and largely self-sufficient states of Southeast Asia. As for the role played by Srivijaya as a maritime power between the seventh and fourteenth centuries, this was to pass to others, to Malacca and ultimately, it could be argued, to Singapore in the nineteenth century. But whichever later state held the role of regional entrepôt and was the focus of trade in the western maritime areas of Southeast Asia, Srivijaya was the first to show how vital the control of the seas could be. Few of the Portuguese, Dutch or British traders and strategists who fought and manoeuvred to gain an ascendancy in the Southeast Asian maritime world realised that they were the successors of earlier maritime empires and none knew of the Srivijayan state, but in a very real sense they were only the latest to follow a very old pattern.

Yet if Srivijaya was adapted to the environment that existed in its heyday, like Angkor it too was unable to survive once that environment changed radically. A vital change for Srivijaya was the development in the thirteenth century of a Chinese maritime trade with Southeast Asia in which the Chinese themselves now sailed in their own trading junks to sell and buy goods in the region. This development upset the balance that Srivijaya had so long maintained, if sometimes in the face of considerable challenge and difficulty. The expansion of Chinese shipping activity was made more dangerous to Srivijaya's interests by the fact that it came at a time when other Indonesian powers were striving to extend a local suzerainty beyond their immediate power centres. Most dangerously for Srivijaya the Javanese land-based states had come to cherish imperial ambitions and saw Srivijaya's weakened condition as an opportunity to strike a deadly blow. Some time in the late fourteenth century the dominant kingdom in Java was able to eliminate the residual challenge of Srivijaya and to bring to an end that state's long history of maritime dominance.

A valid complaint about the kind of history that has just been sketched so superficially in the limited accounts of Angkor and Srivijaya provided in this chapter is that so little place is accorded to ordinary people. We are dealing with courts and kings, with great battles and developments in trade that are linked to regional or even global considerations. The difficulty about this reasonable complaint is that there are few ways to redress the balance. Even when we deal with kings in the classical period of Southeast Asian history it is seldom that a real insight into a personality is provided. There are partial exceptions. The seventh century Khmer king who had his court scribes boast in an inscription that women felt it would be worth rape by the enemy to enjoy the rewards of his smile might be seen as a prototype of the believer in male dominance. Yet even here it is not clear whether one is reading a routine compliment or something that was truly linked to the individual King Isanavarman for whom the inscription was recorded. We can also sense something of the proclaimed personal values of a later Cambodian King, Jayavarman VII (late twelfth and early thirteenth centuries), in both his inscriptions relating to the role he assigned the state and his inscriptions mourning the death of a wife.

No rounded picture of a personality emerges for these rulers, however, any more than it does for the various kings of Javanese kingdoms in the classical period. The names of rulers such as King Airlangga (late tenth century), and Kertanagara (late thirteenth century), or of great officials, such as Gadjah Mada (fourteenth century), are remembered more for the events associated with their names than for any real sense of their personality. And if difficulty is attached to knowing more of such men there are even greater problems when it comes to any attempt to discuss the peasantry, the artisans, and the other groups that did not hold power but yet were vital for the survival of the state.

This problem of history being concerned with rulers, court ritual, and great battles remains with students of Southeast Asian history into the twentieth century. Only in rare instances are we able to see the life of the 'ordinary man' or 'ordinary woman'. There are, for the classical period, some glimpses of that life to be found in the carvings on the Bayon temple at Angkor that show scenes from everyday life in the Cambodia of the twelfth century. While the scenes of cock fights, of ploughing, of women in childbirth, and of gamblers may be typical, the carvings tell us little of the details of life for those who lived at the village level. In the case of Java the great epic poem, the *Nagarakertagama*, dating from the fourteenth century, gives much interesting information about the relationships that existed between the Javanese court of Singasari and the rural villages. We gain, however, little real sense of the villagers themselves from the account. Our sources limit our understanding so that we are forced back to the broader issues, to the problems of Indianization, to the rise and fall of great kingdoms, and to a subject largely omitted in this chapter so far, the cultural and political developments in the one Southeast Asian state that was 'Sinicised' rather than 'Indianised', the state of Vietnam.

Throughout our study of Southeast Asian history Vietnam will remain a state apart, a very different component of the region. So extensive was Vietnamese cultural and political borrowing from its former colonial master, China, that it is sometimes difficult, certainly at first glance, to see the Southeast Asian elements in Vietnamese history and society. Yet those elements were and are present and throughout Vietnamese history there has been a significant tension between the claims of the non-Chinese elements in Vietnamese life and the claims of the Chinese elements, which were associated particularly with the emperor, his court, and his officials. The place accorded women in Vietnamese non-official society, the distinctively non-Chinese language of Vietnam, despite its multiple borrowings from China, and the Vietnamese peasants' migratory urge are only some of the features of that country's history that seem to link it with Southeast Asia rather than China.

At the official level, however, there can be no denying the force of Chinese ideas. China was a model for Vietnamese official life, an armoury from which new weapons could be drawn to combat new problems and challenges as these arose. So much was this the case that an argument could be developed for the greater impact of China on Vietnam than, for example, the impact of India on Cambodia. Like most other arguments over degree, particularly in relation to Southeast Asian history, scholars would adopt differing viewpoints on this matter. They would be in general agreement, however, about the profound importance of China and Chinese ideas for the development of the Vietnamese state.

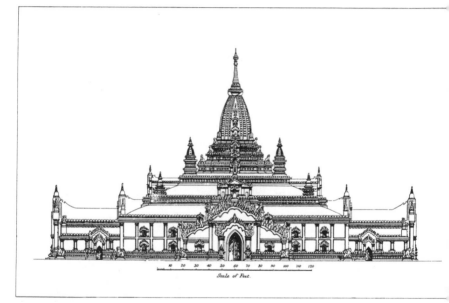

4 The Ananda Pagoda at Pagan
The vast temple complex at Pagan, in central Burma, rivals the Angkor monuments in Cambodia for the richness of its architecture and the extent of the territory covered by its buildings. The most impressive of the temples at Pagan is that built by King Kyanzittha (1084-1113). The Ananda temple represents the high point of Burmese art when, between 1094 and 1287, the Pagan empire was the dominant power in the west of mainland Southeast Asia. *From* A Narrative of the Mission to the Court of Ava in 1855, *compiled by Henry Yule in 1856.*

Equally, moreover, general agreement would also emerge in any scholarly discussion for the proposition that Vietnam, with its independence achieved in 939 AD, continued over the succeeding centuries to work to maintain that independence, if necessary by fighting for it against China. Once again, understanding of Vietnam's relationship with China has been confusing for some observers since Vietnam was, most clearly, one of China's tributary states. This tributary status, despite the strong cultural links between the two countries, did not mean that Vietnam was ready to accept political interference by China in its internal affairs. Tributary status did mean that Vietnam could not readily act outside its borders in a manner likely to offend its great northern neighbour and suzerain.

If Vietnam was a very special Southeast Asian state, by comparison with those other areas that experienced cultural importation from India, its rise to power and emergence as one of the stronger states of the mainland by the end of the classical period in the fifteenth century further emphasises the major changes that were taking place throughout the region as a whole. For Vietnam's rise to power was at the expense of its southern neighbour, Champa. This Indianised state had, on occasion, been able to challenge the mighty Angkorian empire. As late as the twelfth century the Chams were able to sack a temporarily weakened Angkorian state in a successful water-borne attack on the city after their great war canoes had travelled up the Mekong and Tonle Sap Rivers. By the beginning of the fourteenth century, in contrast, Champa's former strength had greatly decayed and the Vietnamese were already involved in a process of annexation and long-term attrition that was to lead, eventually, to the obliteration of the Cham kingdom.

Because so many important changes took place in the thirteenth, fourteenth, and fifteenth centuries, historians have asked whether there might be an identifiable event or series of events that would provide an explanation for the downfall of the great states of classical times and the emergence of the states that were to play more prominent roles in the later history of the region. Notable among the suggestions of such an essential event or series of events is that of the role played by the Mongols of the Yuan dynasty in China. By bringing the downfall of Pagan in Burma, by interfering in developments in the Indonesian Archipelago, and in Vietnam, Champa, and Cambodia, the Mongols, the suggestion runs, created a turbulent situation favourable to change. Other commentators give a different emphasis, pointing to the changes at a little later time that resulted from the arrival of Theravada Buddhism in the mainland of Southeast Asia and of Islam in the maritime regions.

There seems every reason to give some weight to all of these suggestions, so long as no single cause is seen as having been sufficient by itself to alter the political map of Southeast Asia from the late thirteenth century onwards. The importance of the Mongol destruction of the state based at Pagan cannot be overstated. But the role of the Mongols in bringing change to Angkor is much less clear. Theravada Buddhism did involve a notably different set of religious values from the combination of Hinduism and Mahayana Buddhism that it partially replaced in Cambodia. Nevertheless, it is far from certain that an official adoption of these values contributed to the decline of the Khmer state at Angkor. Islam was to have great significance as a unifying factor among the coastal populations of the Indonesian islands. The extent to which its arrival in northern Java and northern Sumatra had any quick, political effect in speeding the decay of the older pattern of state relationships in the Archipelago is more difficult to determine.

Briefly, it is easier to argue that a series of important changes took place and to note that these political changes often ran parallel, or nearly so, with developments in the fields of culture and religion than to argue for general political change as the result of a single major factor, or even series of factors in the history of the Southeast Asian region. The case of Cambodia is instructive in this respect. Since the beginning of the twentieth century there have been a number of attempts to account for the decline of this mighty state in terms of a single, major cause. Some of the earliest of these explanations placed the greatest importance on the arrival of Theravada Buddhism, a more 'democratic' religion, it was argued, than Hinduism and Mahayana Buddhism. Later arguments suggested that a possible reason for the decline of the Angkorian state might have been the spread of malaria as Thai invasions of the Angkor region brought a collapse of the Cambodian irrigation system and so provided stagnant ponds in which mosquitoes could breed. Nowadays such single cause explanations are treated with reserve. The acceptance of Theravada Buddhism by Cambodian rulers might well have been an attempt to shore-up the power of the state rather than an effort to make religion more 'democratic'. The invasions by the Thais undoubtedly were of very great importance, but there seems increasingly little reason to pay very much attention to the idea of a sudden onset of malaria laying the Khmer state low.

Major changes took place in Southeast Asia over a period of more than two centuries as old states were no longer capable of adapting to changed circumstances and as new states proved more attuned to the changed world. To search for causes other than in the broadest range of factors that govern the capacity of individuals and kingdoms to survive or to fail is to court disappointment. Moreover, to place the major historical emphasis on the fall of the old states and the disappearance of certain cultural characteristics, such as the use of Sanskrit, is to minimise the extent to which old values lived on in the new states that were the successors to the powerful kingdoms and empires of the classical period.

In short, the Southeast Asian world that emerged following the end of the classical period owed a very great historical debt to earlier times. Students of modern Southeast Asia may not always be aware of the more complex details of that debt, but they cannot disregard its importance or remain ignorant of the broad lines of development without severely limiting their understanding of more recent issues, of the underlying cultural factors that influence historical developments, and of the basically important fact that Southeast Asia possesses a past no less full of interest and deserving of attention than other areas of the world.

3
Courts, Kings, and Peasants: Southeast Asia Before the European Impact

LOOKING back over a long span of history there is a great temptation to search out 'watersheds', sharp breaks with the past, periods that can be described as the beginning or end of an era. Such an approach to history is both understandable and on occasion justifiable. The danger of such an approach, however, is that it carries with it a very great risk of distortion. Because formerly great empires were overthrown or collapsed in both mainland and maritime Southeast Asia we should not think of those empires as having been completely forgotten by the descendants of the men and women who had once lived at Pagan in Burma, at Angkor in Cambodia, or near the great monuments of central Java such as the Borobodur. Nor should we assume that the kings who ruled over the states of Southeast Asia that emerged in the centuries following the end of the 'classical' period saw themselves as less important, less royal, or less powerful than their predecessors. To put the matter briefly, the bulk of the states making up Southeast Asia in the eighteenth century were not only still essentially traditional in character. They were, just as importantly, states in which the rulers reigned with a clear conviction of the permanence, if not the stability, of the traditional world. Quite certainly, most of the kings and officials of eighteenth century Southeast Asia had no sense of their position being threatened by men from Europe.

This final fact explains why so much attention is given to the eighteenth century in any general survey of Southeast Asia's modern history. Although change when it did come in the nineteenth century as the result of a growing European role in the politics of Southeast Asia was often much slower and less dramatic than some commentators once suggested, the search for 'watersheds' does appear partly justified in relation to the eighteenth century. This century witnessed a significant historical shift from a situation in which most Southeast Asian states maintained a tradi-

5   The Borobodur

The Borobodur monument in Central Java was constructed at the end of the eighth-beginning of the ninth century A.D. Constructed in the form of a huge Buddhist stupa, a conical or domed building, it is richly decorated with low relief carving showing scenes from religious texts (above). Its summit is crowned by a series of smaller stupas, which sheltered statues of the Buddha, and from which pilgrims could look at distant sacred volcanic mountains, such as Mount Merapi (below). *Photographs courtesy of M.C. Ricklefs*

tional existence, essentially untouched by the influence of Europe, to a new situation in which, at the political level at least, Europeans began to exert an increasing influence over developments in the region. The eighteenth century was, therefore, the last century in which the traditional world of Southeast Asia was dominant, if not universal.

The difficulties associated with the use of metaphors such as 'watershed' are immediately apparent, however, when one looks ahead from the eighteenth century to the changes of the nineteenth century that have just been mentioned. So that the question is then raised as to whether or not there were a whole series of 'watersheds' as colonial powers became more and more important in the Southeast Asian region: an 'eighteenth-century watershed', a 'nineteenth-century political watershed', and a 'late nineteenth- to early twentieth-century economic watershed'. Clearly the excessive use of any metaphor robs it of its force and suggestion. Possibly the most helpful way to think of the 'watershed' metaphor is in terms of a series of linked developments in which over a period of perhaps two centuries Southeast Asia was transformed economically, politically, and socially. Viewed with this perspective, the period of the eighteenth century is *part* of the 'watershed' that was represented by the combined political and economic changes of the nineteenth and early twentieth centuries, and ended with the Second World War.

A political map of eighteenth-century Southeast Asia on which the cartographer tried to indicate the boundaries of the various states by use of different colours would appear as an extraordinary mosaic. It is a difficult task even to count how many colours there would have to be on this map. Instead of the ten states that make up late twentieth-century Southeast Asia a cartographer attempting this task for the eighteenth century could not think in terms of less than forty states—kingdoms, principalities, and sultanates—that required delineation. Many of these states were of minor importance. Both on the mainland of Southeast Asia and in the maritime world one would have to find some way of distinguishing between the states of real importance and those which existed at the pleasure of their suzerains or overlords. But however the calculations are made the political map of eighteenth-century Southeast Asia is notably more complex than a political map of the contemporary world. Moreover, the political map of eighteenth-century Southeast Asia, in contrast to a map of the succeeding century, would have one very distinctive feature. The areas showing a colonial presence would be very small indeed. Apart from the northern Philippine islands and much of Java, the European presence in eighteenth-century Southeast Asia was extremely limited, a few trading posts dotted along the coast-lines of the various regions.

What sort of states existed in this still essentially traditional Southeast Asian world? The most distinctive was the Vietnamese state. Throughout most of the eighteenth century Vietnam was politically divided with one great family dominating northern Vietnam while another family dominated the southern areas. Despite this division, and indeed despite the dramatic developments of the last three decades of the century when a major uprising brought temporary unification under rulers who challenged and overcame the power of the great families, the ideal of a politically undivided Vietnamese state survived. This ideal state was thought of as one in which Confucian values were dominant and an administrative system modelled on that used in China prevailed. Yet attachment to Confucian values and a bureaucracy that took China as its example did not mean the Vietnamese were simply a provincial variant on a metropolitan Chinese theme. The rulers of Vietnam, or portions of it when the country was divided politically, copied much but not all from China. Most clearly they did not accept any suggestion that China had a right to interfere in Vietnam's internal affairs, even if it did have the right to demand Vietnam's allegiance as a tributary state.

As a result of the partial Chinese overlay on Vietnam's court and its officials, the state stood apart from its Southeast Asian neighbours in terms of the precision and formality that attached to the government structure. In theory, and to a considerable extent in practice also, the Vietnamese bureaucracy was open to all who could meet the tests of scholarship. In the Buddhist kingdoms of Southeast Asia (Burma, Thailand, Cambodia, and the lowland principalities of modern Laos) officialdom was, in contrast, a quasi-hereditary affair. Being the son of an official was the vital fact that determined subsequent entry into the ranks of the ruler's administration. In Vietnam merit was taken as the guiding principle, even if it often proved the case that the sons of officials had more opportunity to succeed in their learning and so to enter the official ranks.

Vietnamese officials advised a ruler who was spoken of as the 'Son of Heaven', and who was thought to mediate between the physical world and the spiritual world by the correct observance of state and religious ceremonies. Just as the performance of these ceremonies followed a minutely drawn-up set of procedures, so was the rest of Vietnamese official life conceived of as following prescribed patterns. The bureaucracy was a pyramid with the ruler at the apex and with clearly defined links established between that apex and the lowest officials in the provinces who formed the base of this administration. The law was a written code, detailed in form and complete with learned commentaries. Strict rules covered the amount of authority possessed by each grade of official and the qualifications for each grade. And as a further reflection of the character of the state the Vietnamese believed in the necessity of clearly defined borders with their neighbours.

In this, as in so many other ways, Vietnam differed from the other major mainland states of Southeast Asia. For them, in a way that has been discussed in an earlier chapter, the important external cultural influence came from India rather than China. For all of its pervasive importance, however, Indian cultural influence in Burma, Thailand, Cambodia and in the riverine states of Laos, was a less clear-cut and obvious affair. Vietnamese officials dressed in the same fashion as Chinese mandarins. With the exception of some court priests such direct borrowing was not a characteristic of the Buddhist courts of mainland Southeast Asia. In Vietnam, again, official architecture drew directly from China, whereas in the Buddhist states the Indian influence was a more subtle matter, and by the eighteenth century only rarely directly recognisable as a case of cultural borrowing.

The organisation of the Buddhist states contrasted sharply with that found in Vietnam. The pattern of official relationships was in many ways much more complex, in part because it was a pattern lacking the clearly defined lines of authority that were so much part of the Vietnamese system. Where the Vietnamese system sought to control the state in great detail down to the level of the village, the central power in the Buddhist kingdoms followed a very different practice. Control over the more distant regions of the kingdom was readily delegated to provincial governors who were able to exercise almost completely unfettered power, always providing that they did not challenge the king's position as the ultimate arbiter of affairs within the state. If the pyramid is a useful symbol to depict the disposition of power within Vietnam, a series of concentric circles might be taken to represent the nature of power in the Buddhist kingdoms. The state might be considered as the area contained by the largest of these concentric circles, but it was only at the centre, where the smallest of these concentric circles is located, that the king's power was truly absolute. Beyond that central circle—or beyond the limits of the palace to take the real-life example instead of the graphic concept—it was frequently the case that the king's power diminished in a clear proportion to the distance one moved away from the capital. As for the border regions, the Buddhist rulers in mainland Southeast Asia, again in contrast to Vietnam, accepted that these were uncertain and porous. Indeed, given the lack of close links between the centre of the Buddhist kingdoms and the outer regions, as well as the existence of numerous petty centres of power largely independent of their greater neighbours, some writers have argued that to talk of 'states' in the traditional Southeast Asian world is inappropriate. Certainly the states of traditional Southeast Asia, for we will continue to use the term for convenience, were very different from the political units described as states in the twentieth century.

The officials who held power, whether at the centre of the state in the king's palace or in the outer regions, were not men who gained their appointments through scholarship. Birth into a quasi-hereditary family, ability, and an opportunity to gain the ruler's notice all played their part in determining advancement. It would be quite wrong to suggest that the rulers of the Buddhist kingdoms did not have clear ideas on what constituted a good official, for the record is clear that they did. But the standards were much more flexible and much more personal than those that applied in Vietnam. In the same fashion the conduct of business within the state was less set in formal pattern, more subject to the personal likes and dislikes of the kings, at the highest level, or the officials great and small in the provinces away from the capital.

To write in these general terms is to discuss the ideal, or at least the general, rather than to dwell on individual departures from the norm. Notably powerful Southeast Asian rulers of Buddhist states did attempt to impose their control over the kingdom as a whole, just as there were periods in Vietnamese history when the clearly structured organisation of the state was unable to operate and the central power could not control ambitious governors in the regions more distant from the capital. But in the general terms that must be used in any broad historical survey there is no need to hesitate in underlining the great differences that existed between the government of Thailand, to take the example of one Buddhist kingdom, and Vietnam.

The king in Thailand was, like his counterpart the emperor in Vietnam, expected to intercede between the world of men and the spiritual world. But the nature of this intercession, and the role assigned to the monarch involved in the act, was very different. In Thailand, and in the other mainland Buddhist states, the king's semi-divine status reflected the fact that the monarch and the throne he occupied were the centre of the kingdom. Monarchy was the lynch pin that held the Buddhist kingdoms together. Despite his title as the 'Son of Heaven' the Vietnamese emperor had no equivalent status. The Vietnamese emperors were essential to the existence of the state, but they were not the state. The point may be made clearer when it is noted that the Vietnamese were able to accept a situation in which for more than a hundred years during the seventeenth and eighteenth centuries their emperor was no more than a figurehead, a puppet at the beck and call of one of the great families. However limited a king's power was away from the capital in which he had his palace, and however much senior officials might have tried to take advantage of a child succeeding to the throne, the idea of a state existing more as a reflection of its officials than of its ruler was not part of the system to be found in the Buddhist kingdoms.

Common to all of the Buddhist rulers of mainland Southeast Asia was a belief—held both by themselves and their subjects—in their semi-divine, or near-divine, character. The concept of a king possessing magical, divine-like characteristics is a difficult one to grasp, and the more deeply one examines the matter the more complex the issue becomes. For a person seeking to understand Southeast Asia in general terms the following broad points deserve attention. The quasi-divine, magical role played by traditional Buddhist rulers in the states of mainland Southeast Asia involved something more than the concept of 'divine right' associated with Christian rulers in Europe. Such European rulers held an office sanctioned by the Christian divinity. But no matter how elevated the status of these kings and queens, they were not semi-divine or nearly god-like themselves. The Buddhist kings of mainland Southeast Asia, on the other hand, were seen as divine, or partially so. Their position as kings was not only sanctioned by the Buddhist faith, and continuing Hindu religious beliefs, they were in themselves removed from the rest of mankind and credited with possessing powers that only the divine or near-divine could hold.

Once again, this is the ideal picture and if the ideal had prevailed without any qualification there would never have been any family feuds, coups d'etat, and all the other turbulent events that saw kings toppled from their thrones and ambitious men plotting, sometimes successfully and sometimes not, to usurp the monarch of the day. But if the reality was more complicated than the ideal, the ideal was nonetheless maintained. Challengers who succeeded in removing a ruler from the throne immediately tried to claim all of the semi-divine powers of their defeated opponent. What is more, with rare exceptions, those who fought or schemed to overthrow a ruling king did so in terms of their own claim to have a more legitimate right to the throne than the actual monarch. The importance of this traditional historical background for more modern periods in Southeast Asia may already be apparent. Given the immensely elevated status

6   Buddha at Sukhothai
Buddhism was the dominant religion of the Thai states that challenged the
power of Angkor in mainland Southeast Asia in the thirteenth century and
defeated the Cambodians of Angkor in the fifteenth. One of the earliest
of the Thai kingdoms was Sukhothai, its capital some two hundred and
ninety miles north of modern Bangkok. The ruins of Sukhothai are dotted
with great monumental Buddhas, such as that photographed here, which
are still objects of worship.

of traditional Buddhist rulers, there should be no surprise in the fact that a ruler such as the Thai monarch has continued to be a fundamentally important figure in the modern history of Thailand. Traditional ideas of kingship also help to explain why Prince Norodom Sihanouk of Cambodia was for many years able to reap immense political advantage from the fact that he had been Cambodia's king before abdicating his throne in 1955.

Royal figures have also been important in the recent history of the maritime regions of Southeast Asia. If their importance has not been so striking as has been the case for the mainland, the explanation owes something to tradition as well as to the fact that Thailand's monarchy ruled over a country that was never colonised while Sihanouk and his ancestors reigned in a colonial system that allowed at least some of the symbolic importance of the king of Cambodia to be maintained. Unlike the mainland Buddhist monarchies—again excluding Vietnam as a special case—the majority of the rulers of the states in the maritime world were followers of Islam, sultans who acted in the name of their religion as well as their state. As followers of Islam the sultans could not, in strict theory, be other than men with the limitations that such a status involves. Strict theory was yet again qualified, and most particularly in those regions of maritime Southeast Asia that had sustained substantial influence from Indian ideas—in parts of Indonesia and Malaysia.

Nowhere was this more true than in Java where the rulers of the central Javanese kingdom of Mataram were followers of Islam but just as importantly, perhaps even more importantly, inheritors of a rich mystical tradition drawing upon Hindu—Buddhist ideas as well as indigenous Javanese religious beliefs and cultural patterns. The rulers of Mataram *were* more than men in a way that many of the sultans of the coastal and riverine states of maritime Southeast Asia were not. These latter rulers were men with special rights and almost limitless privilege, but they were men all the same. The ruler of Mataram ensconced in his *kraton*, or palace, gave formal acknowledgement to Islam but his kingship is more readily understood as having parallels with the Buddhist monarchs of the mainland than in terms of the patterns to be found in many of the other traditional courts of the islands.

Whatever the religious or philosophical under-pinnings to their exercise of power, the rulers of Southeast Asia in the traditional world of the eighteenth century and the officials who served them were a group apart from the rest of the population. In Vietnam merit could enable a peasant child to move into the official ruling group. Once this change took place the youth or man of the people took on a new role. Even more marked was the division between ruling group and ruled in the rest of the region. Apart from the rarest exceptions, the division between the elite and the rest of the population was almost complete, a profound gap that could only be bridged in extraordinary times or by an extraordinary man.

When using such terms as 'division' or 'gap', however, it is essential to make clear what sort of separation between elite and non-elite is being discussed. The division involved was not one that separated kings or sultans from the peasantry in religious terms, for instance. On the contrary, the peasant quite clearly felt a religious link between himself, his ruler, and the complex religious beliefs he held. This fact is bound up in such basic sayings as 'To be a Burmese is to be a Buddhist'. In terms of traditional Burma one could add 'and to know that the chief patron of Buddhism in Burma is the king'. The essential feature of the division was that of power. In traditional Southeast Asia power was concentrated in the hands of the elite few. No middle group, or class, existed to moderate the stark division between rulers and ruled. Whether power was exercised wisely or not it was in the hands of the few.

Such a situation should not be taken to mean that there were no differences among those who made up the ruled portion of the population in traditional Southeast Asia, for such was not the case. Most importantly in all of the countries of Southeast Asia, including Vietnam, there was a marked difference between the members of peasant society who acted as headmen or village leaders and those who had no role in the determination of policies within a village community. Because the term 'peasant society' is used as a general description there is an easy tendency to think of all peasants being more or less the same: all poor, all farmers, and all with little role to perform in life except to tend their fields and obey higher authority. Such a general picture is unsatisfactory. No peasants in the traditional Southeast Asian world were truly rich, by whatever standards one may apply. But some were a great deal better off than others. These men and their families had gained power and influence in their village communities and once having achieved it seldom let it go. They were the community leaders who acted as 'headmen' and so as go-betweens linking the village with higher provincial authority. Although their material condition may often have been better than that of their fellow villagers their duties as the final link in the chain between the court and the village settlement could often be unenviable as they supervised tax collection, arranged labour contributions, or ensured that men went to war on their distant ruler's behalf.

The application of power by these village leaders differed from country to country, and even from district to district. Given the emphasis that has already been placed on Vietnam's very distinct character, it will not be surprising to learn that village society in that country was dominated and directed by members of a very particular leadership system. Whereas power and executive responsibility generally went hand in hand in the rest of Southeast Asia—a headman held power and exercised it—the situation was different in the complex society of a Vietnamese village. There the more prosperous peasants were a self-perpetuating group, as elsewhere. The difference lay in the fact that the Vietnamese village leaders worked through a group of village officials who had responsibility for the government of the village but were themselves responsible to other more powerful villagers.

So far the survey of Southeast Asian society undertaken in this chapter has dealt with the traditional world that was largely untouched by European power or ideas until the end of the eighteenth century. Yet before the eighteenth century began, and slowly

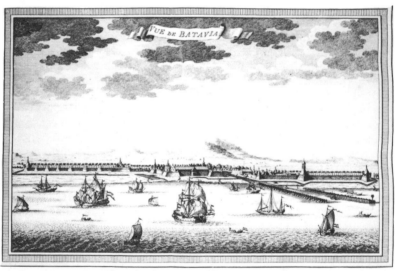

GEZIGT VAN BATAVIA.

7   Batavia in the 17th century
A view of the Dutch colonial city of Batavia, on the northern coast of Java, in the early 18th century. Batavia, modern Jakarta, was well-placed to dominate sea traffic with the spice islands of eastern Indonesia, and it was the trade in spices that originally brought the Dutch to Indonesia. Built on low-lying ground, Batavia was a death trap for many of its European inhabitants who succumbed to malaria or the consequences of appallingly inadequate sanitation. *Photograph from National Library of Australia.*

through that century, men from Europe were beginning to become involved in the affairs of the region and in one notable instance, in the Philippines, to have an important impact on society at large.

The Portuguese, the Spaniards, and the Dutch were the earliest of those from Europe who came to the Southeast Asian region and played a role in its history that remains a matter for continuing debate and reassessment. In the sixteenth century it appeared that the Portuguese as the first upon the scene would establish a dominant role in the region and gain the major share in the rich trade in spices—the commodity that had drawn Europeans to Southeast Asia in the first place. But Portugal's early successes, including in 1511 the capture of Malacca, the great trading city on the western coast of the Malayan Peninsula, were followed by relatively quick decline as the Dutch became the most important European nation trading in the Malay—Indonesian world. But how important? For the merchants of the ports in the Netherlands, the Dutch who lived, and usually after a very short time died, in Indonesia were important indeed as they developed a commercial system that for a period brought great profit to the Dutch state. But the impact of the Dutch outside their base in Java, and their outposts scattered through the islands was minimal until the middle or even the end of the eighteenth century; for some regions of Indonesia the impact did not come until the late nineteenth and early twentieth centuries. In terms of society and its patterns of behaviour, an interesting case has been developed to suggest that Dutch men and women in Batavia (Jakarta) were as much, or more, affected by Indonesian values than the reverse. The interest of such a discussion must not hide the vital fact, however, that the Dutch were still of minor importance to the bulk of the Indonesian population until the middle of the eighteenth century. A similar statement cannot be made in relation to the Spaniards in Philippines.

The Philippines came into historical focus remarkably late by comparison with other parts of Southeast Asia. We know that trading junks from China and Japan visited the Philippines for centuries before the Spanish established themselves in the northern Philippines during the latter part of the sixteenth century. The records of these voyages tell us frustratingly little about the nature of society in the Philippines and as a result our knowledge of life in the Philippines *before* the Spanish arrived depends largely on the information provided by men who wrote *after* the colonial presence had become an established fact.

In the broadest terms, the Spanish came to an area of Southeast Asia in which authority was for the most part exercised over small communities without any central direction. The exceptions to this

general rule were mostly found in the southern islands of the Philippines where the adoption of Islam by traditional leaders had helped
them to organise states that used the unifying force of religion to
incorporate a number of scattered communities into a single
political unit. By the middle of the sixteenth century Islam was
slowly gaining ground in the more northerly islands and had reached
as far as Manila. But this was a coastal phenomenon and the inland
areas remained untouched by the new religion so that the Spaniards
encountered a society in which a large village was the essential unit.
Authority, as elsewhere in Southeast Asia, rested in the hands of a
headman who was through birth and inheritance, or through ability,
more properous and powerful than his fellow villagers.

The absence of central power in the northern Philippine islands,
for the southern islands were never to experience significant Spanish
rule away from a few port centres, enabled the Spanish colonial
power to implant itself in a way unmatched anywhere else in the
region. Unlike anywhere else in Southeast Asia, moreover, the
principal agents for the Spanish advance were not soldiers and
traders but missionary priests. This state of affairs was unique in the
history of Southeast Asia, even though missionary priests played
important roles elsewhere. In the Philippines, however, the link
between the church and the state was of a different order from that
existing during French rule over Vietnam. The church and the state
were inseparable in the Philippines, as they were in other parts of
the world that fell under Spanish colonial control. This distinctive
feature has led some scholars to argue, to an extent convincingly,
that in order to understand Philippine history and society from the
seventeenth century onwards it is necessary to study the Spanish
experience in Latin America.

Whether or not one seeks enlightenment from the comparison of
the Philippine experience with that of the various countries of Latin
America, the impact of Spanish values, particularly Spanish
Christian values, on the peasant society of the Philippines was
profound. The Philippines became the one country in the Southeast
Asian region in which Christianity became more than a minority
religion. The presence of Christian missionaries did not, of course,
bring immediate change to social patterns in the countryside.
Slowly, however, with the combined force of the church and state
lending authority to developments, the Spanish colonial impact
affected the life of the peasantry, giving new and greater power to
the traditional local leaders, yet insisting that power beyond the
village or district level could not pass out of the hands of Spaniards.
The ultimate irony of this situation is well known to Filipinos but all
too often unknown by others. By the early years of the nineteenth

century two hundred years of Spanish rule had brought into being a growing group of native Filipinos whose education fitted them to assume roles in the state and the church that were denied them because they were not Spanish. The resentments this situation caused became the seeds of the Philippine revolutionary movement in the late nineteenth century. Yet there was a further irony again. If the Spanish impact, coming so much earlier and so much more profoundly in the Philippines than elsewhere in Southeast Asia, created a class that resented Spanish political control, it also laid the foundations for a rural economic situation in which centuries of colonial control developed, strengthened, and gave legitimacy to the high degree of social stratification that remains a feature of Philippine life to the present day.

Extended discussion of the Philippines makes the point that the country's experience was in many ways very different from the rest of Southeast Asia—more different, in some important senses, than those features that always remind us of Vietnam's special character. Nevertheless, for the Philippines as well as the rest of Southeast Asia, there was a general pattern to peasant life that allows us once more to enter the risky world of simplification and summary.

Throughout Southeast Asia the basic pattern of peasant life was one in which men and women assured their right to farm land by the act of farming. For most of Southeast Asia the Western concept of land ownership did not apply—Vietnam once again differed from most of its neighbours in the existence of clearly defined private land ownership. A family might work one area of land for many generations but the fields remained the 'property' of the ruler. Such a situation was not so full of difficulties as might be thought at first glance. And so long as the population of the various countries of Southeast Asia remained small there was little pressure on land. If circumstances conspired to make life in one agricultural area difficult through war, famine, or the excessive demands of an overlord, then a family or a village could move on elsewhere to find an alternative region in which to work. They could even move from one country to another. As late as the end of the nineteenth century French officials in Cambodia were amazed to find that peasants moved in both directions across the border between Cambodia and Thailand—a fact that needs to be remembered whenever emphasis is placed on the sense of national identity among a peasant population.

Life as a peasant was seldom easy and at times shockingly harsh. The risk of famine in countries that depended on monsoons to provide the water for irrigating wet-rice cultivation was always in the background. In all but the poorest regions there were occasions

8   Village House in Sumatra
An engraving of a village house in Sumatra. The drawing from which this engraving was made was executed in 1792. Despite the slow increase in European contacts with Southeast Asia by the closing years of the eighteenth century, peasants, such as those seen in this picture, continued to live a life largely circumscribed by the limits of their village and its nearby regions. *From* The History of Sumatra, *by William Marsden, published in 1811, from National Library of Australia*

for village festivals with their accompanying gaiety, but these were the exceptions to a way of life that was plagued by disease as well as involving demanding physical labour.

Although the peasant farmers or cultivators were the most important Southeast Asian group outside of the elite ranks, there were other groups which also deserve attention. In villages of the larger kind and in the minor trading or administrative centres away from the great capitals there were artisans and merchants. Along the coasts of both mainland and maritime Southeast Asia and on the rivers and lakes there were fishermen whose occupation set them apart from the cultivators but who otherwise shared the same values and suffered comparable hardships of life.

The world of the peasant, whether cultivator or fisherman, of the artisan and the small trader was essentially a closed one. No truly autonomous villages existed but the links with the larger world were weak. The more prosperous villager might know a little of the world beyond his village's rice fields, as the fisherman of necessity knew of a world beyond the beach where he landed his catch and pulled his boat out of the water. But the world beyond the village was imperfectly perceived and the likelihood that anyone born into a village would leave it except during war or to live in another village was slim indeed. This fact explains a common theme to be found in the folk tales of many of the countries of the Southeast Asian region. The theme involves the remarkable transformation of a village youth into a great official or even a king through wit, good fortune, or magic—sometimes all three together.

Such a theme gives sharp emphasis to the basic reality of peasant life, the unchanging nature of existence. Life was not necessarily static. Villagers moved in the face of famine or to avoid war. Itinerant traders travelled with their caravans right across the face of mainland Southeast Asia reaching from lower Burma into the highland regions of modern Vietnam. Indonesian traders from Sumatra, the northern ports of Java, and Sulawesi criss-crossed the seas of the Archipelago in their trading voyages. But having ventured abroad they returned to a world that altered little in its essentials from year to year and decade to decade.

Yet change of momentous proportions was not far distant for Southeast Asia as a whole as the eighteenth century drew to a close. Many of the changes that came were the result of the Western impact on the region. During the nineteenth century Thailand alone escaped the experience of colonial rule, and even in Thailand's case the West impinged on the country in a fashion far greater than ever before. But other changes had little if any connection with the advance of the colonial powers. The last three decades of the eighteenth century in Vietnam were marked by political upheaval and by a challenge to established social and economic patterns—just how truly revolutionary the Tay-Son rebellion was in social terms is yet another unresolved historical controversy. The advent of a new dynasty on the Thai throne, the Chakri dynasty, from 1782 onwards, brought a remarkable series of kings to power whose personal energy and ability transformed the state. They did this as much through reinvigorating Thai forms of government as through later selective borrowing from the West.

Changes brought by growing Western influence and changes inspired by outstanding individuals within the ruling groups of the various Southeast Asian states were later to affect the population as a whole. Initially, however, the fact and prospect of change had its greatest effect on the elite. Here, once more, emphasis is given to the division between the rulers and the ruled. It was the ruling class in Thailand who first were aware of the genius that inspired the first Chakri ruler, Rama I, in his profusion of decrees that codified and reorganised life at the court and in his own presentation of the Ramayana legend. It was the central Javanese elite who welcomed the sudden burgeoning of literature from the middle of the eighteenth century. So too the Vietnamese elite were the first to respond to the remarkable epic poem, the *Kim Van Kieu*, that the author Nguyen Van Du wrote at the beginning of the nineteenth century and which has never been superseded as the finest Vietnamese literary examination of the moral dilemmas of human existence.

For the peasant the world went on as before, dominated by the cycle of crop planting and harvest, the seasons of the year, and the awesome events of birth and death. Visualising his physical world in the eighteenth century is difficult in the extreme as even the remotest villages of twentieth-century Southeast Asia have been touched and transformed by the modern world. Entering the spiritual world of the peasant during the eighteenth century is even more difficult an exercise. We may sense something of the complexity of this spiritual world, the blend of animistic beliefs with one or other of the great religions or philosophies—Islam, Christianity, Buddhism, Hinduism, Confucianism—that were followed in the states of Southeast Asia. But even the most sympathetic student can only penetrate a certain distance into the religious world of another culture in another age.

Yet for all of the emphasis that has been given in this chapter to the separateness of existence between ruler and ruled in the traditional Southeast Asian world it would be wrong not to end with an insistence upon the totality of the world within which these two groups lived. For this too was a feature of the traditional world that was soon to come under challenge as new forces and new ideas penetrated the region.

The courts and kings were separate from the cultivators, fishermen, and petty traders over whom they ruled. But all of these groups inhabited a single, unified world. Just as the serf and the feudal lord of medieval Europe both, in very different ways, sensed themselves to be part of Christendom, so the cultivators or fishermen sensed themselves within the same world as their ruler, whether he was an Islamic sultan, a Buddhist king, a Vietnamese Confucian emperor, or a Catholic Spanish governor. To a considerable extent, the history of Southeast Asia from the beginning of the nineteenth century is a history of the changes brought to this assumption of a settled, single world.

4

Minorities and Slaves: The Outsiders in Traditional Southeast Asia

THE 'single world' of the ruled and the rulers described in the previous chapter was a world for those who belonged to the dominant society, whether in a lowly or an exalted fashion. Not everyone who inhabited traditional Southeast Asia, however, did belong, in the sense of being a member of the dominant ethnic group within a state. A relatively small number of the outsiders in the various states that made up traditional Southeast Asia were immigrants or the descendants of immigrants from distant regions, Indians, Persians, Chinese, and Arabs. But minorities of this sort were not really important until late in the nineteenth century. For the mainland of Southeast Asia, and to a much lesser extent in the maritime regions, the true outsiders in the traditional world were the people living in the hills and mountains.

The 'hill-valley' division of traditional Southeast Asian society was of a different order from the division between ruler and ruled in the ethnically unified mainland states or regions. The lowland cultivator was part of the dominant society, even if a very insignificant part. The people who lived in the upland regions were a group for whom the administrative apparatus of the lowland state did not apply and who did not share the values of lowland society.

Yet once again caution is needed when giving a general description for the hill-valley separation was not absolute. The hill peoples of mainland Southeast Asia were outsiders in terms of the operation of everyday government, but they played an important if highly varied role throughout the region. They could supply or be a source of slaves, trade in forest products, or offer special skills such as the training of elephants. In these and other ways the upland minority groups were linked with the dominant society without becoming part of it.

The general picture that is being described and which has changed little until very recent times may seem rather strange in a modern world marked by a very considerable degree of cultural unity—the 'global village' of popular commentary. What has been described would not, however, have seemed nearly so strange to Europeans of two hundred or even one hundred years ago. For the people of the hills and mountains of Europe were long regarded, and regarded themselves, as a group apart. And this was not only the case in Europe as the record of the isolated mountain communities in the eastern United States makes clear.

The variety of minority groups in the upland regions of Southeast Asia was and is considerable. Equally considerable is the variation in their levels of development as compared with those of lowland society. In traditional Southeast Asia many of the hill people were nomadic farmers, gaining an existence through the use of slash and burn techniques—'eating the forest' in their own evocative phrase. They levelled and burnt the trees and found in the resulting ash a temporarily highly fertile site for planting crops. Others were members of essentially fixed societies, farming, with wet-rice techniques, in the high valleys but resistant to any incorporation into the life of the plains.

The ethnic and linguistic links between the people of the hills and those of the valleys were often close, even if this fact generally went unrecognised. In one important case the link was recognised by the hill people themselves. Sections of the great Tai-speaking ethnic group who remained in their mountain valleys rather than joining their linguistic cousins in the lowlands were aware of the common basic language that existed between them so that they too called themselves Tai. But such an awareness does not seem to have been a feature of other groups. The Sedang and the Bahnar hill people of the southern mountains running between Cambodia and Vietnam speak a language that, very roughly, might be described as an early version of modern Cambodian or Khmer. This fact, however, has not led to any sense of shared ethnic identity between hill people and the lowlands majority.

To a considerable extent the popular picture that has persisted for so long of an absolute separation between the upland minorities and the lowland majorities is a result of the almost absolute *social* division between the two groups. Whatever the links involving the interests of government and trade, there was a near absolute social division that was summed up in the words chosen by the dominant societies to describe the peoples of the hills. Without exception the words are pejorative, laden with disdain and emphasising the social and cultural gap that separated the two groups. Uplanders were *moi* to the Vietnamese, *phnong* to the Cambodians, and *kha* to the Laotians. The words can all be translated as 'savage' or 'barbarian', and as enshrining Rudyard Kipling's concept of a 'lesser breed without the law'.

Social division, in the very broad sense the term has in this case, may have been almost absolute, but, as already noted, it did not prevent contacts between the dominant and non-dominant groups. The hill people performed a variety of functions for the lowland societies. Who else could provide their knowledge if a lowland army wished to move across the hills and mountains to strike at any enemy? Who else could guide the slave-raiding parties from the lowlands to the most remote regions and aid in the capture of men, women, and children whose primitive society set them furthest apart from those dwelling on the plains?

These tasks were irregular, as was the employment of levies from the hills to fight as soldiers in the armies led by lowland rulers. The importance of this soldierly role may be gauged from the appearance in Cambodian folk literature of a man from the hills who is the hero of a successful battle against invaders. Other tasks were more regular. Until the French stopped the procedure, because they saw it as an example of slavery, a minority group in southwestern Cambodia had the hereditary task of supplying the Cambodian court with cardamom seeds. In return for this tribute the Pear or Por hill people were allowed to live largely undisturbed in their malaria-infested environment.

Beyond such practical tasks the link between the peoples of hill and plain could be magical. While the traditional world of Southeast Asia still retained its essential character in the eighteenth century both the Vietnamese and the Cambodian rulers accorded a special magical role to two Jarai sorcerers living in the chain of mountains lying between the two countries. These 'kings' of fire and water were sufficiently important for the Cambodian monarch to send them gifts, a procedure that seems to have been curiously parallel to his act of sending tribute to the rulers of both Thailand and Vietnam. The explanation appears to lie in terms of a belief in the great magical power of these sorcerers and of their distant link with the most sacred component of the Cambodian royal regalia, the *preah khan*. This was a famous sword that was also described as the 'lightning of Indra', the king of the Hindu gods. In more scientific terms the status attributed the two 'kings', and the tenuous links maintained between other royal families and particular groups of hill peoples might be regarded as testimony to the long-forgotten shared origins of groups that now lived in isolation from each other.

Most of the observations about upland and lowland peoples that have been made so far relate to those states of mainland Southeast

Asia in which there was a clearly dominant ethnic group, the Vietnamese in Vietnam, the Cambodians (Khmers) in Cambodia, the Thais in Thailand, and to a much lesser extent the Laotians in Laos. The picture was very different in other areas. On the mainland the situation in Burma stood in sharp contrast to its neighbours. Despite its long history, Burma has seldom been a unified

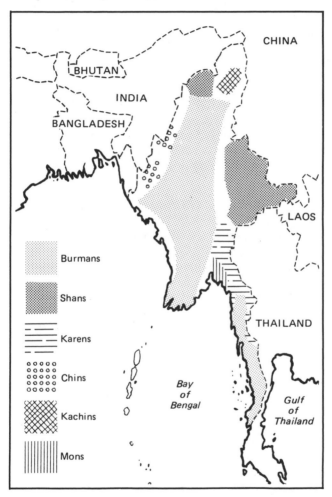

Map 4 A Simplified Ethnolinguistic Map of Burma
Among the countries of mainland Southeast Asia, Burma is distinctive because of the high proportion of ethnic minorities within its borders. More than thirty per cent of Burma's population is made up of minority groups.

state. The Burmans have dominated the major river valleys, but the populations of the upland regions that fall within the frontiers of Burma have seldom readily accepted the government the Burmans have tried to impose on them. Indeed, from the first recorded history of Burma to the present day tension between different ethnic groups has been a recurrent feature. It has been a feature because of the very considerable size of the indigenous minorities. The Shans, Kachins, Karens, and Chins, to mention only the most prominent of the non-Burman groups, make up approximately one-third of the entire population—the Shans and the Karens alone account for something like 16 per cent of Burma's total population.

Minorities of this size underline the much greater ethnic unity of Thailand, Vietnam, and Cambodia. In each of these countries the indigenous minorities are less than 20 per cent of the total population. Such a figure did not always prevent clashes between the dominant and the non-dominant groups in the past but with the preponderance so clearly established in favour of the major ethnic groups there has never been any real question as to where power lies.

The indigenous minorities in Thailand, Vietnam and Cambodia could accurately be described as outsiders. But the term takes on a different meaning in relation to Burma. There the Shans, Karens, and others were outsiders too, but outsiders who again and again showed they were able to resist any attempt by the Burmans to impose their Burman will upon them. In making this distinction there is a very necessary qualification that must be added. If in Thailand, for example, there was no question of where real power lay and which group exercised it, there was also another aspect to the upland-lowland relationship. Throughout the historical period, indeed until quite recently, lowland governments have not generally found it necessary to become involved in the day-to-day government of upland areas. Provided the populations of those areas did not act against the interests of the state then they were best left to govern themselves. Such a policy was possible in the states where the upland peoples were not seen as a threat. It was impossible, in Burman eyes, when the upland peoples posed all too clear a threat to the dream of Burmese unity.

The pattern of ethnic relationships that existed in mainland Southeast Asia in traditional times had no real parallel in the maritime regions. Although the inhabitants of the maritime world, from the Malayan Peninsula to the Philippine islands, spoke a series of languages that have a common linguistic root, the geographical character of their environment encouraged fragmentation rather than unity. The large island of Java gave scope for the development of sizeable states, such as Majapahit in the fourteenth and fifteenth centuries. Yet even Majapahit and the earlier Sumatran-based empire of Srivijaya had little ethno-linguistic unity beyond their centres. As students of Southeast Asia have repeatedly emphasised, the maritime regions of Southeast Asia have an ethnic pattern very different from the mainland. Instead of there being a general pattern of dominant majorities and non-dominant minorities, the population of the maritime world is much better seen as composed of an intricately related series of ethnic groups. Only comparatively rarely was there a situation in which one clearly defined ethnic group dominated another, minority group. Rather, territory was associated with groups of people who had a clear picture of their own identity and of their separateness from others. This was true whether one talks of the Bugis seafarers of Sulawesi, the Sundanese of West Java, or the Dyak tribesmen of the interior of Borneo. In the geographically fragmented and often environmentally difficult world of maritime Southeast Asia the establishment of large territorial states was mostly impossible and the survival of smaller states and of many tribal areas was the norm.

There were, and are, some limited instances of primitive hill populations whose level of development set them apart from the larger ethnic groups of the maritime world. These peoples, to be found in scattered groups from the Malayan Peninsula through the Indonesian Archipelago and in the Philippines islands are the descendants of some of the earliest inhabitants of the region. Always small in numbers and described as negritos by ethnologists they never represented a challenge to those other ethnic groups whose life was lived in the lowlands.

The real division in the maritime world was not between hill and valley dweller but rather between those who followed a pattern of life linked with a permanent base, whether for farming, fishing, or trading, and those who still pursued a nomadic life combining hunting and slash and burn agriculture. In the mainland world the nomadic cultivator was, of necessity, an uplander, but such was not the case in large areas of maritime Southeast Asia. Moreover, for the bulk of the nomadic groups of the traditional maritime world there was no sense on their part, or on the part of others, that they were linked to state systems of more settled peoples.

The experience of being an outsider in traditional Southeast Asian society was in general determined by ethnic and geographical factors. But there were other outsiders who need to be considered in any survey of the region. These were the men, women, and children whom European visitors so readily described as 'slaves'. There were indeed persons whose position in society in traditional Southeast Asia combined all of the deplorable features that are usually conjured up by the word 'slave'. These were persons who were in a very clear and special fashion outsiders, persons who could never share in the benefits of established society. They were the property of their owners, to be treated and disposed of as their owners pleased, with no hope of release for themselves or for their children, who were automatically slaves from the moment of their birth. Prisoners of war and the persons seized in slaving expeditions were the groups who most usually filled this role.

Beyond these persons, for whom the fact of being a slave was a harsh matter with no prospect of relief, there were other groups whom Western observers also described as slaves but who, more accurately, deserved other descriptions. Western visitors to the traditional world of Southeast Asia seldom understood the difference, for instance, between the 'true' slaves, condemned to a life of servitude, and those persons who had voluntarily, but temporarily, given up their freedom in order to meet a debt or other unfulfilled obligation. These debt bondsmen were not outsiders in a true sense, though clearly the treatment they received at the hands of their masters varied greatly from place to place and from period to period.

Perhaps more importantly for our understanding of the complex nature of traditional Southeast Asia there were other groups of persons who occupied indeterminate positions as hereditary servants of rulers or great officials. These men and women did not live outside the societies in which they performed their tasks, but they had no choices open to them; their position in life and the tasks they pursued were pre-ordained by birth.

Even the briefest review of those who were the outsiders in traditional Southeast Asia lends emphasis to the complexity of a region that began to experience a substantial impact from the West from the end of the eighteenth century onwards. Yet an awareness of that complexity should not blind an observer of Southeast Asia to the possibility of general judgements nor to the fact of there being some general themes in the history of the region. For all of the contrasts that exist between mainland and maritime Southeast Asia, between regions that have adopted Islam as a religion and those who follow Buddhism, or another religion, there are equally important unifying features to be considered.

All regions of Southeast Asia at the beginning of the eighteenth century were still dominated by a pattern of life that had altered little for many centuries. Industry, in a Western sense, was non-existent, and artisans were only a small proportion of the total population. Outside of the ranks of the rulers, their officials, and those who provided the services the elite demanded, there was little if any buffer between those who governed and the cultivator, the fisherman, and the petty trader.

This was a world that placed a high value on order, the observance of proper relationships, and the maintenance of due respect for traditional procedures. It was a world, as a result, that was also vulnerable to the efforts of those who were not Southeast Asians to change it. For the men of the West frequently did not work by the Southeast Asian rules. Even when they thought they were doing so this was seldom really the case and resultant change was often as great as if deliberate attempts had been made to introduce new ideas and techniques.

The traditional Southeast Asian world of the eighteenth century may have been one that felt it had answers to its own problems, whether these were of peace and war, the relationship of man to the universe and the gods that controlled it, or the need to find proper patterns of behaviour towards different groups inside and outside society. These were no longer the only problems that had to be answered as the West increasingly began to impinge upon the daily life of an ever-growing number of Southeast Asians. To a considerable extent the history of Southeast Asia from the beginning of the nineteenth century can be seen as a long drawn-out debate or argument, and sometimes battle, over the issue of how Southeast Asians could find answers to the problems posed by the new challenges they faced. Some of the answers were the result of a conscious search for solutions. Some of the problems have never been fully answered. Challenge, in brief, became the keynote of the nineteenth and twentieth centuries—challenge to traditional dispositions of power, to the acceptance of traditional values, and to the traditional pattern of economic life. As these challenges developed so was the traditional Southeast Asian world slowly but inexorably undermined.

5

The European Advance and Challenge

THE question of how important the European role has been in the history of Southeast Asia has been one of the great preoccupations of those who have studied the region since the Second World War. Like many scholarly debates there have been times when the real issues have been obscured by the dust of combat as advocates of particular points of view have been unready to see that theirs was not the only opinion that deserved consideration. At the heart of the controversy was the issue of what factors were really important in shaping the course of Southeast Asian history. As the debate developed most scholars came to agree that Southeast Asian factors were the most important. And it was recognised that in the past non-Southeast Asians when writing about the region had frequently been prevented from giving full weight to the Southeast Asian factors as the result of their own, usually Western, values.

Now that the dust has settled, however, there is additional general agreement that the period of European colonial activity cannot be dismissed as an unimportant episode in the broader history of Southeast Asia. What is now accepted as an important qualification to older ways of looking at the history of the region—ones that emphasised the role of Europe and so came to be called 'Eurocentric'—is that the nature of the European impact was highly varied and the force of its impact was very uneven. Recognition of these facts, combined with an awareness of the rich and important history of Southeast Asian states and their populations that form the true stuff of Southeast Asian history no matter what the period under examination, has permitted a more balanced picture of developments to emerge. And this more balanced picture certainly takes account of the European role even if in a rather different fashion than was the case thirty or even twenty years ago.

One example will make the point clear. Before the Second World War it was quite common for history books to refer to Dutch rule over the Indonesian islands as if this had been established in a firm fashion for some hundreds of years. The Dutch had arrived in Indonesia in the early seventeenth century and so, general histories often suggested, these islands had been a Dutch colony for three hundred years. The errors of such a presentation are glaring, but the erroneous simplification had wide currency. The idea of a Dutch colony established for three hundred years takes no account of the fact that large areas of modern Indonesia did not fall under Dutch colonial control until late in the nineteenth century and even later, in the present century. Moreover, the type of history that was preoccupied with the Dutch role seldom, if ever, gave any significant attention to the Indonesian role in the history of their own islands. Indonesians formed the background for Dutch action instead of being seen as vital participants in the clash between two cultures that was part of a much larger *Indonesian* history.

None of this means that Indonesian history can be written without giving attention to the role of the Dutch. They in Indonesia, as was the case for the Spaniards and Americans in the Philippines, the French in the Indochinese region, and the British in Burma and Malaya, were important participants in the historical development of the country. In some aspects of history the European role was vital in determining developments of far-reaching historical significance. The establishment of international boundaries in the Southeast Asian region was one such case. But in other aspects of life the part played by the European was much less important than it was once thought to have been. French officials in Vietnam, for instance, were often depicted in histories of that country, written before the Second World War and by their countrymen, as presiding over the implantation of French culture among the Vietnamese population. The error of such a view was most clearly revealed in the extent to which Vietnamese revolutionaries were able to strengthen their capacities to challenge the French through the promotion of literacy in the Vietnamese language. French language and culture, all French claims to the contrary, never supplanted indigenous values and the indigenous language.

As much as anything else, we are dealing here with a question of focus. The older histories of the countries in Southeast Asia tended to have a narrow focus. They looked at the parts played by European governors and officials in Southeast Asia rather than at the whole of the scene. When the focus changes from this narrow approach to a broader view the Europeans do not disappear but they assume a different place within the overall Southeast Asian world. The Europeans become only one group of the many seeking to advance their position, and a group moreover that was often notably ill-informed about the societies within which they worked.

A further example reinforces the point being made. As the eighteenth century drew to a close the Dutch had been established in Batavia (Jakarta) for nearly two hundred years. Much of Java was linked with the Dutch East India Company through trading agreements or the Dutch appointment of senior provincial officials responsible to the alien power. Yet to think of Java as a region that was 'Dutch' in any political, let alone cultural, sense would be an extravagant nonsense. Not only did Javanese cultural life continue virtually unchanged from centuries before, the Dutch colonial rulers still had remarkably little knowledge of the region over which they claimed uncertain control. Not until after the beginning of the nineteenth century did a European power in Java come to know of the existence of one of the world's great Buddhist monuments, the giant stupa of Borobodur near the central Javanese city of Yogyakarta. And this discovery was made not by the Dutch but by the British when, during the Napoleonic Wars, they played a colonial role in Java.

What, then, did the Europeans achieve as they asserted their political and economic power in Southeast Asia? The European powers became, at the most fundamental level, the paramount powers of the region. This political development was accompanied by one of the most important features of the European advance into Southeast Asia: the creation by the colonial powers of the borders that, with minor exceptions, have become those of the modern states of Southeast Asia. At the same time, the Western advance called into question old values and ways of conducting government, since the success of the European powers in gaining control served as a testimony to the inadequacies of past systems. To understand these political developments, and the shifts in power and thought that were involved, the time has come for a country by country survey of the establishment of colonial rule that ended forever the traditional world described earlier.

The Mainland States

Burma

Up to the end of the eighteenth century Burma had not been the target of major European expansion. Beset by its chronic problems of ethnic disunity over the centuries Burma in the second half of the eighteenth century seemed to have found new life under the vigorous leaders of a new dynasty, the Konbaung. Under the founder of this dynasty, Alaungpaya (reigned 1752–60) and his successors, most particularly Bodawpaya (reigned 1782–1819), Burma achieved a measure of internal unity and was able to lessen, if not entirely eliminate, the external threats posed by its neighbours. Relative success in these fields, however, only solved one set of problems facing the Burmese states. The other set of problems was posed by the slow expansion of British power into areas of northeastern India that had previously been regarded by the Burmese as falling within their sphere of influence.

Here was an almost textbook instance of a clash between alien and Southeast Asian values. Eighteenth-century Burmese rulers regarded the areas of Assam, Manipur, and Arakan lying in or to the west of modern Burma as a frontier zone in which their interests should prevail. They did not, in general, seek to maintain strict control over these regions. What was expected was that Burmese interests should be paramount and that no place should be allowed to those who might challenge those interests. Such a view was quite the reverse of that held by the officials of the British East India Company whose power was extending over an ever wider area of India. The idea of frontier zones as opposed to clearly delineated borders was foreign to them. Equally inexplicable in their eyes was a political system that allowed the rulers of Burma to claim paramountcy over these regions lying between India and Burma, on the one hand, while accepting no responsibility for the conduct of the inhabitants of this region so long as Burmese interests were not involved. If, the British argument ran, raiding parties from Assam, Manipur, or Arakan struck into territories under East India Company control, then the Burmese court was responsible and should act to prevent its 'subjects' from behaving in this way.

There was no meeting of minds. What was more, the problem of the frontier zones was not the only issue in dispute between Burma and the British. Other irritants involving differing views on the rights of British traders—or to make the point more clearly, the lack in Burmese eyes of those rights—and the appropriate level of diplomatic interchange slowly but surely poisoned relations and led to the disastrous decision by Burma's ruler, King Bagyidaw (reigned 1819–37) to confront the British by invading Bengal.

The tragic result for Burma was the British advance into Lower Burma, the capture of Rangoon, and then the imposition of the Treaty of Yandabo in 1826 that gave the East India Company control of Arakan and Tenasserim.

For more than twenty years this was the limit of the British advance and in the Burmese capital at Ava complex domestic political concerns were of greater importance than the annoying but not unbearable British presence in Arakan and Tenasserim. Once again, however, totally different views of how government and business should be conducted led to a confrontation between the Burmese and the British.

The parallel between developments in Rangoon in the early 1850s and those in Canton in the years 1839–42, when Britain fought the First Opium War, is striking. A Burmese official in Rangoon, seeing foreign merchants as interlopers, did not hesitate to seek personal enrichment through persecution of the aliens, believing, at the same time, that Burmese prestige was enhanced by this evidence of his unassailable power. His judgement proved fatally wrong as the British in India came to see events in Burma as a test of strength with significance for their role in the East as a whole. At first without authorisation but later with approval from London British troops fought the Second Burma War that led to the occupation of Lower Burma, an area of considerable agricultural and timber potential.

Once again there was a pause in the British advance. Having established themselves in Lower Burma by 1853 the British were content to wait and the Burmese court found it impossible to muster sufficient military power to evict the British or even to present a united diplomatic front as chronic domestic rivalries continued despite external danger. By the 1880s Burma had become important to Britain not only as a potential source of wealth but also as an element in Britain's rivalry with France for spheres of influence in Asia. It is far from clear how much of this was apparent to the Burmese court, its ruler and officials. For some officials British traders were still seen as providing an opportunity for personal enrichment and the humiliation of foreigners. For others in the court at Mandalay issues of protocol often seemed more important than those of power—though it should be made clear that the British just as much as the Burmese attached great importance to the question of whether or not foreigners should wear shoes in the presence of the king.

By the beginning of 1886 Britain had captured Mandalay and proclaimed control over those areas of Burma not previously occupied. Although much hard fighting took place over the next few years, often accompanied by harsh punishment of those captured by British forces, 'British Burma' had come into existence and a western border was delineated between Burma and India. What might have happened if the Burmese leadership had better under-stood the nature of the challenge they faced can never be answered. The harsh, though accurate judgement must be that the Burmese leaders as prisoners of their own view of the world were unable to see that the values to which they attached so much importance were meaningless to the British.

Vietnam

Like Burma, Vietnam came under colonial rule in a series of steps. But unlike Burma the imposition of French rule was completed in a period of twenty-five rather than nearly sixty years. And in a fashion similar to Burma, also, Vietnam's ruler and court at times behaved in a fashion that suggested there was no true understanding of the nature of the challenge presented by the French.

The search for similarities should not be carried too far, however, since Vietnam was a very different state from Burma at the time of the first invasion by French forces in the late 1850s. Quite apart from the great cultural differences between the two countries, Vietnam in the 1850s seemed set on an ever-rising path towards success. There were internal difficulties but the state was unified and expanding. Whatever the political and cultural differences between the two states, there was a shared fatal flaw in the governments of Burma and Vietnam. In neither case was there any general appreciation of the power and the determination of the European invaders.

The French saw Vietnam as a springboard for trade with China, little realising that Vietnam's geographical location next to China did not mean that any significant trade passed between one country and the other. When French forces invaded Vietnam, hoping for trade, pledged to protect Christian missionaries, and jealous of British colonial advances elsewhere, the Vietnamese court could scarcely believe what was happening. The Confucian order had not prepared the ruler and his officials for a development of this kind, despite their awareness of events in China as the Western powers imposed their presence upon the Chinese state. As a result the Vietnamese, once they found they did not have the material strength or the diplomatic capacity to chase the French from the country, adopted a policy that had little more than hope as its justification. With the French occupying a large, fertile area of southern Vietnam between 1859 and 1867, the Vietnamese in the capital at Hue hoped that the invaders would advance no further even if they did not go away.

Their hopes were notably astray. The French intended to stay and went on in the 1880s to extend their colonial possessions to include all of Vietnam. In doing so the French did more than establish a new colonial empire in the East. They played a significant part in accelerating the developing intellectual crisis in Vietnam. The

Vietnamese state at the time of the initial French invasion at the end of the 1850s was a paradoxical combination of dynamism and stagnation. Vietnam's continuing territorial advance into the lands of the western Mekong River delta was the clearest evidence of the state's persistent dynamism. But this was a dynamism that existed alongside the unreadiness of the bulk of the official class to recognise how great a threat the West could pose. A very few voices were raised to argue the existence of threat and the need for change, but until the full import of the West's challenge was revealed by the establishment of French colonial rule throughout Vietnam the conservative element remained dominant.

The geographical shape of Vietnam was not determined by the French in a fashion that was to be the case with the impact of colonial rule in other parts of Southeast Asia. In part this was so because of the long concern that Vietnamese rulers and officials had always shown to delineate their country's borders. Nor, unlike the maritime regions, was France instrumental in creating a new state where none had existed previously. But in posing a military threat and then imposing an alien colonial government the French played an important part in the destruction of the old Vietnamese order. In their subsequent unreadiness to share power with the Vietnamese and consider the possibility of independence for their colony the French did more: they set the stage for one of the most powerful revolutions in Southeast Asia's history.

Cambodia

By comparison with Burma and Vietnam, Cambodia was a minor state in the mainland Southeast Asian world. Little remained of its former greatness, so far as power was concerned, and even its great temple ruins had by the middle of the nineteenth century passed out of Cambodian control to lie within the territories of the king of Thailand. That Cambodia survived at all was a reflection of the unreadiness of the rulers of Thailand and Vietnam to push their rivalry to its ultimate conclusion. Having clashed in a series of protracted campaigns fought across Cambodian territory earlier in the nineteenth century the Thais and the Vietnamese concluded that their best interests would be served by permitting Cambodia's continued existence, in vassal relationship to both the neighbouring courts, as a buffer zone between them.

We can only speculate what might have happened if the nineteenth century had not been marked by France's advance into Vietnam and subsequently into Cambodia. Yet while it can only be speculation, the likely lines of historical development that might

9 High ranking Vietnamese mandarin
Vietnam is part of Southeast Asia, but culturally distinctively different
through the influence of China. In traditional Vietnam this Chinese
influence was visually apparent in the architecture of palaces and temples,
and in the clothing of officials such as this high ranking mandarin. *From the*
Tour du Monde *1878*

10   Vietnamese soldiers
By comparison with the rulers of other traditional states of Southeast Asia,
the Vietnamese emperors differed in maintaining a standing army. The
existence of this army, and a belief in the power of their Confucian
ideology, misled the Vietnamese rulers and their officials into thinking they
could withstand the onslaught of French colonialism. In the event, soldiers
such as those shown here were no match for the much better armed French
soldiers who gradually conquered the whole of Vietnam between 1858 and
1886. *From the* Tour du Monde *1878*

have affected Cambodia do not seem difficult to trace. Without the French advance it seems hard to think of Cambodia being left for long to play its buffer zone role. Eclipse as a state seemed—though it can never be argued in any certain fashion—the most likely fate in store for this painfully weak country.

The decision of the French in Vietnam to extend control over Cambodia beginning in the 1860s may therefore be seen as ensuring the state's survival. Not only the state's, moreover, for by treating the ruler of Cambodia in such a way that he managed to remain as the symbolic leader of the nation the French also were instrumental in boosting the prestige of the royal family and the officials associated with the court. In this their actions were in striking contrast to what happened in the two other countries already surveyed in this chapter. In Burma the British brought the monarchy to an end. In Vietnam the French undermined the authority of the royal house so that no Vietnamese emperor could ever again command the loyalty that was demanded and received in pre-colonial times. But in Cambodia as a result of both planning and the lack of it the French helped the traditional royal leadership to remain important politically.

Laos

As the British and French pursued their aims in the rest of mainland Southeast Asia, two areas remained outside the general pattern of developments. The most important of these was Thailand, the one country in the whole of Southeast Asia that was able to avoid the experience of colonial rule. The other area was that region of the mainland that has come to be known as Laos.

No such entity existed in the nineteenth century. The region that is today called Laos was composed in the mid-nineteenth century of a confusing pattern of minor states, none of them able to act in any truly independent fashion. In the traditional Southeast Asian manner these petty states were vassals of more powerful overlords; on occasion a state would have more than one suzerain.

In a very real fashion the fact that a state of Laos came into existence was the result of colonial action, more specifically colonial rivalry. As the nineteenth century drew to a close rivalry between the French and British on the mainland of Southeast Asia was intense. With the British established in Burma and the French controlling Vietnam and Cambodia, the question of where spheres of influence would lie was a matter for prolonged, and sometimes emotional, debate. Thailand both benefited and lost from such a situation. The benefits flowed from the fact that so long as Thailand remained as an independent state between the British holdings in Burma and the French holdings in Indochina the advantages of a buffer state to the two imperial rivals helped to preserve Thailand's existence. But Thailand's benefits had to be weighed against the losses that resulted from the concessions necessary to preserve the goodwill, or tolerance, of the rival European powers. So while Thailand remained free of colonial control it was at the cost of many concessions that ceded some at least of Thailand's independence to foreigners. Foreign powers were able, for instance, to gain highly advantageous trading terms in Thailand and to insist, as they had done in China, on the right of their subjects to extra-territorial privileges should they become involved in both civil and criminal legal cases.

What was possible for Thailand was denied to the Laotian states. Without unity of their own, the vassals of various overlords, and subject to increasing disorder as Chinese refugees and bandits spilled out of China into the region south of the Yunnan-Kwangsi border, the Laotian states appeared an attractive prospect for colonial advance. The opportunity was seized by the French and between 1885 and 1899, through a combination of individual audacity, great power manoeuvring, and reliance on dubious claims linked to Vietnam's past suzerainty over sections of Laos, the French established a colonial position in Laos. More clearly than anywhere else in mainland Southeast Asia this was a case of the European advance bringing into existence a new state, one that despite great political transformations has survived to the present day.

Thailand

Thailand's distinction in avoiding the experience of colonial control has already been stressed many times. Yet this success did not mean that Thailand was unaffected by the great changes that accompanied the colonial advance into the rest of Southeast Asia. Along with Vietnam, Thailand was one of the two notably successful states of mainland Southeast Asia. Unlike Vietnam, however, Thailand was able to build upon its historical success to survive without experiencing colonial rule. Many factors combined to make this possible. One of these has already been mentioned in discussion of developments in Laos—the fact that Thailand came to be seen by the rival European powers as a buffer zone between their conflicting interests. But there were other more positive reasons for the Thai achievement. Most importantly, Thailand gained advantage from the leadership of remarkable kings and officials.

The contrast between Burma and Thailand is particularly striking in this regard. Facing a new and alien threat from the British, Burma's Buddhist kings and officials found it almost impossible to appreciate the nature of the challenge, let alone to formulate a means of resisting it. In Thailand, on the other hand, inquiring minds from the king downwards were already seeking to understand the nature of European power and the scientific and technical learning that formed an essential part of that power.

King Mongkut (reigned 1851–68) was one of the most outstanding of all Thai rulers and a vitally important architect of Thailand's plans for avoidance of foreign rule. Mongkut's strategies involved positive efforts to acquire Western knowledge and diplomatic concessions that prevented an opportunity arising that could have been used by one or other of the European powers as an excuse to impose foreign rule. His approach was followed by his son and successor, King Chulalongkorn (reigned 1868–1910). Both monarchs were remarkable men and fortunate in the calibre of their senior associates whether these were other members of the royal family or officials in the Thai court.

Yet despite the great talents of Thailand's leaders the challenge of the European powers could not be evaded entirely. French determination to consolidate their colonial position in the Indochinese region led to Thailand losing control of territories along the Mekong River in the Laotian region and of the western provinces of Cambodia that had been regarded as part of Thailand for over a century. These losses of Thai territory took place around the turn of the century. A little later, in 1909, Thailand conceded control over four southern Malay states to the British. These states—Perlis, Kedah, Kelantan, and Trengganu—then became associated with the British colonial empire in the Malayan Peninsula and form part of the modern state of Malaysia.

In short, if Thailand never experienced colonial rule in the fashion of its Southeast Asian neighbours it was nonetheless very much affected by the European advance. It lost control of territory and had to make substantial concessions to foreign interests. Despite this, Thailand presented a singular contrast to the rest of Southeast Asia in the late nineteenth century. Thai leaders followed policies that revealed a remarkable capacity to gain the greatest benefit from the new and intrusive element of European power. Only in Thailand did an independent Southeast Asian state seek to gain the benefits of modern science and technology through the employment of foreign, European advisers.

The Maritime States

Indonesia

When discussing the mainland region of Southeast Asia and the challenge posed by European imperialism the time span involved for the establishment of colonial states is at most some sixty years. For Indonesia the period during which the Dutch established an empire was in excess of three hundred years. Not surprisingly, with a slow advance of this sort spread over so many years, the character of the challenge posed and the response it evoked varied tremendously. Having made this point it is as well to remember, as emphasised later in this chapter, that the major period of Dutch advance in Indonesia took place over a period of about sixteen years at the end of the nineteenth century.

The Dutch came to the Indonesian Archipelago as traders. To pursue their initial goals it was sufficient to gain control of the major ports of northern Java and the principal commercial centres of the other islands engaged in the spice trade. Slowly, however, and in a fashion that has certain distinct similarities with developments in India, the Dutch East India Company became as much a territorial power as a trading venture. When Javanese rivalries led to the collapse of the kingdom of Mataram in the eighteenth century the Dutch had already become sufficiently involved in manipulating the internal affairs of Java to be vitally interested in playing a part in overseeing the establishment of Mataram's successor states, based in the central Javanese capitals of Yogyakarta and Surakarta (Solo).

By the middle of the eighteenth century the Dutch East India Company could claim to exercise political control over most of Java. But this political control was tenuous in character and there was no accompanying impact in terms of Dutch culture or technology. There was, however, an economic impact as the Dutch, working through the Javanese elite and through Chinese tax agents, developed an ever-increasing number of ways to raise money and extract the maximum agricultural production for the Company's benefit. The burden of this economic impact fell on the peasantry. But for the peasantry as well as for the elite economic changes did not mean there were any sudden transformations of their traditional world, its values, and its hierarchy.

The same was essentially true in the limited number of areas away from Java that sustained the Dutch impact before the nineteenth century. Challenge to established relationships and systems of values were part of the history of the nineteenth and twentieth centuries as the Dutch slowly and intermittently expanded their control over the Indonesian Archipelago. This expansion was in part a response to a growing market for tropical products in Europe and in part a response to the increased activities of other foreign powers in the Southeast Asian region.

From the Dutch point of view the pressures of economic demand and foreign competition meant that it was no longer sufficient to maintain a loose control over the scattered islands, working from a limited number of bases and in association with local rulers. Instead the Dutch government in the Indies—for the Dutch East India Company had been abolished at the end of the eighteenth century—now sought to establish closer control and more uniform administration. These aims on occasion led to sharp conflict with local forces and in areas of Sumatra most particularly the Dutch had to fight for decades before they were able to achieve dominance at the end of the nineteenth century. In Bali, too, Dutch control was only achieved after bitter resistance was overcome.

By the early twentieth century the basic structure of the Dutch East Indies had been established. As the result of conquest and treaty the Dutch claimed control over all of the Archipelago stretching from Sumatra in the west to the western part of New Guinea in the east. Only the tiny Portuguese colony located in the east of Timor escaped the Dutch net. The Dutch flag now flew above a strikingly diverse series of islands in which levels of cultural development ranged from the distinctive and refined world of Java to the modern stone age still found in New Guinea. In such a diverse region of the world the impact of an alien European force had to be equally diverse, ranging from the increasing impoverishment of the peasantry in central and eastern Java to the implantation of Christianity in such sharply differing regions as the Toba highlands in Sumatra and the outer Indonesian island of Ambon.

More than all of the other changes and developments that came with Dutch rule the eventual establishment of foreign control over all of the islands of modern Indonesia brought something else. This was the possibility for the varied population groups in the Dutch East Indies to think of their common interests and a future common national identity. In more distant historical times there had been rulers who thought in terms of a *Nusantara*, an empire of the islands. As a result of foreign rule the outlines of such an empire were established, and in a clearer and firmer fashion than had ever seemed possible before. The final creation of the Indonesian Republic was the work of Indonesians. But this work was accomplished within a framework that in considerable part was laid down during the period of Dutch colonial rule.

Malaysia, Singapore and Brunei

No less than Indonesia the modern state of Malaysia finds its geographical origins in the colonial period. In traditional times the present state of Malaysia was part of the wider Indonesian-Malay world. Malay sultans ruled in states of varying size along the sea coasts of peninsular Malaya, the northern regions of the great island of Borneo and in eastern Sumatra, an island that came under Dutch control. Non-Malay peoples inhabited the hinterland of both the Peninsula and Borneo. In traditional times the areas now occupied by Malaysia formed a region of shifting power and alliances. The northern states of peninsular Malaya were linked in vassal relationships with the rulers of Thailand while the southern states of the Peninsula had ties with sultanates in areas that now form part of Indonesia.

European expansion into this region was a slow and haphazard affair. The Portuguese capture of Malacca in the early sixteenth century was not followed by any major further advance into the area of modern Malaysia until the late eighteenth century. By that time the Portuguese had been replaced by the Dutch as the rulers of Malacca and the first British settlement in the territory of modern Malaysia had been established on the island of Penang, in 1786. Settlement of Singapore followed in 1819 and by the 1830s the British had advanced to the point that they held three settlements on the fringe of the Malayan Peninsula, Singapore, Penang, and Malacca where they had now replaced the Dutch.

These settlements were not only on the fringe in a geographical sense, they also had a fringe character in terms of their relations with the Malay states of the Peninsula. The Straits Settlements, as the three British colonial bases came to be called, were *in* but not *of* the Malay world that surrounded them. In all three the population grew not so much as the result of migration by Malays, though some took place, but rather through the influx of Chinese, and later of a lesser number of Indians. Nevertheless, as the years of the nineteenth century passed, links between the British settlements and the Malay sultanates of the Peninsula grew. The southern Malay state of Johore became, in economic terms, a close partner with, if not an integral part of, Singapore. All three units of the Straits Settlements played roles as bases from which merchants and traders, tin miners and labourers gradually began to transform the economic structure of the Peninsula. To a considerable extent the usual proposition was then reversed and the flag followed trade into Malaya so that, as trade and commerce developed, Britain came first to achieve a political paramountcy in the region and then, subsequently, to build

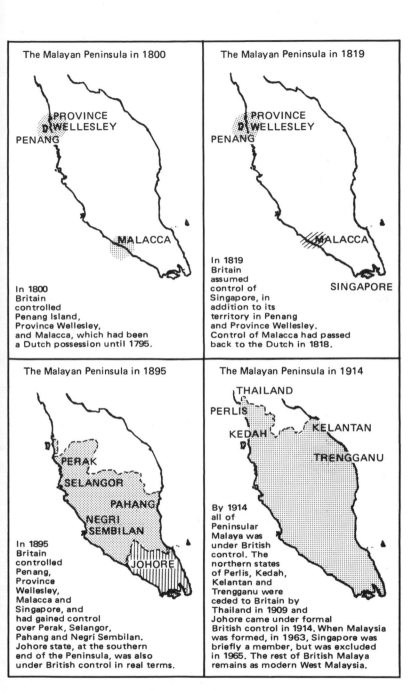

The Malayan Peninsula in 1800

PROVINCE
WELLESLEY
PENANG

MALACCA

In 1800
Britain
controlled
Penang Island,
Province Wellesley,
and Malacca, which had been
a Dutch possession until 1795.

The Malayan Peninsula in 1819

PROVINCE
WELLESLEY
PENANG

MALACCA

SINGAPORE

In 1819
Britain
assumed
control of
Singapore, in
addition to its
territory in Penang
and Province Wellesley.
Control of Malacca had passed
back to the Dutch in 1818.

The Malayan Peninsula in 1895

PERAK
SELANGOR
PAHANG
NEGRI
SEMBILAN
JOHORE

In 1895
Britain
controlled
Penang,
Province
Wellesley,
Malacca and
Singapore, and
had gained control
over Perak, Selangor,
Pahang and Negri Sembilan.
Johore state, at the southern
end of the Peninsula, was also
under British control in real terms.

The Malayan Peninsula in 1914

THAILAND
PERLIS
KEDAH
KELANTAN
TRENGGANU

By 1914
all of
Peninsular
Malaya was
under British
control. The
northern states
of Perlis, Kedah,
Kelantan and
Trengganu were
ceded to Britain by
Thailand in 1909 and
Johore came under formal
British control in 1914. When Malaysia
was formed, in 1963, Singapore was
briefly a member, but was excluded
in 1965. The rest of British Malaya
remains as modern West Malaysia.

Map 5   The Making of Modern Peninsular Malaysia

on that paramountcy to ensure direct political control of affairs.

The process that led to the final emergence of British Malaya in the first two decades of the twentieth century need not be detailed here. By the time of the First World War British control, with some degrees of variation, extended over the whole of peninsular Malaysia in addition to the Straits Settlements. Together the two political conglomerates formed an economic whole and a more or less unified political entity. But whatever had been achieved in these terms the result of colonial advance in the area of modern peninsular Malaysia had not been the achievement of unity in other terms. Chinese immigrants predominated in the Straits Settlements. In the sultanates of peninsular Malaya the Malays retained special rights as the 'people of the country' but they did so against a background of economic advance on the part of other communities, the European and the Chinese. Here was a very special result of the European advance into Southeast Asia. Britain's colonial efforts in peninsular Malaysia drew new geographical boundaries that were to become the basis of a later new state. But within those boundaries the same colonial power followed policies, for the most part without thought, that led to the creation of new problems that are still being worked out today.

The importance of the European powers in the creation of new boundaries is abundantly apparent in relation to peninsular Malaysia, but nothing could make the point more plainly than the developments that took place in Borneo, in the areas that have come to constitute East Malaysia (modern Sarawak and Sabah) and Brunei. As part of the general colonial advance of the nineteenth century Europeans considered the possibility of gaining economic and strategic advantage in northern Borneo. This was done at the cost of further diminishing the already declining power of the Brunei sultanate, which once had extensive power along the coast of Borneo and over parts of the Sulu Archipelago. In the event the areas that have now been incorporated in the modern state of Malaysia were brought under a measure of European political control by two of the most unusual colonial powers to operate in Southeast Asia, while Brunei was left as a small enclave, becoming a British protectorate in 1888.

In Sarawak the agent of colonial advance was not a government but an individual, James Brooke, the first of the 'white rajahs' about whom so much has been written. In Sabah, by contrast, the colonial power was a commercial venture, the Chartered Company of North Borneo. In each case the peculiarities of the colonial 'power' led to very distinctive developments within these two territories. Yet the fundamental thread that has linked so much of the commentary on developments in the maritime world was there nonetheless. In Sarawak and Sabah, as elsewhere, the very existence of the later post-colonial states was the partial result of the European advance. Where no comparable state had existed before and no boundary lines had been drawn, the nineteenth century, even in these two eccentric cases, witnessed the establishment of new political entities.

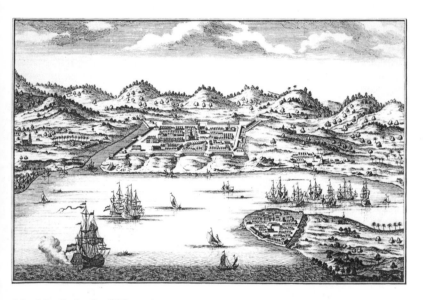

11 Manila in the 17th century
The Spanish established their colonial headquarters for the Philippines in Manila in 1571. By the mid-seventeenth century Manila, as seen in this engraving, was a substantial town. Trade was Manila's lifeblood. Silver and gold from the Americas was exchanged for goods brought to Manila from East Asia, with the commerce handled by Manila's large resident Chinese population. Power, however, was firmly in the hands of the Spanish, with the State and Catholic Church working hand-in-hand to further political control and the conversion of the population.

The Philippines

Much of what has been written in this chapter concerning the importance of the European impact in establishing the territorial boundaries of Indonesia and Malaysia applies with equal force to the Philippines. The long period of Spanish rule over these islands was vitally important in delineating the boundaries of a state where neither boundaries nor any entity equivalent to the modern Philippines existed previously. Yet just as the Dutch in Indonesia moved much more slowly than is often recognised to establish control over the whole of the modern Indonesian state, so was the Spanish achievement of control in the Philippines a slow affair. And not only slow; it was also incomplete. Although Spanish power in the Philippines was able to dominate most of the lowland areas of the northern Philippines by the middle of the eighteenth century, the highland areas remained regions apart. Moreover, the southern, Muslim areas of the Philippines never came under real Spanish control. Repeated Spanish attempts to dominate the fiercely independent sultanates of the southern regions failed. Spanish control was achieved in some major ports such as Zamboanga, but the Sultan of Sulu and his less powerful counterparts never submitted to Spanish rule. The seeds of contemporary Muslim separatism in the southern Philippines were sown long ago.

But while the Philippine's experience of the European challenge had the similarities with Indonesia and Malaysia that have just been noted, the imposition of Spanish rule provided an additional element in the history of those islands that did not exist elsewhere. This vitally important element was Catholicism. Conversion to the religion of the invading European colonial powers took place elsewhere, most particularly in Vietnam. But nowhere else in Southeast Asia did the religion of the colonialists become, in a broadly universal sense, the religion of the colonized. (Once again stress must be given to the fact that it is the northern Philippines that is being discussed.)

At a wider level one might see the implantation of Catholicism as reflecting the more general fact that Spanish rule in the Philippines gave the northern islands a new framework for society. Building upon the village structure of pre-colonial times the Spaniards created a new, non-indigenous system. To suggest that this system removed all indigenous elements from Philippine society would be an error. But it would be equally erroneous not to recognise that the administrative and economic, as well as the religious, structures instituted by the Spanish had the most profound effect.

The historical irony that marked the Philippine reaction to Spanish rule has been recorded in an earlier chapter. Filipinos became dissatisfied with Spanish rule when it became clear that the colonial power would not allow *Indios* — the non-Spanish inhabitants of the islands — to enjoy the same civil and ecclesiastical rights as the Spaniards did themselves. Yet the *Indios* who claimed these rights were the products of Spanish schools, seminaries, and universities. The Spaniards who ruled in the Philippines had created a situation with no real parallel elsewhere in Southeast Asia. Their colonial subjects began the revolt against Spanish rule in the nineteenth century because they were, in effect, excluded from being Spanish. In their resentment of the barrier placed in the way of their becoming Spanish the Filipinos established their own national identity, one that nonetheless remained inseparably linked with the experience of Spanish rule and the importance of Catholicism.

The attention given in this chapter to such administrative matters as the establishment of states' borders must be seen as only one facet of a complex whole. The colonial powers may be correctly seen as having established borders where none existed before, and their actions, whether good or bad, self-interested or altruistic played a part in shaping the new nations that were to emerge in Southeast Asia. Such developments were not, it is useful to remember, confined to one area of the world. The institution of new borders and the establishment of new nations were associated with the years of colonial rule in Africa as well as in Southeast Asia.

Beyond these administrative matters, however, other processes were at work that have only been mentioned briefly so far, but which will receive more consideration as the history of Southeast Asia is traced into more modern times. Colonial powers delineated the areas of states and played a part in shaping the character of their populations. In the final analysis, nonetheless, the indigenous inhabitants, the Southeast Asians themselves, determined how they should live and by what standards. This must be constantly remembered when the challenge and the advance of the Europeans into Southeast Asia is being considered.

6
Economic Transformation

IN the preceding chapter great emphasis was placed on the impact of the alien European colonial forces that established themselves in Southeast Asia. The advance of the colonial powers began as early as the sixteenth century, but developed most importantly during the nineteenth and twentieth centuries. And, as the previous chapter underlined, the nature of the European impact was complex and varied. It was more than this; it was also paradoxical. Southeast Asians found they were controlled by alien newcomers who were strangers to the culture and values of the region and they came, some sooner and some later, to resent this control and so to fight against it. Yet the same control that evoked resentment also played its part in establishing the political map of Southeast Asia as it exists today. The room for argument about the true importance or the true cost of European expansion into Southeast Asia is almost limitless. The kind of balance sheet that is prepared to record 'good' and 'bad' will vary from individual to individual, time to time, and most certainly nationality to nationality. What there can be no doubt about, however, is that there *was* a European impact on the societies of Southeast Asia and that this impact had enormous consequences. One of these many consequences, that has only been mentioned briefly so far, was the economic transformation of Southeast Asia.

Although Southeast Asia's economic transformation from the seventeenth century onwards involved the essential participation of its indigenous population, there is no way of avoiding the conclusion that great change took place because of decisions taken by the colonial administrations that ruled over all but one of the countries in the region. In terms of the interests of the indigenous populations, many of the changes that took place were negative and it was rare indeed that the colonial powers placed the interests of the indigenous population above their own. But whatever the motivations and the nature of the results,, Southeast Asia experienced massive economic change, particularly during the nineteenth and twentieth centuries. This chapter's concern is to provide an outline of those changes.

To fly above modern Southeast Asia on a clear day is to be struck by the great contrast between areas of land that have been brought into agricultural or mineral production and those that have not. Whether on the mainland or in the maritime regions the work of man as he has transformed the landscape stands out clearly. Vast ricefields spread about river deltas. Open-cut mining leaves bleached scars on the ground below. The repetitious patterns of rubber and oil palm plantations are clearly differentiated from the chaotic world of still uncleared jungle. It is staggering to realise how much of this landscape did not exist one hundred years ago. Rubber plantations, to take what is perhaps the most striking example, are essentially a development of the twentieth century. A relatively small number of plantations were begun in the late nineteenth century, but the great expansion of rubber-growing began in the twentieth. It took place either as the result of European investment or, when smallholder rubber grown by Southeast Asians was involved, in response to the demand of the European or American capitalist world.

The expansion of rice-growing in Southeast Asia is another example of the tremendous changes that took place from the nineteenth century onwards and owed much, though by no means all, to the onset of European colonial control. The massive efforts that transformed the Mekong River delta in southern Vietnam from a maze of swamps and undirected water courses had begun before the arrival of the French in the early 1860s. As change took place in the last two decades of the nineteenth century and the early decades of the twentieth it was still Vietnamese, for the most part, who both contributed the labour and, for a very limited few, reaped the financial benefits of the transformation that was achieved. But the fact that such vast change took place depended in considerable measure on the European control that made the draining and cultivation of the delta both possible and profitable. This same European, more particularly in this case French, control also permitted a series of social developments to take place that led to deep resentment of the economic system that emerged. For the changes in the Mekong delta region did not bring the economic enrichment of the many but of the few.

This fact points once again to the other side of Southeast Asia's economic transformation that was all too often ignored while

European powers still held sway in the region. When the term 'transformation' is used it carries with it, for many persons, the suggestion of 'progress'. Change has often in the past been seen as good in itself, particularly when it could readily be seen to involve the expansion of areas under cultivation, the introduction of new crops and plantation products, and the establishment of a new infrastructure where there was none before. Yet each of these transformations had not one effect but many. At very least it is essential in seeking to understand how Southeast Asia's economy changed so rapidly from the nineteenth century onwards to ask 'Who benefited from this transformation?'

In order to answer the question and to understand the importance of the nineteenth and twentieth centuries it is essential to realise that the economic activity that accompanied the expansion of European colonial control of Southeast Asia was very different from that of traditional times. Certainly, there was abundant economic activity in traditional Southeast Asia. The great empire of Srivijaya was a forerunner of later maritime states that sought to gain wealth through a monopoly of the sea routes and the markets. Even in such states as Angkor, where participation in external commerce was a minor part of national life, complex internal economic patterns were developed to meet the cost of maintaining and staffing the many monastic institutions that formed such a vital feature of Cambodian life. Malacca before it fell to the Portuguese in the early sixteenth century was a flourishing international entrepôt. Chinese and Japanese junks traded into the 'southern seas'. Caravans of merchants wended their way across the heart of the mainland regions and inter-island trade in the maritime world was as much a part of life in pre-colonial times as it continued to be once the European presence was established.

The prospect of becoming involved in the existing pattern of trade and of so gaining wealth was, after all, one of the single most important factors bringing the Europeans to Southeast Asia. They wanted to gain a part, the largest part indeed, in an existing spice trade that promised vast riches. That the Iberians, the Portuguese and the Spanish, wanted more need not delay us long at this stage. They wanted converts to Christianity, it is true. But this hope never excluded the possibility of gaining wealth through trade, though in the case of the Spanish in the Philippines there were sad disappointments when it was found how little opportunity existed for the development of profitable exports, in the early stages of Spanish rule at least.

For a period, in the sixteenth and seventeenth centuries, the Portuguese and then the Dutch succeeded in their aims. They gained a monopoly of the spice trade in Southeast Asia, more exactly in Indonesia, and so controlled the supply of these commodities for the European market. In doing so, however, they commenced a process of peasant impoverishment in the Indonesian world that has left its marks to the present day. The Dutch aimed at complete control of the spice trade and worked to achieve it through destruction of spice trees outside selected areas. Having begun as aliens working within an existing trading system the Dutch, through their technological and organisational superiority, then began to alter that system significantly. Whole islands that had once formed an integral part of the traditional pattern of trade were suddenly removed from participation. Even where production was still permitted, trees were destroyed to meet short-term Dutch efforts to maintain high price levels. Already Southeast Asia's economic activity was being linked to the European market economy in a way that had never existed before.

As the Dutch succeeded in controlling the spice trade in cloves and nutmeg in the eastern part of Indonesia, and the pepper trade in much of the western regions, so during the eighteenth century did they go on to exert a growing control over the production and marketing of agricultural crops in Java. Coffee, most particularly, became the object of Dutch regulation. Working through local rulers and Chinese agents, the Dutch themselves were at one remove in this process. But it was they who determined upon the system of 'forced deliveries' that required a set amount of the crop to be made available to the East India Company under threat of severe corporate punishment of villages if the goods were not forthcoming. At the same time the Dutch expectation was that the Indonesians who furnished the goods so much in demand in the European market would provide a market themselves for the manufactured goods, particularly textiles, that could be brought to Southeast Asia in Dutch ships.

It would probably be an error to suggest that Java, the Spice Islands, and the other sections of Indonesia that had become part of the Dutch colonial economic system had been plunged irretrievably into economic disaster by the beginning of the nineteenth century. Nonetheless, a pattern of economic development had been clearly established that placed the interests of the exploiting power, and its agents, above all else. And the role of the bulk of the population in this pattern was clearly, and disadvantageously, determined. Such a pattern was to be reinforced as the economy of Indonesia, and the whole of Southeast Asia, became more diverse and more closely attuned to a broad range of European interests in the nineteenth century.

The nineteenth century was the age of Europe's industrialisation. That technological revolution played a major—many would argue *the* major—part in accelerating the search for colonial possessions overseas. Colonies, in the simplest form, were seen as essential elements in the economic pattern that required the supply of raw materials to the industrial countries of Europe. Once processed these raw materials could be sold to the markets of the world, including, if possible, the colonies from which the processed materials originally came. Seen in retrospect the whole system appears quite remarkably unbalanced in Europe's favour. A Southeast Asian, in Burma, Vietnam, or the Philippines, for instance, was expected to play an uncomplaining part in a process that enriched his colonial masters but offered little reward to him or his fellows. The fact that an imbalance existed and that this did not trouble the bulk of the Europeans concerned with the colonies may be hard to believe, but it was certainly true. An essential feature of the expanding imperial age and the economic developments that went with it was a belief on the part of the Europeans involved that what they were doing was right and proper. For most of them questions of equity simply did not arise. They saw the world in different terms and thought in grandiose fashions so that a mid-nineteenth century Frenchman saw nothing unrealistic or unreasonable about the proposition that 'nations without colonies are dead'.

His observation avoids an examination of a whole range of questions, not forgetting the issue of whether or not those who were colonised wished to undergo this experience. As a statement of the kind of drives that urged men on to develop rubber estates, to exploit tin mines, and to grow copra palms, the Frenchman's view cannot be ignored. And Southeast Asia, like Africa, could supply many of the materials that became, during the nineteenth century and early twentieth century, essential to the needs of modern Europe and America. Tin from Malaysia and Indonesia could help meet the industrial nations' demand for cheap tinplate and the bearings so essential to the development of fast-running factory machinery. Rubber from Southeast Asia as a whole, but particularly from Indonesia, Malaysia, and French Indochina, could help meet the multiple needs of societies that expected constant improvement in a range of items from motor car tyres to surgical equipment. Copra from coconut palms could play a major part in the vast expansion of the soap industry as rising standards of living in Europe and America made personal cleanliness the norm rather

12   Rubber Plantation
A rubber plantation in Malaysia. The discovery that rubber could be grown profitably in much of Southeast Asia was a major factor in the modern economic transformation of the region. *Photograph courtesy of* Far Eastern Economic Review

than the exception.

Since Southeast Asia in the nineteenth century came to meet new demands from Europe it will be readily understood that a new kind of economic relationship developed between Southeast Asia and the industrial world during that century. The old system, characterised by the Dutch-monopolized spice trade, faded into unimportance as the new pattern developed. Rather than survey this pattern country by country, a more useful approach is to consider the economic changes that took place in terms of some of the principal industries, or commodities involved.

Rubber

The existence of natural rubber had been known for centuries before scientific advances in the nineteenth century permitted the development of a stable substance, largely unaffected by temperature changes, that was rapidly recognised as having a vast range of uses. The problem remained of finding a reliable source for this product since initially it was available only at high prices and in erratic quantities from South America.

Mostly as a result of British efforts, the possibility of growing rubber in Southeast Asia was discovered. Since this discovery did not take place until the last two decades of the nineteenth century it must be noted that rubber was not, in itself, one of the initial causes for the dramatic advance of European power into Southeast Asia in the second half of the nineteenth century. Other economic factors had been at work before rubber came to play its part, but once established rubber plantations became a vital justification for colonial endeavour. For in one of those notable conjunctions between supply and demand the discovery that rubber could be grown profitably in the Southeast Asian region coincided with the sudden expansion of demand of the early twentieth century that culminated in the period of the First World War.

Vast areas of the Malayan Peninsula, of Java and Sumatra, and of Vietnam and Cambodia were brought under rubber cultivation. Here was transformation indeed, for many of the areas that were planted with rubber had not been cultivated previously. Some sense of the size of developments involved is provided in even the briefest review of statistics. West Malaysia (peninsular Malaysia) had no rubber plantations—not even the exploitation of wild rubber in its various forms—before the 1880s. Yet by the beginning of the 1970s rubber plantations accounted for nearly 65 per cent of all cultivated land, with one-third of the agricultural work force engaged in the plantation industry. This is the most dramatic example of all, but it reflects a pattern that developed elsewhere, even if on a smaller scale. Where once land lay uncultivated, or covered in jungle, new plantations were established.

Such vast enterprises required large investments of capital and this fact ensured that the ownership of large-scale rubber holdings was in the hands either of foreigners or of that very small group within the indigenous community who could provide the investment capital necessary for establishing a plantation and then waiting at least five years for production to begin. Initially, therefore, the rubber industry was controlled by large investors and the benefits to Southeast Asians themselves were limited. Even in the field of labour, the employment opportunities in Malaya went to non-indigenous workers as the plantation companies imported indentured labourers from India and Ceylon (Sri Lanka). In Vietnam the bulk of the labour force was indeed Vietnamese but this guaranteed no real personal or social gain since the conditions under which plantation labour was recruited and subsequently used were the basis for repeated complaint and justifiable scandal.

Yet for all of the lack of benefit to Southeast Asians associated with the establishment of much of the rubber-growing industry, developments from the 1920s onwards redressed the balance to some degree. For it was from that decade onwards that the small-holder began to play an important part in the production of rubber. While they could never challenge the role played by the great plantations, the smallholders were able to grow rubber as part of their broader agricultural activities and to reap unexpected benefits as a result. To illustrate the point by statistics again, it has been calculated that by the end of the 1930s well over 40 per cent of the rubber being produced in Malaya and Indonesia came from small-holders. In the closing years of the 1970s the smallholders in West Malaya (the former British Malaya) had improved their share of the market to above 50 per cent. Such an advance took place against opposition from the large plantation interests. In British Malaya and even more particularly in the Dutch East Indies—the role of the smallholder was much less important in French Indochina—legislation discriminated against the small grower in favour of the large plantations. There could be few more sharply defined demonstrations of the extent to which, under the colonial regimes, the economic interests that colonial governments believed should be served were not those of the indigenous inhabitants.

Tin

Tin mining had been a part of Southeast Asia's economic life for millenia before it assumed sudden new importance in the nineteenth century with the growth of demand in Europe and America. Although deposits of tin are found elsewhere in the region, it was in Malaya (West Malaya) that the industry developed to its greatest degree. There, from the 1870s onwards, the establishment of British political control over the Malay states enabled the rapid expansion of already existing Chinese tin-mining enterprises. In the twentieth century Chinese dominance was challenged by European capital and the greater technological efficiency of the extraction methods used by the large Western firms that now sought to gain a major share of the industry. Although the Chinese share declined, this section of the industry with its reliance on labour-intensive methods was never overwhelmed by the capital-intensive Western firms which relied on the tin dredge for extraction of the metal.

In contrast to the situation that existed in the rubber-growing industry, the competition that has just been described was between two different sets of non-indigenous groups, the Europeans and the immigrant Chinese. The exploitation of tin by Chinese mining groups, with the sanction and for the partial benefit of local authorities, had been going on in Malaya for centuries. Only with the establishment of a British colonial presence in Malaya, however, did the situation favour a very considerable expansion of Chinese mining activity. The final resulting situation, before the Second World War, was that Malaya's tin-mining industry remained in the hands of groups, whether Chinese or European, who were considered outsiders by the Malays who regarded themselves as the only true owners of the country known as British Malaya.

Rice

The rubber plantations were largely dependent on imported labour. The tin industry was in the hands of non-indigenous groups. But in the development of the most important Southeast Asian export crop of all, rice, the role of the indigenous peasant was absolutely vital. This did not mean, for the most part, that the final result in terms of the peasants' interests was startlingly different from other aspects of the economic development of Southeast Asia. Unlike the plantations and the mining enterprises, however, in rice growing the Southeast Asian peasant was essential.

Rice had been exported from Southeast Asia before the onset of a full-scale colonial advance in the mid-nineteenth century. But the volume of the exports was small, and internal movement within a single country, from a rice surplus to a rice deficit area, was certainly more important than any export trade that was carried on. Moreover, rice was not generally grown for export. The bulk of the rice produced before the nineteenth century was for subsistence, to feed the peasant farmer and his family. Only if conditions were particularly favourable and yields higher than expected was a surplus available for disposal outside the growing area.

An increasing world market in the second half of the nineteenth century provided the stimulus for rapid expansion of Southeast Asia's rice-growing areas that were capable of developing export surpluses: the Mekong River delta region in southern Vietnam; the Chaophraya (Menam) River delta in central Thailand; and the Irrawaddy River delta in Burma. In Vietnam and Burma the expansion of the rice-growing industry took place within a colonial context. In Thailand, by contrast, the almost equally rapid expansion occured in an independent state. The differences between the colonial and non-colonial experience are worthy of attention.

Just as the development of large-scale rubber plantations represented a tremendous physical transformation of the countryside as well as an economic development of great importance, so too the expansion of the main rice-growing areas of Southeast Asia changed the landscape. In the deltas of the Irrawaddy, the Chaophraya, and the Mekong a bare 100 or 120 years ago rice growing took place on a sparse, scattered basis. In a real sense these were untamed frontier lands. Seen today the deltas offer a vision of immense agricultural richness and are a testimony to the millions of anonymous peasants whose labour drained the swamps, built the canals, and brought the rich soil into crop production. In the face of such evidence of agricultural richness the fact that these deltas, most particularly in Burma and Vietnam, became regions of major economic and social inequality demands an answer.

Put simply but accurately the promise of the open agricultural frontier eluded the peasantry of Burma and Vietnam because they were not equipped to supply more than their labour. To grow rice was an age-old peasant activity and one that the peasants carried out with tireless efficiency. But in the developing conditions more than labour was required. Expansion of the area under cultivation may, at first, have seemed a golden opportunity to the small peasant cultivator. As never before it appeared that there could be a chance to break the cycle that had kept the peasantry what they were—subsistence farmers living in the shadow of want. But the financial demands of the expanding rice-growing industry were beyond the peasant. Capital was required for seed, for equipment and to employ the labour necessary to ensure that the harvest was collected with a minimum of delay. With great luck an individual Burmese or Vietnamese peasant did occasionally overcome the problems involved in such a situation. In general, however, the tide ran against the small peasants' interests.

Almost from the beginning of the dramatic expansion of the rice-growing area in southern Vietnam the peasants found they had no role to play on the developing large holdings other than as tenants, at best, and as simple labourers, at worst. Interestingly enough, the hopes of individual Frenchmen that they would be able to acquire and control the great rice-growing areas of southern Vietnam proved as ill-founded as the different hopes of the peasants who sought to change their lot. The real beneficiaries of the expansion of Vietnam's rice-growing capacities, and its participation in the expanding export trade, were a relatively small number of rich Vietnamese landowners and the Chinese rice merchants and shippers of Cholon, Saigon's twin city. The Vietnamese landowners, their interests closely linked with the French colonial power, were able to command both the capital and the labour necessary to bring the previously unproductive regions into production. The Chinese merchants and shippers, who also controlled the vital rice mills in Cholon, provided an unsurpassed commercial network that no one, European or Vietnamese, could successfully challenge.

In the Burmese case the situation was a little more complicated and the eclipse of the peasant from other than a labouring role took a little longer. But the general pattern was essentially the same. One notably different element existed in Burma as the result of that country's administrative link with British India. As Britain established its colonial control over Burma, the new territories came under the general administration of India, despite the substantial cultural differences dividing the two countries. As 'part' of British India, Burma was open to virtually unrestricted immigration from India and many of these Indian immigrants were to play a major, and, most would argue, negative social role in the development of the rice-growing industry in Lower Burma. Although it is true that the availability of rural credit owed much to Indian money lenders, it is equally true that the long-term trend was one in which Indians slowly drove out the Burmese from many of the essential sections of the rice industry, including the basic role of labourer. Burmese landlords remained an important element in the overall scheme of things, but like the Vietnamese landowners who profited from the Mekong delta rice fields they were separated in almost every sense from their workers.

For both Vietnam and Burma the weaknesses and the dangers that had accompanied this economic transformation of the rice industry during colonial times were dramatically and tragically revealed in the Great Depression of the 1930s. Once the export markets of the world collapsed so were the weaknesses within the rice industry starkly revealed. Although the major landowners were able to weather the storm through reliance on accumulated savings or by drawing on reserves of capital, no such choice lay open to the labourer who suddenly found himself without funds and without work. The social costs of such a situation had immediate consequences in riots and protests. In the long term the political consequences were of a more formidable character.

In very considerable contrast to the description of events in Vietnam and Burma was the history of the rice industry in Thailand. To suggest that no peasants suffered in the expansion of rice growing in the Chaophraya delta region of Thailand would be to ignore reality. Few, if any, major economic changes take place without some human cost. Yet if there were losers in this massive development there were certainly far fewer than elsewhere and the social costs were notably smaller. Like Vietnam and Burma, Thailand in the mid-nineteenth century possessed a vast area suitable for rice growing that had not previously been developed. Unlike the other two countries that have been examined, however, exploitation of this formerly untilled area was the essential prerogative of the peasant. Just why this should have been so is not always clear, but the main reasons are not hard to find. The fact that Thailand was not a colony of an external power—whatever limitations the external powers might have succeeded in imposing on Thai freedom of action in some fields—was of cardinal importance. The Thai government was not accountable to a distant parliament, ministry, or electorate that expected its colonies to pay. Instead the control of agricultural development was in the hands of the Thai monarch and his close advisers. It was they rather than foreign commercial interests who determined the broad pattern of developments which saw the peasants retaining land ownership and the size of land holdings much more restricted than in Burma and Vietnam. The availability of capital was important in Thailand too. Once again the role played by Chinese rice millers and merchants was essential for expansion. Yet, unlike the other two expanding areas geared to the export market, the relationship between the peasants and the merchants in Thailand could be accurately described as involving a sense of partnership rather than exploitaiton.

Other Export Commodities

Rubber, tin, and rice were among the most important of the commodities exported from Southeast Asia. But there were many more that contributed to the character of the region's economy, in particular its increasing dependence on capital investment and the use of wage labour. The development of copra plantations, for instance, followed the pattern set by the rubber industry, though on a much smaller scale. A range of other crops proved suitable for plantation development including tobacco and coffee, and most importantly sugar. This last crop developed as a major export item in Java and the Philippines. Drawing on the local population for its labour supply the sugar industry played a significant part in shifting the balance of peasant labour away from subsistence farming to paid employment. In doing so the sugar-growing industry was yet another factor aiding the great economic changes of the nineteenth and twentieth centuries. The development of Southeast Asia's oil industry was less labour intensive but required very substantial capital investment. As early as the 1880s oil was being produced in Burma. Subsequently, from the second decade of the twentieth century onward, oil production was an important export commodity from the Indonesian island of Sumatra and from the territories of Sarawak and Brunei in northern Borneo.

So far the emphasis in this chapter has been on one broad aspect of the general economic transformation that took place in the nineteenth and twentieth centuries. Many other changes and developments occurred that were of great importance, including changes in the infrastructure. But there is still an important general question that arises: how widespread were the changes that were taking place? Should we imagine a situation in which, from some time in the second half of the nineteenth century, Southeast Asia was 'gripped' by economic change, so that no part of life was untouched by the kind of developments that have already been described?

Quite clearly such was not the case. In the more remote areas of the Southeast Asian world the inhabitants were largely, if not totally, unaware of the momentous changes that were occurring elsewhere. Even in less remote regions, and most particularly in the rural villages, much of life went on with only the most limited effects being felt from the economic developments associated with the expansion of Southeast Asia's export economy. Village cultural life, to take one of the most notable examples, demonstrated an extraordinary resilience to outside pressures, even when these were geographically not far distant. Increasingly, however, recent research has laid stress on the extent to which the economic transformation did reach down and affect a quite remarkably broad range of Southeast Asian life, whether this was the intention of the ruling colonial administrations or not.

The development of an export-oriented economy not only posed the possibility of an alternative to subsistence farming, it also introduced those who were prepared to engage in wage labour to the concept of a cash economy. This, for most of the rural population of Southeast Asia, was a totally new element that replaced traditional barter arrangements. The development of a cash economy went hand in hand with the slow but steady growth of a demand for consumer goods on which to spend wages. And this pattern was such as to encourage the spread of petty retail business, usually run by one or other of the two major immigrant groups in Southeast Asia, the Chinese and the Indians.

Developments of this sort were most obviously associated with areas in which the establishment of plantation industries had immediate and easily observable results. There were, however, other results that were less easily observable. To a considerable extent their existence has only come to be recognised by scholars who have been able to review the past with the benefit of accumulated knowledge and the perspective that time affords; which does not mean that Southeast Asian peasants were unable to recognise the problems in a less academic fashion at the time. It is now clear, to take one of the best-known examples, that as the economic transformation of Java took place, and as there was a simultaneous major growth in the rural population, the Indonesian peasants who lived on that island responded by a process that has been called 'agricultural involution'. Instead of seeking to escape from the increasing difficulties of rural life by migration—one of the methods adopted elsewhere—the peasant methodically set to work to grow more and more on what was, proportionately, per capita, less and less space. This effort may have been admirable in terms of the determination displayed. In terms of the social costs that it exacted it was highly negative in character. The already harsh conditions of normal existence became worse. The value of land increased to benefit not the average peasant but the moderately well-to-do rural dweller. And the downward spiral of rural poverty was followed at an increasing pace.

Developments in Java are perhaps the best known of those important changes that were taking place in the background of economic transformation but which were often misunderstood or ignored at the time. A much less well-known example, that also reflects some general developments, may be taken from the history of Cambodia. This country, in great contrast to Java, was untroubled by population pressure throughout its modern history. Yet even here, in a country that did not develop large-scale plantation industries until after the First World War, the existence of a colonial presence led to economic changes that profoundly affected the life of the rural population. The institution of new taxes, the establishment of new authorities within the village structure where none had existed before, and the requirement for men to engage in unpaid labour on the state's behalf disrupted the traditional rural scene. Only as the full impact of French policies in rural Cambodia have begun to be understood has it become possible to understand why rural discontent in Cambodia in 1915 and 1916 was sufficiently strong to involve protest action by perhaps as many as 100,000 peasants.

So change as the result of economic developments was indeed widespread, but it was also very uneven. The views of some earlier economic analysts who thought in terms of there being two separate economies—one linked to the world market and the other a closed 'native' economy—operating in Southeast Asia were incorrect. Certainly there were broad divisions within the economic life of the various countries of Southeast Asia. These broad divisions were, however, interrelated so that the life of the subsistence farmer as well as that of the wage labourer on a plantation was affected by the economic changes that were taking place.

The development of cities provides one instance of the broad impact of general economic change. In the early nineteenth century the number of cities of any size in Southeast Asia was very small. Royal capitals, such as Bangkok in Thailand, or Yogyakarta in central Java, had populations that were numbered in tens of thousands, not hundreds of thousands. Even the older colonial capitals such as Batavia (Jakarta) and Manila after centuries of an alien presence had populations of less than 200,000. Saigon, in 1820, had a population of about 180,000, but it was unquestionably the largest settlement in Vietnam, a country that the French in the 1860s accurately described as being almost entirely without cities.

The great cities of modern Southeast Asia, in short, date for the most part from the nineteenth century, in terms of their possessing a character as metropolitan centres with vital links to the wider world. Singapore, to take perhaps the most dramatic example of all, was a tiny Malay fishing settlement at the time of its foundation in 1819, probably with less than two hundred permanent inhabitants. Its rapid growth during the nineteenth century was chiefly due to immigration from China in response to a rapidly expanding economy. As *the* great entrepôt for the Southeast Asia region as a whole Singapore's development was a vivid reflection of the economic changes and developments that were taking place. It was the transshipment point for goods coming into the area and for those goods that were sent to ports in the rest of the world. And after the opening of the Suez Canal in 1869 Singapore's role as a link between Asia and Europe was strengthened as the time required for a voyage to or from Europe was sharply reduced.

Just as the growth of cities was a feature of the nineteenth century, so too was the expansion of the infrastructure, the roads, canals, and other forms of communication so essential to modern economic life. The effect of the new road and rail systems introduced in the nineteenth and twentieth centuries varied greatly from country to country. In some cases, moreover, the long-term and unplanned effect was just as important as the immediate intentions for which a particular communications artery was constructed. The case of the roads built in peninsular Malaysia is a good example of such a development.

Before the last decades of the nineteenth century almost all communication in Malaya was by water. Instead of the modern road and rail systems that carry traffic north and south, particularly on the west coast of the Peninsula, transport moved slowly on the sea and in an even more restricted fashion along the rivers that ran down from the central mountain range to the coast. The construction of a road and rail network took place to carry the growing quantities of tin and rubber that were produced as economic transformation played its part in this region. At first there was little benefit to the population in general as the result of this new communications system, for it was specifically designed to serve particular and mostly alien commercial interests. Yet with the passage of time the expanding communications system came to be important for the Malay peasantry as well, and finally to serve the interests of those peasants. Settlement patterns in Malaysia, in Vietnam, Cambodia, and elsewhere in Southeast Asia, changed to take account of the new infrastructure that developed in the nineteenth and twentieth centuries and made ease of movement an expectation for large numbers of the population. Comfort may not be the most striking feature of travel by bus or third-class train in the region, but no one who has used such transport in modern Southeast Asia can doubt the importance and relative ease of the travel that has become such an accepted feature of daily life.

There can be no room in anything less than a full-length study of Southeast Asia's economy to provide more than the briefest mention of some of the other features of the vital transformation that began in the nineteenth century. A longer examination of the economic changes would need to dwell on the development of the banking system. Space would need to be found for discussion of the contrasts of developments from country to country and region to region as well as the broad similarities that have been given emphasis in this chapter. And attention would certainly need to be paid to complex questions concerning the interplay of economic and political forces—a point that will be examined later in relation to the rise of nationalism.

From the middle of the nineteenth century onwards, the broad lines of development are clear, as is the importance of those developments. Southeast Asia in a period of less than one hundred years changed from being a region in which exports played a relatively minor role and subsistence farming was essentially dominant to a vital area in the world economy as a whole as its exports met European and American demands that had been fuelled by the changes following the industrial revolution. As Southeast Asia's export economy developed so did more general economic and social change penetrate into almost every level of society, leaving only the most remote regions and populations untouched. The growth of great metropolitan cities, the rise of exports and the development of a cash economy, the institution of new communications systems, all these are products of economic change in a period beginning a bare hundred years ago. Indeed, during the years between the mid-nineteenth century and the outbreak of the Second World War Southeast Asia's economy underwent greater change than at any other time in the region's entire history.

7
The Asian Immigrants in Southeast Asia

ALMOST anyone who visits Southeast Asia for the first time will be struck by the variety of ethnic groups encountered in any of the major cities of the region. The 'mix' of ethnic groups will vary considerably from city to city. But there is scarcely an urban centre in which a visitor will not readily recognise the wide range of differing groups that make up the city population. Sometimes the clues to the existence of differing ethnic groups will be in terms of physical appearance. Descendants of dark-skinned Tamil immigrants from southern India and Sri Lanka (Ceylon) are quickly identified as different in appearance from the descendants of immigrants from China or, indeed, northern India. At other times the fact of ethnic diversity is made apparent through the clothing worn by one set of immigrants rather than another, or in contrast to those worn by the descendants of the original inhabitants of the country in which the immigrants now live. Other indications of ethnic differences abound. The places of worship of one group are usually in stark architectural contrast to those of another. A visitor has no difficulty, in Singapore for instance, in seeing the difference between a Malay mosque, a Chinese or Indian temple, or the imported European architectural style of a Christian church, the religious symbol of yet another immigrant community.

Technically, of course, the term 'immigrant' applies only to the first generation of settlers who left their own lands to come and live in a foreign country or region. In using the term in this present chapter, an extended meaning is being given to the word. In discussing immigrant communities this chapter will focus on the important phenomenon of modern Southeast Asian history that involved those groups of settlers who established new communities that were, for generations, regarded as being in but not really part of the country in which they were located. To put the matter another way, difficult though it may be to believe in the second last decade of the twentieth century, most of the ethnic Chinese living in Malaya (peninsular Malaysia) in the 1930s were not regarded as permanent settlers. The majority of the Chinese population had not at that stage been born in Malaya and, so far as their political interests were concerned, China rather than Malaya was where these interests lay. A similar series of comments could be made about the Indian immigrant community in the same colonial situation. The majority had been born in India rather than Malaya and those in the Indian immigrant community with political interests directed these, almost exclusively, towards India.

Even the brief amount of information provided so far will alert a reader to some of the most important features of Asian immigration into Southeast Asia. The major immigrant groups involved came from China and India, though as will be made clear later in this chapter there were very considerable variations within these two broad ethnic groups. Large-scale immigration from India and China into Southeast Asia is a relatively modern development, dating from the second half of the nineteenth century in most cases. And finally, though far from exhaustively, many of those who made up the immigrant communities in Southeast Asia settled in cities or were involved in occupations linked to the commercial centres of the region.

Immigration in its various forms is as old as Southeast Asia's history, in fact older. During prehistoric times successive waves of immigrants moved southwards through mainland Southeast Asia so that the area of modern Cambodia probably experienced two major immigrant waves before the Khmer or Cambodian ethnic group established its political dominance in the fifth and sixth centuries AD. (Some scholars would argue that what was involved was the passage of new cultures rather than of people; for the moment the matter is unresolved). In the maritime regions of Southeast Asia, also, there were broad movements of population in prehistoric and early historic times. Specialists still argue about the nature and direction of these movements. Part of their significance and scale may be grasped from the fact that outposts of Indonesian culture may be found in as distant a location as the island of Madagascar lying off the east coast of Africa.

As prehistory blends into history so do we become aware of another form of migration—a much more limited and selective form of population movement than the large-scale changes that appear to have taken place, for instance, when Australoid peoples were succeeded by Indonesian peoples moving through the Southeast Asian mainland several thousands of years ago. The migration in question involved the limited but very important movement of priests and traders from India into the early states of Southeast Asia. These men, for few if any women were involved, were not part of any massive wave of population movement. Instead, by their command of specialist knowledge, they came to fill vitally important roles in the emerging Southeast Asian states and so to implant the Indian cultural contribution to Southeast Asia's historical development that was discussed earlier in this book.

In general, however, the Southeast Asian classical world does not seem to have been one marked by large-scale voluntary migration. A limited but highly important number of Indians settled in the area and made their mark. From an early time, too, there were Chinese visitors to Southeast Asia, some of whom became settlers. Writing about Cambodia at the end of the thirteenth century, but in all probability describing a situation that had existed for some hundreds of years, the Chinese diplomat Chou Ta-kuan reported on his countrymen that he saw in the Cambodian capital at Angkor. They were mostly sailors who had settled in Cambodia and become traders, marrying local women with their descendants becoming, we must presume, thoroughly absorbed within the population in a generation or two.

The advance of the ethnic Thai into the territories of modern Laos and Thailand was a major instance of migration that did take place in the latter part of the classical age. Just what was involved in this migration is a subject for the familiar controversy associated with so much of Southeast Asia's history. Did the advance of the Thai people into the fertile lowlands of Southeast Asia involve a mass movement of population? Or was the process more subtle, involving the spread of the Thai language and culture by an elite that succeeded in imposing a new, Thai identity on others?

The answer is less important for the moment than the contrast the Thai case provides with the rest of Southeast Asia. Leaving aside the forced movement of large numbers of persons from one area to another as prisoners of war, Southeast Asia by the end of the classical period was not an area in which major migrations any longer occurred. Developments involving Vietnam once again were an exception. From the achievement of independence from China in 939 AD the Vietnamese population slowly but surely moved southward into territories that had been controlled by Champa and Cambodia. This *nam-tien* (southern march, or advance) was still in progress when the French colonialists arrived in the nineteenth century. For the rest, what had begun to develop very slowly was the type of immigration Chou Ta-kuan saw at Angkor: the settlement of individuals and families in response to the opportunities

13   Singapore Malays, Chinese and Indians

Three faces of an immigrant society — Malays, Chinese and Indians in Singapore.

Singapore provides the most dramatic example of an immigrant society in Southeast Asia. Sparsely settled by less than two hundred Malays when Raffles took possession of Singapore for Britain in 1819, it is today a thriving state of more than 2½ million. Chinese compose 77 per cent of the population, Malays 15 per cent, Indians 6 per cent, and the balance of 2 per cent other races.

In these photographs, Malays are seen returning from Friday prayers, Chinese watch traditional theatre, and Indians stand by their doorway in the predominantly Indian Serangoon Road area.

these person saw in foreign lands. Some of these immigrants were quickly absorbed into the existing population. Others, most notably the communities of traders associated with a great port city such as Malacca, maintained their very sharply defined ethnic identity. At the height of Malacca's power and fame in the fifteenth century there were major communities of Chinese, Arabs, Indians of different regions, Indonesians, and Persians, to mention only some of the cosmopolitan inhabitants in the city. It is almost certain that most of these people living far from their homelands did not think of Malacca as their home. They might die or have children in Malacca, but their home remained in a distant region across the sea.

This continued to be the attitude of the great majority of non-indigenous Asian communities living in Southeast Asia until very recent times. Individual immigrants might become important within a particular state so that their descendants blended completely into what had been a new culture for their ancestor. The Thai kingdom provides such a case in which a Persian family settled in Ayuthia in the seventeenth century and rose by the nineteenth to be among the most powerful in the land. In addition there were others who did not conform to the general pattern. The Baba Chinese of Malacca were such a case in point. These descendants of immigrants lived in a special world that was half Chinese and half Malay, never completely one nor the other. But perhaps as their most distinctive characteristic they did regard themselves as permanent settlers in Malaya.

In a somewhat similar way the Chinese *mestizo* community in the Philippines, and most notably in Manila, came to be a group that sank deep roots into what had originally been an alien land. This mestizo community was already important by the eighteenth century and the descendants of the mixed alliances involving Chinese and Filipinos played a vital role in Philippine life that continues to the present day.

Yet despite these and other exceptions to the general pattern, including the refugees from Ch'ing rule in China who fled to Vietnam and settled there in the seventeenth century, the situation throughout Southeast Asia had a broadly uniform character. In the port cities and to a much lesser extent in the urban centres of the interior there were small immigrant communities engaged in commerce that was, for the most part, shunned by Southeast Asians themselves. Of these immigrant communities the Chinese were by far the most important. The range of Chinese business and financial interests were immense, but their numbers by comparison with later stages of full-scale immigration were limited. At the end of the eighteenth century the number of Chinese in and around Batavia

(Jakarta), to take an example, was about 22,000. This figure, more-over, related to one of the two major colonial cities in the whole of Southeast Asia—the other was Manila. Outside of these two cities the numbers were much smaller.

Change came in the nineteenth century, and as the result of many factors. Nowhere was the impact of Asian immigration more obvious than in the British colonial possessions that came to be known as the Straits Settlements (Penang, Malacca, and Singapore) and Malaya. And of these Singapore provides, perhaps, the most dramatic if atypical example of how Asian immigration into South-east Asia in the nineteenth century transformed the previously existing political and demographic balance.

When Thomas Stamford Raffles took possession of Singapore for the British Crown in 1819 his actions 'removed' a sparsely populated haunt of fishermen and pirates from the surrounding Malay world. He claimed a legal basis for his actions in terms of the agreements he concluded with one of the parties in a succession dispute involving the Johore sultanate, within whose territory Singapore island lay. Leaving these justifications aside, Raffles' aim of making Singapore the centre for international trade in Southeast Asia had a very immediate consequence. Manpower was needed to turn Singapore into an entrepôt and the hundred or two hundred Malay fishermen on the island were neither inclined nor sufficient in their numbers to provide this. The Chinese, and to a lesser extent Indians, were ready to do so. Singapore's census figures tell the story. Within five years of its foundation Singapore's population had risen to more than ten thousand. Malay numbers had increased so that this group exceeded four and a half thousand—a notable increase on the situation in 1819 and a figure representing more than 40 per cent of the total population. But the trend for the future was already clear in the fact that Singapore's Chinese population was already nearly 3,500 persons (over 30 per cent) where previously there had been no Chinese settlers at all.

Within twenty-five years of Singapore's foundation the Chinese in the British colony represented an absolute majority of the total population. Of the 52,000 residents in the mid-1840s, no less than 32,000, or 61 per cent, were Chinese. Descriptions of Singapore written in the mid-nineteenth century make very clear how dependent the growing settlement was on the labour and services of the immigrant Chinese. It seemed that scarcely a trade existed that was not filled by the newcomers from China. And as the years passed a growing number of immigrants became men of substance, as wealthy and even wealthier than the European businessmen who had also found excellent prospects in Singapore.

Through being a barely inhabited island Singapore was a special case in the Southeast Asian region as a whole. Nowhere else in the region experienced the same combination of commercial success and Chinese immigration that eventually formed the basis for a new state in which the descendants of ethnic Chinese were and are the dominant ethnic group. Yet if the Singapore experience must be noted as unique, this should not diminish the importance and significance of Chinese immigration elsewhere in South-East Asia in the nineteenth century. In Singapore's neighbour, peninsular Malaysia, for instance, the size of the Chinese immigration into that country during the second half of the nineteenth century and up to the beginning of the Second World War created political problems that are still acutely present today.

In the mid-nineteenth century the political map of the Malaysian—Singaporean world was very different from that known today. Britain administered its three territories of Penang, Malacca, and Singapore. But what was to become British Malaya, the Peninsula, lay outside British control. The growth of Singapore was, by the middle of the nineteenth century, playing a part in changing the British reluctance to become involved in the often complex affairs of the various Malay sultanates of the Peninsula. The sultanate of Johore, separated from Singapore by less than a mile of shallow water, was one of the first of the Malay states in the Peninsula to develop important links with Singapore. In economic, if not political, terms Johore by the middle of the nineteenth century might be described as Singapore's hinterland. Although many decades were to pass before Johore became the essential supplier of much of Singapore's fresh water and produce, this role was foreshadowed in the steady expansion of agriculture by Chinese settlers with close links to Singapore. In the middle of the nineteenth century, most particularly, Johore was a base for the production of gambier, a plant used to produce black dye, and for growing pepper.

Chinese agricultural settlement in Johore, important though it was, was much less significant than another Malayan industry that developed rapidly from the middle of the nineteenth century. From the 1850s onwards there was a rapid expansion of tin mining and for this Chinese labour and Chinese capital became vitally important. Tin had been mined in Malaya for centuries, but in an essentially limited fashion. As the Western world moved more and more quickly into the industrial age, however, the growing demand for tin changed the old pattern of limited exploitation of Malaya's vast reserves of the metal. But there was a problem: who was going to mine the tin?

Already by the 1850s the Malay sultans, their noblemen and chiefs, had recognised the value of Chinese labour and recruited Chinese workmen either directly from China or through agents in Singapore. By the 1860s, as demand for tin continued to grow, so did the number of Chinese tin miners in Malaya increase, and with them Chinese merchants and businessmen. Tin mining was not an activity that Malay peasants found attractive so that if the Malay rulers and aristocracy wanted to expand the tin-mining industry the easiest way to do this was to expand the Chinese work force.

This policy presented problems. The Chinese miners were not regarded as permanent settlers by the Malays nor did they think of themselves in these terms. Equally, the miners did not think in terms of the rulers of the Malay states as having any authority over them. Such authority as they recognised was exercised by clan associations, self-help groups, and most importantly by secret societies. This state of affairs had profound implications for Malaya, for the Chinese miners, numbering in the tens of thousands by the 1870s, became a major factor in the increasingly unsettled conditions in the Peninsula. As Malay factions in the various sultanates quarrelled over succession disputes Chinese secret societies clashed with each other over the right to exclusive mining privileges in one area or another. Not surprisingly, moreover, the disputes of the Malay aristocracy came to involve the contending Chinese groups. When to this already dangerous and unstable situation was added an increase in piracy along the coast of the Peninsula one begins to understand the point of the arguments that were increasingly heard in Singapore calling for Britain to play a part in the political affairs of the Malayan Peninsula. For the Peninsula was, by the 1860s and 1870s, an important market for commercial firms based in Singapore and Singapore was, in turn, heavily involved in the tin-mining industry.

When British involvement did take place from the mid-1870s, one of the clearly seen results was the continuing influx of Chinese workers and merchants. The new colonial presence succeeded in establishing law and order and in doing so created a more stable environment for commercial activity of all kinds. As towns grew up in Malaya they were, on the west coast of the Peninsula, over-whelmingly Chinese in character, Ipoh, Kuala Lumpur, Seremban, and dozens of other smaller settlements were centres for Chinese commerce both large and small. Yet, difficult though it may be to believe a hundred years later, the Chinese who came to Malaya in the late nineteenth and early twentieth centuries saw themselves not as immigrants who had left their homeland permanently but rather as persons who, however long the stay might be, were only temporarily living in a foreign land.

Only if this is understood is it possible to explain the nature of the Chinese community in Malaya before the Second World War and the policy, or lack of policy, of the British colonial government towards that community. As late as the 1930s the overwhelming majority of the Chinese in peninsular Malaya had either been born in China or were the children of parents born in China. The political interests of the Chinese community lay, for the most part, outside of Malaya in China itself. Rather than pursuing political activity connected with Malaya the great issue dividing the community was the clash between the Nationalist and Communist Parties in China. Living in Malaya, the bulk of the Chinese continued to think of China as their home, as a place to return to die, and as the country from which they would draw their cultural values and which would shape their political opinions.

The Second World War was to bring an abrupt end to this situation. Then, after that war had ended, the momentous changes in China that followed the victory of the Chinese Communist forces meant that the old relationship between communities of ethnic Chinese overseas and the Chinese state could never be the same again. But by the time the Second World War interrupted the apparent colonial calm of Southeast Asia the Chinese population resident in Malaya had grown to be nearly 40 per cent of the country's total population, a formidably large proportion and one that was increasingly seen as a threat by the politically conscious Malays.

Why were Chinese immigrants so important in Malaysia and, if on a smaller scale, in so many other areas of Southeast Asia? How does an historian, or any other scholar, explain the repeated success of the Chinese communities in Southeast Asia in a wide range of commercial and other undertakings?

There is a temptation, not always avoided in the past by those trying to find answers to these and similar questions, to retreat into mystifying generalisations about Chinese 'commercial skill' or the 'innate capacity' of the Chinese to succeed in business by really trying. The attraction of such answers is obvious—broad, general answers to big questions, without too much complicated analysis. A more helpful and accurate set of responses to the questions can be offered, but a warning should be given. These more accurate answers, particularly if they are explored in any depth, are complex and even difficult to understand. The study of China has always been the study of a world apart by a group of scholars whose mastery of the Chinese language sets them apart from their fellows. To some extent the same comment is true for those who study the *Nanyang* Chinese, the Chinese of the southern seas with their wide variety of dialects, and the present writer's readers should be aware that he has no specialist knowledge in this field.

The effort of explaining the success of Chinese commercial activity in Southeast Asia may be lessened by noting one vital fact that is often forgotten. A large proportion of the Chinese immigrants into Southeast Asia came, worked, and died as coolies—labourers, working for low wages and doing hard, physically demanding work. The success of the Chinese immigrants who were businessmen should not be allowed to obscure the existence of the poorly paid and often ill-treated labourers. Other Chinese immigrants worked in occupations far removed from the upper ranks of the commercial world, as market gardeners or as kitchen hands, as carpenters and as clerks. In brief, success in business and access to great wealth was not a universal feature of life for the Chinese immigrant in Southeast Asia.

For those who were successful some general and straight-forward explanations are possible. Chinese immigrants in Southeast Asia filled roles in society that others would not or could not fill. The situation in Vietnam during the period of French colonial rule makes this point clear. When the French invaded southern Vietnam in the late 1850s and then captured Saigon in 1861 they encouraged Chinese settlement because they knew that Chinese businessmen could play a commercial role for which no one else in the colony—French or Vietnamese—was equipped. What was true in Vietnam was true elsewhere. Chinese immigrants were ready and able to undertake tasks that Southeast Asians themselves either shunned or for which they lacked training and expertise.

The role of a rural shopkeeper provides a good example of the kind of position that a Chinese immigrant occupied but which was, in general, shunned by Southeast Asians themselves. The Southeast Asians, with some notable exceptions, did not regard commercial endeavour as an attractive way of life. Moreover, even to engage in the business of small-scale shopkeeping in a rural area required capital and an understanding of a cash economy. Chinese immigrants did have notable advantages here. Even if a man of ability did not possess capital of his own he could often gain access to funds through family or clan connections. And once he possessed funds his knowledge of the workings of a cash economy enabled him to become not simply a vendor of goods but in addition to engage in a broad range of business, selling on credit to farmers in return for a share of their crop and lending money. It is easy enough to see why Chinese immigrants were, on occasion, the subject of resentment. A successful shopkeeper with interests extending into the rice industry, most particularly, could become a vital and sometimes oppressive figure.

Resentment of Chinese immigrants was also felt, on occasion, because of the links they had with colonial governments. As the presence of colonial governments became more and more a matter of resentment among the peoples of Southeast Asia, so did that resentment come to encompass those Chinese immigrants, in particular, whose livelihood was closely linked with the alien, European authorities. In Indonesia, for instance, there was bitter resentment of the Chinese who acted as tax collectors and as the agents for the colonial government's opium monopoly.

Feeling against the Chinese immigrant communities in Southeast Asia was more acute in those regions where a variety of social and religious factors made any prospect of assimilating the immigrants into the existing Southeast Asian community extremely difficult, if not impossible. Only in Cambodia, Thailand, and the Philippines has there been major assimilation of Chinese into existing Southeast Asian societies. Elsewhere, with Vietnam as a partial exception, assimilation has been limited, even rare. For the Indonesian and Malaysian regions of Southeast Asia the reluctance of the Chinese immigrants to embrace Islam has been a major barrier to assimilation. In Cambodia and Thailand, by contrast, the national religion of Buddhism provided a flexible framework within which immigrant Chinese found it possible to begin the assimilation process that was then carried through by subsequent generations. The Catholic church in the Philippines may not, perhaps, be described as flexible in the same way as the Buddhist church in Thailand or Cambodia, but without Islam's dietary restrictions and with, in practice if not always in strict theory, considerable tolerance towards widely varying degrees of religious observance, Catholicism in the Philippines played a vital role in the assimilative process.

As late as the middle 1960s it was still possible to see the process of assimilation at work in Cambodia. The experience of each family had its distinctive features but the case that is described in the following paragraphs may fairly be designated as representative of a process repeated elsewhere hundreds upon thousands of times.

In the Cambodian seaport town of Kampot the important pepper trade was dominated by a few families. One of these families still, in the mid-1960s, had a founder member alive. He, now in his nineties, had come to Cambodia with his brother in the late 1880s. They were then in their early twenties and had left their native Chinese island of Hainan to settle in an area where Hainanese had begun to develop the cultivation of pepper before the end of the eighteenth century. This old man, who spoke no Cambodian, was the great-great uncle of the youngest member of the family, three generations removed from the immigrants of the 1880s. And this young man in his early twenties spoke virtually no Chinese, was legally Cambodian, spoke Cambodian as his first language, and was indistinguishable to an outside observer from the many thousands of other Cambodians whose ancestry included ethnic Chinese forebears.

To see the oldest and youngest members of the family together was to have the reality of assimilation forcefully demonstrated. An equally striking insight came in the vast shop-house that accomodated three generations. Depending on the generation involved, there were subtle clues to the balance existing between 'Chineseness' and 'Cambodianess'. Buddha images, in the Cambodian style, rested near to strips of red paper painted with Chinese characters in

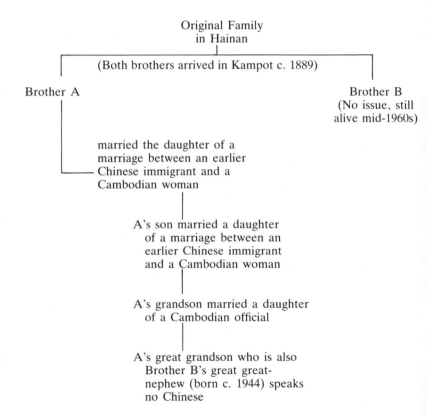

Original Family
in Hainan

(Both brothers arrived in Kampot c. 1889)

Brother A

Brother B
(No issue, still
alive mid-1960s)

married the daughter of a
marriage between an earlier
Chinese immigrant and a
Cambodian woman

A's son married a daughter
of a marriage between an
earlier Chinese immigrant
and a Cambodian woman

A's grandson married a daughter
of a Cambodian official

A's great grandson who is also
Brother B's great great-
nephew (born c. 1944) speaks
no Chinese

gold that offered the traditional wishes for health, wealth, longevity, and fecundity. Of the dwellers in the shop-house perhaps no more than half could read these characters. A glance at a simplified family tree emphasies the subtle but steady change from being Chinese to becoming Cambodian in the family just described.

Whether welcomed or resented, assimilated or kept as a community rigidly apart, the Chinese immigrants into Southeast Asia played a major role in the region's history. Their economic role was most obvious but time and again that economic role was one that had important political implications. Above all, the presence of large numbers of unassimilated Chinese in their immigrant communities was, whatever their role beforehand, transformed into a major political problem once the Second World War and the establishment of the Chinese People's Republic in 1949 meant that a return to their homeland was, for the great majority, a personal and a political impossibility.

Mention has already been made of the fact that the Chinese were far from being the only immigrant community in Southeast Asia. Some of the other immigrant communities were of minor importance in the broad history of the region, however important individual members of a particular ethnic group may have been. The scattered immigrant communities from parts of the Middle East are a case in point. Other immigrant communities were important in particular areas but not in others. In Cambodia and Laos, for instance, the French encouraged Vietnamese migration since the Vietnamese were ready to undertake the clerical duties required by the French colonial administration and engage in small-scale commerce that only very rarely attracted Cambodian or Laotian interest. Of all the immigrant communities, however, only one other ethnic group played a part in economic life that even approached that played by the Chinese. This was the overseas Indian community; a community, moreover, that, like the Chinese, can be discussed in general terms only so long as due weight is given to the great variations within it.

Although we are aware of Indian immigration in Southeast Asia dating back to the early period of written records, major Indian immigration into the region did not begin until the nineteenth century. As was the case with Chinese immigration, Indians came to Southeast Asia to fill positions that could not or would not be filled by Southeast Asians themselves. And like the Chinese who immigrated to Southeast Asia the bulk of the Indians who came to the region did so because the chances for employment appeared better than in their native land.

Although Indian immigrants established themselves throughout the Southeast Asian region, their numbers were greatest in Burma and the Malaysia—Singapore region. The reasons for this situation are readily recognised. India was administered by a British colonial government and emigration from India was mostly to other British colonial possessions. The bulk of the Indians who migrated were labourers, particularly plantation labourers. But Indian labour became important in other spheres too—in road building, and in railway work. Right up to the present day the importance of Indian labour can be readily seen in the fields just mentioned by any visitor to Malaysia.

Like the Chinese, however, Indian immigrants into Southeast Asia worked in a wide range of occupations. Some were recruited in India to occupy military and police positions that their caste or religious group had traditionally occupied in India. Others, among them the money lenders, came of their own accord to practise a profession that frequently led to resentment when local Southeast Asian peasants found themselves deeply in debt to an alien. The activities of Indian money lenders in Burma were among the reasons for the very great resentment felt by the Burmese towards the Indians, a resentment that led, after Burma's independence, to a mass expulsion of Indians from the country.

Like other immigrants into Southeast Asia in the expanding economic circumstances of the nineteenth and early twentieth centuries, there were some who prospered mightily. Indian immigrants and their first-generation descendants became successful businessmen, lawyers, and doctors. Yet while it is difficult to supply very satisfactory figures, it is quite clear that a smaller proportion of Indian immigrants into Southeast Asia rose to the towering heights of commercial success attained by some Chinese. The explanation for this difference seems fairly clear even if a great deal more research into the question still needs to be done. Indian commercial success in Southeast Asia appears to have been very much at the family level. As the result of a system of values that included reluctance to become engaged in business ventures involving joint stock operations, Indian commercial success was never so far-reaching as for the Chinese.

Asian immigration into Southeast Asia was one of the most important features of the great economic changes that took place from the middle of the nineteenth century. The immigrants provided the physical muscle, the energy, and later the finance for much of the development that took place as Southeast Asia moved firmly, if unevenly, away from the traditional past. In Singapore, where the state that ultimately emerged at independence was dominated by ethnic Chinese, and in Malaysia, where the Peninsula of Malaya came to have a population that was more than a third ethnic Chinese, the arrival and settlement of Chinese was and is of vital importance. Indian immigration into Malaya and Singapore was less numerous and correspondingly less significant. That it was, nonetheless, vitally important is beyond dispute, just as Indian immigration into Burma was of great significance also.

As has been made clear, however, immigration into Southeast Asia has not been free of problems and resentments. The point has been made several times that the immigrants filled the jobs that Southeast Asians shunned or for which they lacked the skill. This was true, but times changed and Southeast Asians came to resent the difficulty in gaining access to jobs held by immigrants or their descendants once they—the Southeast Asians—had gained the skills or training they previously lacked. At the same time, and as part of the long and often turbulent process leading up to independence, Southeast Asians often came to see the Asian immigrants in their countries as an integral part of the colonial regimes ruling over them. When, as in Burma, this perception was added to sharp resentment of the dominant economic role many Indian immigrants had attained the stage was set for reaction and retribution once independence was achieved.

There is real difficulty in ending any discussion of Asian immigration into Southeast Asia without introducing a note of tragedy. For all of the many who prospered, and continue to prosper, and despite the very special experience of Singapore, Asian immigration into Southeast Asia had always had a risk of tragedy associated with it. For the early immigrants in the nineteenth century it was the tragedy that would overtake them if they died in a foreign land. For later immigrants and their descendants there was the special and very personal tragedy of finding that they 'belonged' neither in the land of their ancestors nor, in the eyes of many Southeast Asians, in the new land where they had been born and established roots. On occasion the sense of tragedy linked to Asian immigration has become powerfully apparent in the forced deportation of Indians from Burma or the large-scale killing of Chinese in Indonesia in the 1960s when to be Chinese was to be regarded as a Communist.

The contrast between the experience of the Asian immigrants into Southeast Asia and those immigrants from Europe who travelled to America and Australia is instructive. For the European in the nineteenth century America and Australia offered many challenges, but never the challenge of established states, however weak or locked into traditional ways of life those states might have been.

The Asian immigrant by contrast was caught up in a process that led to the transformation of states. Unlike his European counterpart the Asian immigrant often found he could not become a full member of the state. The Asian immigrants were vital for the economic transformation of Southeast Asia but for the most part, with Singapore as the notable exception, they were not to be among its political masters.

8

The Years of Illusion: Southeast Asia Between the Wars, 1918—1941

FOR those who give Southeast Asia more than passing thought, the years between the First and Second World Wars present a striking paradox. On the one hand these were the years that have provided the basis for some of the most widely held views of the nature of Southeast Asia in the period of colonial rule—'British Malaya', the 'Netherlands Indies', 'French Indochina', have repeatedly been seen as being at the height of their success during these years. Our sense of Southeast Asia gained through novels and travel books, in some cases through family association, owes much to this period, so that the image of the European planter or official, his white tropical suit spotless or stained and shabby according to his personal character has become more than a figure in a Somerset Maugham short story and, instead, an historically significant and representative reflection of an age. In the same way, the 1920s and 1930s have, in the imperfectly formed image of popular memory, been seen as a period when Southeast Asians, 'natives' in the terminology of the times, were stereotypes: self-effacing and industrious peasants, faithful servants, courtly but ineffective princes, rare and occasionally heroic rebels against modern colonial rule and the virtues that went with it.

On the other hand, and here is the paradox, knowledge of the interwar period at a deeper level, that penetrates below the easy generalisations of popular literature and travellers' tales, suggests a very different world from the image still having widespread currency. For all that we may think of the 1920s and 1930s as the heydey of colonialism, a time when, with the exception of Thailand, all of the countries of Southeast Asia were under foreign European or American rule, these were years when the foundations of colonial rule in Southeast Asia were under very considerable strain. Sometimes this was recognised by those who exercised colonial rule. For others the threats to the colonial position were hardly realised.

115

Whatever the degree of awareness that was present, however, the interwar years were marked by two notably contradictory characteristics: at the very time when external powers held their most extensive presence in the region, new and essentially internal forces were beginning to operate that would help ensure the end of all the colonial regimes.

By the end of the second decade of the twentieth century Southeast Asia possessed a pattern of boundaries that has changed little up to the present. Various territorial adjustments in the early years of the century brought to an end some long-standing disputes, and colonial expansion had virtually reached its limits. On the mainland there was a British colonial government in Burma; France ruled over Vietnam, Cambodia, and the Laotian states, with the sum of these possessions being described as French Indochina; and Thailand, alone, preserved a tenuous independence. The modern states that exist in the Southeast Asian mainland have, with only limited change, inherited the boundaries observed in the colonial years. The same is true for the maritime regions, though rather more qualification is required when discussing their case. The territories of the Netherlands Indies were to become Indonesia. In the same way the boundaries of the Philippines under Spanish and then American colonial control became the boundaries of the independent Philippine state. But in modern Malaysia's case there was no single predecessor state uniting the territories that now constitute that country. Britain ruled over the Malayan Peninsula and Singapore. In Borneo, however, there were two of the more unusual examples of European control to be found in Southeast Asia. In what has become the Malaysian state of Sarawak rule by the Brooke family lasted until the Second World War. And in modern Sabah, a chartered trading company provided the apparatus of government, following in the pattern, if on a much smaller scale, of the British East India Company. Even if Sarawak and Sabah were administrative oddities, however, their links to Britain were clear and the eventual formation of an independent Malaysia between 1956 and 1963 provided another example of a modern state assuming the boundaries laid down and stabilised during the period of colonial rule.

With stable borders and the conclusion of the most terrible war in history the European powers that controlled the colonised states in Southeast Asia looked forward to a period of governmental calm and economic expansion. So far as the second of these hopes was concerned, the experience of the early 1920s seemed to match and even exceed their expectations. The economic expansion of Southeast Asia that had begun in the closing decades of the nineteenth century had transformed the region and left it ready to meet the demands of the peace-time boom that followed on the heels of the war. With Southeast Asia as a prime source for rubber, rice, and tin, the export earnings of those who controlled the plantations, mines, and paddy fields rose rapidly. Southeast Asian rubber made the tyres for a Western world that had now come increasingly to depend on motor transport. Southeast Asian tin played a vital part in manufacturing, both in end products, such as those involving tinplate, and as a component in specialist industrial equipment. The rice grown in Southeast Asian countries fed populations from India to Europe. And in this period of widespread economic expansion the other export products of Southeast Asia enjoyed a comparable expansion.

If colonial officials hoped that a period of increased economic activity would be matched by a lack of overt resentment of or reaction to their alien rule by the populations they governed, these hopes initially seemed justified. In the early 1920s calm did seem to be the general, though not absolutely complete, order of the day. Whether this calm grew out of a period of expanding economic activity is, at very least, open to argument. Just as much weight would have to be given to the proposition that it was not until the mid-1920s that modern political movements began to develop in Southeast Asia that looked beyond the basic goal of regaining independence from foreign control and towards the eventual establishment of a new state governed in accordance with new, even revolutionary political theory.

This development, so often discounted and dismissed as insignificant at the time, was what made the 1920s so important. Colonial governments had encountered resistance before. The Dutch had fought bitter colonial wars as they expanded their hold over the Indonesian islands in the nineteenth century. In Burma the so-called programme of 'pacification', pursued by the British for many years, had been a testimony to the reluctance of large numbers of the population to submit to foreign rule; while in Vietnam the record of resistance to the French was almost continuous, ebbing and flowing according to circumstances, but never absent for a significant period. Before the First World War, however, all of the movements that had resisted foreign rule in Southeast Asia had been *essentially* traditional in character.

The change from traditional resistance to modern anti-colonial challenge has usually been described as the growth of nationalism. Such a description, however accurate it may be from some points of view, is unsatisfactory as an explanation in itself because it begs a great many questions. If one talks about nationalism, what is being described? And was the rise of Southeast Asian nationalism a process similar to or significantly different from the rise of nationalism in Europe or Latin America?

Rather than giving a detailed account of the controversies that this issue has generated, a more positive approach is to look at the areas of general agreement that have been reached among those who study Southeast Asia—always accepting that there is no absolute identity of views concerning such a complex and, on occasion, emotion-charged subject. Most scholars now agree that the political movements that emerged to challenge the existing colonial order after the First World War were different, in important ways, from those that had existed in the nineteenth century. To see the fact of difference does not mean that those who sought independence from their colonial rulers in the 1920s and 1930s disregarded the more traditional opposition to colonial rule of other centuries. Rather, the modern generation of Southeast Asians who opposed colonial rule saw themselves building upon the traditions already established by their countrymen, but doing so in a way that took account of changed social, economic, and political factors.

The development of the modern Indonesian independence movement provides a particularly instructive example of an awareness of the past being joined to a new political programme that was directed both at ending colonial rule *and* towards creating a new Indonesian state. The men who emerged into prominence as advocates of Indonesian independence in the 1920s were very much aware of the efforts of the men and women who had fought against the Dutch expansion of control in such campaigns as the Java War (1825–30), the Paderi Wars in Sumatra (1820s and 1830s), and the Acheh War, again in Sumatra (1872–1908). But for a man such as Sukarno, who was to become the first President of Indonesia, the campaign waged against the Dutch had new elements that had not been dreamed of by the earlier anti-colonial leaders. First and foremost, for Sukarno and the other leaders of his generation who emerged into prominence in the 1920s, a clear link was now proclaimed between independence from foreign rule and the establishment of a new Indonesian *nation* where none had previously existed. This new nation, incorporating all of the peoples and territories ruled over by the Dutch, was acknowledged to be a diverse entity—the Indonesian national motto is 'Unity in Diversity'—but it was to be united by more than a rejection of colonialism. Unity was to be forged through an acceptance of new political values, some from Indonesia's own past, some from Europe, where the ferment of the nineteenth century had brought forth a host of new political theories and immense practical change in the disposition of actual political power.

In a loose but accurate sense, the new nationalism that emerged in Indonesia and elsewhere in Southeast Asia did combine the old and the new, something of the values of the West as well as the values of Southeast Asia itself. Nationalism asserted that populations and territories ruled as colonial possessions had their own independent right to existence, to the pursuit of national goals that were the preserve of one particular group of peoples living in one particular area. The colonial powers, unsurprisingly in terms of the values of the times, opposed these demands for basic change in political control. Moreover, the obstacles that lay in the way of achieving the nationalists' goals often seemed formidable and frequently led the colonial administrators to dismiss the force of the new movements. For the nationalists themselves, a faith in their ideals enabled them to believe that political power could be gained and that apparently unfavourable and even impossible odds would be overcome.

Still the question remains: why did the growth of this new national spirit take place in the 1920s and 1930s and not before? Some historians would reject the basis for this question, preferring to stress the way that old forms of anti-colonial resistance were transformed into new nationalist efforts. For most observers, however, there not only seems to have been a significant difference between traditional and more modern anti-colonial movements. There also seem to be some readily identifiable explanations for why change came when it did. Central to most explanations is the fact of *awareness*. By the 1920s, and increasingly thereafter, there was a new sense of awareness among an ever-growing number of Southeast Asians that the colonial relationship that dominated their lives was not beyond question but, rather, open to challenge. In a country such as Vietnam, where a sense of national identity had a long history, the sense of awareness was particularly marked by an embrace of new political theories that were seen as offering a programme for ending their country's colonial status. In other countries, perhaps most particularly Indonesia, where a new sense of national identity developed very much as a consequence of the colonial experience, it may be argued that it was this awakening of a national awareness, more than the adoption of one rather than another political theory, that was most important. Throughout Southeast Asia, including Thailand which never experienced a formal colonial relationship, the twenties and thirties saw an awakening of interest concerning the nature and purpose of government.

In stressing the growth of this sense of awareness with all of the different paths that were followed by the new nationalist leaders in the different countries of the region, attention is again focused on Southeast Asia's role as a receiver and adaptor of external theories and concepts. Political ideas relating to Socialism, Communism, Democracy, and a host of other theories and concepts, did not develop in Southeast Asia, however much these theories came to be used and adapted. And here, moving beyond the global explanation of awareness, the importance of the 1920s and 1930s is more readily understood.

Europe achieved its modern political configuration—the delineation of state boundaries and the consolidation of national units—in the eighteenth and nineteenth centuries. This process was accompanied and followed by an outpouring of writing on political theory. By the early twentieth century the debates that continue today were already joined between those in favour of revolutionary solutions to political problems and issues and those who sought a variety of evolutionary approaches. Not surprisingly, Southeast Asians who had become dissatisfied with their colonial status looked to the great body of Western political thought to see whether it contained answers to their political dilemmas.

It was an unsurprising decision since one of the results of the major political changes that took place in Europe in the nineteenth and early twentieth centuries was the growth of a body of opinion—never particularly large but always significant—that insisted that opportunities for education should be extended to the populations in the colonised states. With education, for a few at least, came the opportunity to read of the momentous political changes that had taken place in Europe and of the political forces that had brought those changes. No exaggeration is involved when it is observed that once a significant number of Southeast Asians were exposed to Western education the development of a new nationalist spirit received one of its most powerful boosts. Moreover, education and changing administrative and social patterns led, by the beginning of the twentieth century, to the development of a new and significant class, the intelligentsia. Although arguments may be developed to suggest that such a class had long existed in Vietnam, both in that country and elsewhere in the Southeast Asian region the new class that now emerged was distinguished from its predecessors or precursors by a political as well as an intellectual commitment. For the first time there was a significant group of educated Southeast Asians who questioned the position of their rulers—the colonial powers—in terms of political theory, and who were able to see themselves as part of a wider intellectual community concerned

14 Ho Chi Minh
Ho Chi Minh was one of the most remarkable of the Southeast Asian
revolutionaries who challenged colonial rule. Living as an exile from
Vietnam for thirty years of his life, he embraced Communism in the belief
that it would provide the revolutionary philosophy that would drive the
French from his country. *Photograph courtesy of* Far Eastern Economic
Review

to debate, discuss and act in the hope of attaining their nationalist
goals.

Exposure to Western education and through it to new political
concepts took many forms. For some the exposure came in a formal
sense, through schooling and study, sometimes culminating in years
spent in Europe. For others an understanding of Western political
ideas came through less formal, but no less important, contacts with
the West. The careers of Mohammad Hatta of Indonesia and Ho
Chi Minh of Vietnam provide examples of the very different ways
that Southeast Asians came to know Western political theories and
to see in them a way to end colonial rule in their countries. Hatta,
seen by the Dutch as a model Indonesian student, spent nearly ten

years of his early adult life studying economics in Holland. He was an outstanding student. He was also a man who increasingly found it impossible to reconcile the political ideas that prevailed in Holland with those existing in Indonesia. When he returned to Indonesia in 1932 his advocacy of independence for his countrymen led to his imprisonment by the Dutch colonial authorities, an imprisonment that lasted until his release by the Japanese during the Second World War.

Ho Chi Minh's acquaintance with the West came in a very different fashion. Unlike Hatta, Ho was never seen as a model student by the French. Instead he was the troublesome son of a minor official who had refused to cooperate with the colonial government. He left Vietnam at an early age to work as a member of a ship's crew and found his way to Europe and to a changing series of low-paid jobs in London and Paris. It was in Paris that he slowly became acquainted with the revolutionary literature of those who had adopted Marx, Engels, and Lenin as their guides to political philosophy and action. Convinced as he became that Communism offered the answer to the problems of the world, and most particularly those of colonised peoples, Ho became one of the founder members of the French Communist Party. This fateful step was to lead him along an extraordinary path of personal hardship, imprisonment, and eventual partial triumph in his battle against French rule in Vietnam.

For those in the colonised regions of Southeast Asia who came to learn of the nature of government in the West, whether through personal experience or from books and the accounts of their fellow countrymen, the most striking realisation was how contradictory were the patterns of life and behaviour that applied in Europe and the United States and those that applied in the colonies. In this regard a well-known saying about the British in India could equally be applied to the Europeans and Americans who lived their lives in Southeast Asia in the 1920s and 1930s. All Englishmen, the saying went, were *sahibs* east of the Suez Canal. The very fact of being a white man, in other words, transformed individuals who in their own countries might have been of very humble status into 'lords'. There is abundant evidence to show the ease with which Europeans in the colonies of Southeast Asia readily slipped into a pattern that presumed their moral elevation above the 'native' masses and ensured their conditions of existence were fitting to such an elevated status. Dutchmen and Englishmen, to take two examples, found no more difficulty in regarding themselves as *tuans* (*tuan* is the word for 'lord' or 'master' in Indonesian and Malay) than did their counterparts in India. This was a situation that more and more came to cause resentment. And this resentment was further fuelled by the growing realisation that the economic benefits of the colonies accrued overwhelmingly to the distant metropolitan states and to the alien members of the colonial community and those who had joined their interests to them. Awareness of the inequities of colonialism was, for the bulk of those active in the developing nationalist movements, increasingly focused on these two features: the social and political dominance of the alien colonists over the indigenous population and the economic dominance of those colonists.

When the obvious link between the various colonial political systems and the economic situation in the colonies was discerned, thoughtful Southeast Asian nationalists asked whether Western political and economic theory might offer an answer to the problems they confronted. There should be no surprise that for some an apparent answer to the problem of how to gain independence was seen in Communism. More than sixty years after the event it is difficult to sense the profound international concern and excitement that accompanied the 1917 Communist Revolution in Russia. What was seen by the conservative politicians of the West as a terrible illustration of what could happen if too much power fell into the hands of the workers was, of course, viewed very differently by underprivileged and disadvantaged groups throughout the world. For some men and women in Asia—not just in Southeast Asia—the Russian Revolution offered not merely the spectacle of a corrupt, authoritarian monarchy being overthrown by a political group that acted in the name of the workers of Russia. It was seen as an event that signalled much more: the imminence of revolution throughout the world, but most particularly in their own colonised situation.

How inaccurate that view was is apparent many years later. For some Southeast Asians, however, the promise of independence through Communist revolution seemed very real in the 1920s and 1930s. The force and appeal of the revolutionary philosophy of Communism in Vietnam provides the best known example. But Communism had an important following in Indonesia and played a small but significant role in the Philippines also. In British Malaya Communist organisers were active in the Chinese community, but developments in that colony were very different from elsewhere in the Southeast Asian region. The Chinese community in British Malaya in the 1920s and 1930s still saw its interests as inextricably linked with the Chinese homeland. Since this was so, those who supported Communism did so not in terms of challenging British authority but rather in terms of raising funds and providing support for their Communist countrymen in China.

Why was it then that only in Vietnam did a Communist party emerge as the leader of a nationalist independence movement? There is no simple answer to this question, but an attempt to provide *some* of the answers has much to tell us about the development of modern Southeast Asia. Of all the countries of Southeast Asia only Vietnam and Indonesia were forced to fight a protracted war in order to achieve independence from their colonial rulers. These wars, fought after the Second World War had ended, may be seen as a reflection of the determination of France and Holland to try and maintain their colonial empires at a time when other European powers had accepted that the age of colonies either was passing or had passed. The wars of independence fought in Vietnam and Indonesia after the Second World War may also be regarded as the logical extension of the situation that had existed in those countries during the 1920s and 1930s. For in both Indonesia and Vietnam the colonial governments had made very clear their position that independence was simply not a possibility that would be considered for the Indonesians and the Vietnamese despite the growing and insistent demands that independence should be granted.

But what was different about the Vietnamese experience when it is compared with the events in Indonesia? Why did the Communists become the leaders of the nationalist resistance to the French while in Indonesia the Communist Party was only one of the various groups that combined to form the anti-Dutch nationalist movement? Part of the answer may be given in terms of leadership and personalities. The leaders of the small but determined Vietnamese Communist Party were men of exceptional talent. There were able and dedicated Indonesian Communists also, but the talent of non Communist Indonesian nationalist leaders was at least equal to that of their Communist allies. Another contrast between the Vietnamese and Indonesian situations lay in the nature of their respective colonial regimes. Both the French and the Dutch colonial regimes were repressive, but it is arguable that the repression in Vietnam was fiercer than in Indonesia. Although the Dutch did not hesitate to exile such men was Sukarno, Hatta, and Sjahrir, and to imprison hundreds of other less eminent nationalists, it seems correct to note that repression in Indonesia was never so complete as in Vietnam under the French.

To argue that because of the severe political repression that operated in Vietnam only the Communist Party could survive and eventually succeed because of its clandestine nature and organisational capacities would fall far short of a satisfactory explanation. Repression in Vietnam during the 1920s and 1930s did eliminate or render impotent other political groupings. And the Vietnamese Communist Party was aided in its efforts to survive by its secret character—a bitter complaint of the French security services was of their failure to penetrate the inner ranks of the party's leadership. But there was more to the party's slow progress to power than this. For the party leaders and their followers Communism seemed to provide both a political theory and a programme for action that was particularly appropriate for the conditions that existed in Vietnam,

5   President Sukarno
President Sukarno was the first leader of independent Indonesia. Active as a revolutionary from the 1920s, Sukarno was a man of remarkable talents mixed with personal weaknesses. Between 1946 and 1965 Sukarno dominated Indonesian domestic politics and played a prominent role in international affairs. *Photograph by Derek Davies courtesy of* Far Eastern Economic Review

where the colonial economic system seemed to fit quite remarkably well into the exploitative pattern described in the writings of Marx and even more particularly Lenin. Nonetheless, it is as well to remember that, although the Communists had established themselves as the leading nationalist group in Vietnam by the end of the 1930s, they were still far from being in a position to seize power.

The Indonesian nationalist opponents of the Dutch were not close to power either, at the end of the 1930s. But if they shared this experience with the Vietnamese, there was much else that was profoundly different. The Vietnamese Communists had emerged as the leading political force in a country that had a long tradition of national identity and in which the old absolutist values of a Confucian society had first been under threat and then shown to be inadequate to meeting the challenges of colonialism and the changing nature of the modern world. By contrast, the development of a sense of Indonesian identity was essentially a modern phenomenon in a society marked by all manner of pluralist tendencies. Moreover, if it is possible by simplifying greatly to speak of twentieth century Communist political theory and practice filling the void left by the collapse of traditional Confucian values in Vietnam, no such parallel could be found in Indonesia. As Indonesian nationalists formulated their plans for the future they did so in a situation in which traditional cultural values and both traditional and modern religious values had not proved to be failures. A Vietnamese might mourn the passing of a society in which Confucian values had had their place but he had to seek something to replace them, most particularly because even those who regretted the passing of the old order would usually admit its inadequacies. Most Indonesians, on the other hand, did not see their varied and rich cultural heritage or their Islamic religion as the cause of Dutch colonialism or as the reason for the failure of their countrymen to expel the Dutch. Instead, and not even excluding the Communists so far as cultural values were concerned, Indonesia's nationalists drew strength from their heritage and saw it as having at least as much importance as Western political theory.

Consider Sukarno. He embodied so many of the characteristics of his countrymen, and particularly of his fellow Javanese, that one begins to understand why a man who could be seen by unsympathetic outside observers as a caricature was, to his fellow Indonesians, a reassuring figure in whom an almost endless range of personal, cultural, and political traits were harmoniously combined. Sukarno's defence of his nationalist position when the Dutch put him on trial in 1930 is a remarkable testimony not only to his energy in reading a vast and varied range of political writings but also to his readiness to look for a path to Indonesian independence incorporating the widest scope of ideas on the state and its character. In Indonesia, for the most part, those who opposed the Dutch did not feel the need for an absolute set of political principles of the kind associated with Communism. Nationalism in Indonesia accommodated a range of political beliefs rather than becoming, as in Vietnam, a movement that was, essentially, synonymous with Communism.

The very considerable contrasts between Indonesia and Vietnam serve as a timely reminder of the slow progress of Communism elsewhere in Southeast Asia. In Thailand, for instance, the gradual transformation of the traditional Thai state that owed so much to the energies of two remarkable kings, Mongkut (1851—68) and Chulalongkorn (1868—1910), reached its culmination in the 'Revolution' of 1932. This 'Revolution' did indeed represent a major change in the system of governing Thailand, for from that date onward the Thai king was to occupy the position of a constitutional monarch rather than to be, in theory at least, an absolute ruler. The aims of the 'revolutionaries' who insisted on this new state of affairs—they were mostly younger men in the civil service and military, many with experience abroad—were far removed from Communism. Instead, with the various European models as guides to follow, they looked for a means to end a situation in which the nature of the Thai political system depended so much upon one man, the king. What followed the 1932 'Revolution' in Thailand could hardly be described as the implementation of democracy. It was, however, an important shift in power and this shift was sufficient to meet the interests of those who, in the late 1920s, had feared that the ruler, King Prajadhipok, would not take account of the political aspirations of those outside his tight royal circle. The political changes that took place in Thailand, however, were achieved within a society in which a prevailing sense of unity about the throne and within the Buddhist religion provided a basis for stability very different from some other parts of Southeast Asia.

The limited success of Communism elsewhere in Southeast Asia need not, however, be seen only in terms of the capacity of some nationalists to achieve change peacefully while others sought change through violent means. Just as the monarchy and the Buddhist religion were a unifying factor in Thailand, so were other 'models' seen as offering alternative answers to the dilemmas of the emerging nationalists. Long before the success of the 1917 Russian Revolution, Southeast Asians had been struck by the success of the Japanese in challenging and defeating the power of Tsarist Russia in the Russo-Japanese War of 1905. In a similar way the Chinese Revolution of 1911 presented an example of revolutionaries in an Asian country successfully achieving great political changes. For some the success of the Japanese state and of the Chinese revolutionaries were models to be followed closely. For others the success had a more general importance. Japan's defeat of Russia showed that Asians could triumph over Europeans just as the Chinese Revolution showed that major political change could be achieved by those seeking to institute revolutionary goals even in the most traditional of circumstances.

Beyond these general examples provided by particular events, there were longer-term influences that played a significant role in stimulating the development of nationalist policies and which might also be seen as having provided alternative rallying points to Communism. To write in these terms is not to suggest that the role of Islam in Indonesia and Malaysia, or of Buddhism in Burma, during the 1920s and 1930s was something consciously developed in opposition to the challenge of Communism. Rather, the existence of Islamic and Buddhist movements in these countries meant that there were already important rallying points about which nationalist thought could develop *before* consideration was ever given to the possibility of finding an answer to the problems of a colonial existence through the adoption of Communism as a guide for both theory and action.

More than usual difficulty attaches to writing about the history of religious movements in Southeast Asia. Religious experience is such a personal matter that an historian often finds it hard to do much more than emphasise the barest outlines of developments. Accepting that this difficulty exists, it is nonetheless possible for an outsider to sense something of the force and impact of the Islamic movements that were important in Indonesia and Malaya during the first four decades of the twentieth century and to see their significance for the development of nationalist politics. Islam, particularly Reformed Islam that stressed the basic teachings of the Koran, gave an impetus to the growing awareness of community felt by certain groups in Indonesia. Finding spiritual comfort and support from their religion these Indonesian followers of Islam also found that shared belief formed a basis for shared political and economic aims. The first truly important national organisation in Indonesia was the Sarekat Islam, established in 1912, originally an association of Indonesian *batik* cloth merchants who first came together in 1908 (with a slightly different name) to advance their interests in the face of competition from Chinese dealers and who found a basis for unity in a shared religious faith. For many Indonesians who joined

Sarekat Islam in its early, essentially economic phase, and for others who through the 1920s and 1930s associated themselves with one or other of the various Islamic organisations that emerged in those years, their religion became more than a statement of personal faith and belief. The fact of being a follower of Islam became a political statement as well. To be a follower of Islam was to be identified with all the other members of an Indonesian community whose interests were separate from, and indeed opposed to, both the Dutch with their political power and the Chinese merchants who controlled so much commerce in the islands.

In Malaya from the beginning of the twentieth century Islam played a similar, if less significant, role in emphasising the common interests of followers of this faith throughout the Peninsula. Although those who had experienced the impact of Reformed Islam, often in the course of study in the Middle East, argued for its importance in efforts to bring a social renovation to Malaya, religious organisations did not have the same impact in the slowly developing course of Malay (*not* Malayan) politics in the 1920s and 1930s. In the face of British Malaya's development as a multi-racial society in which there were major Chinese and Indian immigrant communities, adherence to Islam was only one of the factors that made up the sharply increasing sense of Malay identity that set politically conscious Malays apart from the Chinese and Indians. The realities of economic life as much as membership of the Islamic faith spurred men to find some way of matching a sense of Malay identity to the need for gaining some significant share of economic progress. Nonetheless, if Islamic movements did not have the same impact in Malaya in the 1920s and 1930s as was the case in Indonesia, they may perhaps be judged to have had a longer-term effect than was realised at the time. In contemporary Malaysia, with Malay political dominance apparently firmly established, Islam plays a major role as a factor unifying the differing political and social interests within the Malay community.

Among those for whom nationalist politics were important in Burma during the years between the World Wars, Buddhism provided a central rallying point. While it would be misleading to paint a picture of Burma in the 1920s and 1930s that suggested the level of agitation for independence from colonial rule was of the same order as that found in Vietnam or Indonesia, there was an active nationalist movement and no account of it could neglect the Buddhist element present. Buddhism not only was seen as setting Burmans apart from alien non-Buddhists, including non-Buddhist Asians such as the Indians who had flocked to Burma once British colonial rule was established; the religion also provided an administrative framework for the nationalists to spread their ideas. Propaganda in favour of independence could be circulated within the monkhood and anti-colonial strategy could be discussed at Buddhist councils. Just as was the case for dedicated followers of Islam in Indonesia, the Burmese Buddhist activists found in their religion an affirmation of national identity as well as a basis for spiritual comfort.

So far in this chapter the overwhelming emphasis has been on the emergence of nationalist movements in Vietnam and Indonesia with only a limited amount of attention paid to developments in other parts of Southeast Asia. The reason for this apparently lopsided approach is very simple. In the rest of Southeast Asia the nature of nationalist movements was either very different from those found in Vietnam and Indonesia, or, as was the case in some countries, nationalist movements simply did not exist in any significant fashion. Cambodia and the Laotian states in the 1920s and 1930s could accurately be described as barely affected by nationalist activity before the Second World War. In both these countries, in very considerable contrast to Vietnam, the other French colony in Indochina, traditional society and the traditional ruling class were preserved under the control of a French administration. French rule brought changes to Cambodia and Laos, but these were not of a kind to bring forth the nationalist reaction found elsewhere.

Consider the contrast between Cambodia and Indonesia. In the former the real impact of French colonialism was not felt until the beginning of the twentieth century. The King of Cambodia continued to reign and to remain for the overwhelming majority of his subjects the almost divine centre of their world. Western ideas and Western education had only barely penetrated Cambodia before the Second World War, and the impact of the French-controlled colonial economy had little clear effect on the bulk of the population. In Indonesia things were very different. Although much of what was traditional in Indonesian society survived in the 1920s and 1930s, the impact of the Dutch colonial regime, particularly in Java, was profoundly greater than the French impact in Cambodia. It was certainly the case that royal courts also remained important in Indonesia in the inter-war period, but whatever their significance the alternative focus of a modern outward-looking city existed in Batavia (modern Jakarta). Western education had had an impact in Indonesia by the end of the 1930s that was of an order that simply could not be compared with the situation in Cambodia where by 1939 fewer than a dozen Cambodians had completed the equivalent of a French secondary school education.

Cambodia, Laos, and to some extent Malaya, showed the degree to which an alliance of interest between members of the traditional ruling class and the colonial power could act to inhibit the development of nationalist activity. The alliance involved did not just relate to personal concerns such as a measure of power and wealth. In the political and social climate of the 1920s and 1930s it was possible for Cambodian and Laotian kings and princes, and for Malay sultans, to feel that their countrymen were benefiting from the operation of the colonial system. Who else but the French, a Cambodian prince might well have argued, would ensure that the Vietnamese did not expand to subjugate Cambodia? Who else but the British, in the view of Malay royalty, could be relied upon to bolster Malay interests in the face of the energetic and resourceful economic competition of the Chinese?

The Philippines presents a very different case. Like parts of Indonesia the Philippines, particularly the northern islands of the country, had experienced a long-term colonial impact. Of all the countries of Southeast Asia the Philippines can lay claim to having developed the earliest modern nationalist movement, for the attempted revolution against Spain at the beginning of the twentieth century possessed distinctly modern characteristics in its aims. Nonetheless, the Philippines remained in a colonial relationship with the United States until the end of the 1930s with remarkably little manifestation of nationalist resentment of this position. The explanation for this state of affairs may be found in the following two broad sets of facts. On the one hand the United States government, however much some of its citizens may have acted like the colonisers of other nations, made clear from the start of its rule over the Philippines its firm intention to grant independence to the country. There were periods of hesitation as to eventual timing and the policy was pursued with greater and lesser enthusiasm by various individuals. But the basic commitment to granting independence was always there. On the other hand the Philippine elite, the group most likely to furnish the nucleus of a nationalist movement should there have been any doubt as to the eventual intentions of the United States, not only believed that independence would come, but just as importantly found that their personal economic interests were served perfectly well by the system that evolved under American control. Once again, though in very different circumstances from those existing in Cambodia and Laos, there was an alliance of interest.

To what extent, throughout the Southeast Asian region, did the prospect of independence for the colonised countries seem near or far towards the end of the 1930s? Not only does the answer to this question vary from country to country, but equally obviously the answer varies whether one looks at the problem from the point of view of Southeast Asians or colonisers. From some points of view it is, perhaps, easier to attempt to recreate the assessments of the colonisers rather than the Southeast Asians, though even in this case the fact of very considerable variation from colony to colony and from individual to individual must be stressed.

One of the chief factors that helped to convince many Europeans that the age of colonial rule still had many years to run was the nature of the challenges that were mounted against colonial governments during the years between the two world wars. With the exception of a period of sustained Communist-led resistance to French rule in Vietnam in 1930−1, all of the other challenges that were posed to colonial governments were essentially short-term in character and relatively easily overcome. Not only that, the various challenges that did emerge, including the Communist-led risings against Dutch rule in the Netherlands Indies, had a sufficient number of traditional overtones, sometimes including reliance on magic and adherence to millenarian expectations, for the colonial powers to dismiss them as having little modern political, let alone nationalist, significance. The Saya San rising in Burma in 1930−1 appears to have been stimulated in part by economic conditions that owed their existence to the fact of British colonial rule over Burma. But although the British-controlled administration became the target for Saya San's followers, they tried to achieve a traditional aim through traditional methods. The former Buddhist monk, Saya San, was to be installed as a new 'king' of Burma by peasants who were ready to confront the firearms of the police with antique weaponry and a belief in magic amulets that would protect them from bullets.

The protesters against Dutch rule who followed the lead of second-echelon Communist activists in Java and Sumatra in 1926 and 1927, and briefly succeeded in convincing the colonial authorities that there might indeed be a serious threat to Dutch control, were only a little more attuned to the realities of the modern world. As in Burma the case can be convincingly made that colonial rule had brought about the general conditions that had led to a sense of distress and disorientation being felt by sections of the Indonesian population. But the hopes held for the success of these risings in Java and Sumatra by the followers, if not the leaders, were far removed from the expectations of those thoughtful nationalists who recognised that eventual independence would entail costs as well as benefits. Men such as Hatta, Sukarno, and Sjahrir thought about the theory and practice of government of the new state that would be instituted after independence. The participants in the 1926–7 risings in Indonesia thought of the abolition of all taxes, of free taxi rides in the urban areas, and of Kemal Attaturk, the reforming Turkish dictator, suddenly appearing in Indonesia to lead the movement for independence after descending from a great aircraft.

These developments in Indonesia and Burma, as well as such affairs as the rare instances of Malay protest against British administration in Malaya and the Sakdalist peasant movement in the Philippines in the 1930s, could not be seen by the alien colonial administrators as posing any true threat to their rule, however troublesome such events might be at the time. The same observation could not be made about the Communist challenge to French rule in Vietnam in 1930–1 that has come to be known as the Nghe-Tinh Soviets. For nearly a year French control over sections of two provinces in north-central Vietnam was resisted by adherents of the Vietnamese Communist Party who succeeded for a time in setting up their own soviet-style administration. Only after the French Foreign Legion was sent to the area and given an almost completely free hand to subdue this challenge to French authority by any means, including the routine execution of nine out of ten prisoners, were the Nghe-Tinh Soviets brought to an end. Even in this instance there were some French officials who fell prey to their own propaganda, choosing to believe that the challenge that had confronted them was more reflective of the supposed 'debased' character of 'Asiatics' than of any true spirit of nationalism or a desire for the establishment of a more modern society.

Despite the unwillingness of colonial officials to believe that early independence was a real possibility for the populations of the various colonised regions of Southeast Asia, the 1930s seem, nonetheless, to have been a period of considerable unease or at least uncertainty for these alien administrators. For all of the insistence of a man such as Governor General de Jonge in the Netherlands Indies that the Dutch would still be ruling over their colonial subjects for another three hundred years, there were other more hesitant estimates about the future. In British Malaya the remarkable failure of the colonial administration to think about the future was slowly changing by the end of the 1930s, and with this change came the first tentative thoughts about possible independence at some undefined date. In Burma the British administration, conscious of developments in nearby India and confronting a slowly increasing demand for an end to the colonial regime from Burmese nationalist groups, was also no longer able to pretend that independence was not an eventual possibility. Nonetheless, no clear timetable for independence had been considered. In the countries of French Indochina attitudes towards the future were very different according to location. In Cambodia and Laos the French saw little to suggest that nationalism would undermine their rule. Vietnam, however, was a different matter. Opinions vary on the extent to which there was a French awareness of the size and force of the Communist-led opposition to their rule. Possibly, in a brief survey, no better summary can be provided than the observation that there were significant sections of the French colonial administration in Vietnam—most notably the security services—and certainly a range of individuals who doubted the public official stance that French rule in Vietnam was likely to last for the indefinite future.

Only in the Philippines, with little if any serious consideration being given to the possibility of Japan's armed expansion southwards, were the 1930s a time when Southeast Asian politicians could look forward confidently to an independent future and plan and bargain for that future with the colonial power. Unlike the other colonial administrations in Southeast Asia, the United States officials in the Philippines in the 1930s were working within a structure that had accepted the inevitability of independence.

The other side of the story is more difficult to describe. In particular it is hard for an outsider to strike a balance between an awareness of the burning conviction that drove Southeast Asian nationalists on towards their goal of independence and the effect upon their aims of the often tremendous obstacles placed in their way by the colonial authorities. How close to independence and national emancipation could the Indonesian political prisoners languishing in exile feel during the 1930s? And what were the inner estimations of Vietnamese held in the jails and prison colonies of Indochina? Despite the memoirs that some of these prisoners have published after their release there must be real uncertainty as to their actual judgements of the likely progress of efforts to achieve freedom from colonial rule. Whatever doubts or difficulties of judgement remain, however, the fact of these nationalists' conviction in the rightness of their cause and in the eventual inevitability of their success must be recorded. They may have been uncertain about the speed with which they would obtain their goals, but they never doubted their ultimate attainment of success.

The suggestion has already been made that the 1920s, and more particularly the 1930s, were years of uncertainty. There was uncertainty of various kinds, political, social, and economic, and this atmosphere of doubt and indecision must be remembered when the inter-war years are considered and put against the still wide-spread picture of the period before the outbreak of the Second World War being a time of colonial calm and untroubled European dominance. To the extent that uncertainty did reign, this state of affairs might help to explain why so many Southeast Asian nationalists could look to the future with confidence even if the colonial powers still appeared to have a monopoly of physical power.

Southeast Asia did not escape the effects of the Great Depression that burst upon the Western industrialised world at the beginning of the 1930s. The dramatic slow-down of the economies of the Western nations had an equally dramatic effect on the countries of Southeast Asia with their export industries that were so dependent on Western demand. The Great Depression may often be thought of in terms of Wall Street brokers plunging to their deaths as the market collapsed, or of men, both skilled and unskilled, forming huge dole queues in the cities of the industrialised world. But it should also be thought of as a time when the markets for tin, and rubber, and rice collapsed so that the export economies of Southeast Asia were temporarily crippled and employment opportunities for hundreds of thousands of Southeast Asians were eclipsed.

Political uncertainty and economic difficulty were not the only deeply unsettling factors at work in Southeast Asia before the Second World War. The problem of overpopulation in certain areas of Southeast Asia, notably in Java and in parts of Vietnam, was already apparent. And with overpopulation came the threat of famine. Eye-witness accounts of areas of north-central Vietnam at a time of famine in the early 1930s still make harrowing reading today. Skeletal figures fought each other for a handful of potatoes in the provinces of Nghe-An and Ha-Tinh when famine ravaged that area in 1930.

Social inequalities had been sharpened by the period of colonial rule and an awareness of this situation was a further cause for unease and uncertainty. Southeast Asian nationalists were not only aware of the dominance of their alien rulers in economic matters, they were aware also of the growing inequalities that existed between the small numbers of their own countrymen who did profit from the presence of colonial rule and the vast mass that did not. Convincing arguments have been put forward, moreover, to suggest that at least some of the public signs of discontent that emerged in parts of Southeast Asia in the inter-war years were a reflection of the sense of frustration that existed among sections of the population which believed they were prevented from participating in an economic advancement that was rightfully theirs.

The changes that took place during the 1920s and 1930s are not always easy to summarise. Nor were these changes always recognised as taking place either by the people of Southeast Asia or by the outsiders from Europe or America who had come to live in and rule over the region. But changes of very great importance did take place. The growth of nationalism may have been unequal throughout the region, but however uneven the subsequent events of the war years themselves were to show that in every colonised country of Southeast Asia the force of nationalism was such that in no case was it possible to put back the clock, to return to how things had been before the war began.

The population of Southeast Asia was, by the end of the 1930s, one that knew more of the outside world, of the extent to which the colonial powers depended on their distant possessions for prosperity, and of the inequalities present in a colonial situation. To write in these terms should not be regarded as meaning that we should have a view of *all* Southeast Asians straining for independence and poised for revolution just before the Second World War began. Quite clearly this was not the case. But the numbers of Southeast Asians who had come to believe change must take place had grown substantially. And even among those, such as the peasantry, for whom modern political issues remained outside their knowledge, an awareness that change had occurred was present. The slow but important extension of education, the expansion of the modern economic sector into wider and wider areas of each country, the dim but definite awareness of developments elsewhere in the world, whether the momentous events taking place in China or the constitutional developments in India, all of these and many others were factors making for change or the desire for change.

How much of this was clear to the colonisers as they reviewed their position over a 'sundowner' at the end of the day may remain a matter of debate. Did the Dutchman with his 'genever' or the Englishman with his whisky and soda sense what was happening, sitting in his club or on his bungalow verandah as the sharp tropical change from day to night took place? Perhaps only a perceptive minority ever did. For the others, who believed change was far away, the illusion of continuity blinded them to the great changes that had taken place in just over twenty years.

9
The Second World War in Southeast Asia

DURING the years between the First and Second World Wars men could still believe that colonial rule in most of the countries of Southeast Asia had an unlimited future. An independent Philippines was not regarded as too far distant, it is true, and Thailand, of course, had retained its independence. But for the rest of Southeast Asia, including Burma where there was inconclusive discussion about future self-government, the future, for the colonial administrations at least, was charted in terms of their continuing, alien rule. Even for the most optimistic and dedicated of Southeast Asian nationalists, at the end of the 1930s, there could be little expectation of a sudden disappearance of the colonial powers. Only when this general state of affairs is appreciated can we begin to sense why it was that the Second World War had such a shattering impact on Southeast Asia, on Southeast Asians, and on the colonial administrators who served in the region. The Japanese invasion of Southeast Asia transformed the region and its politics and the years between 1941 and 1945 must be judged as among the most momentous in modern Southeast Asia's history.

Why then has so relatively little been written about this period? Although the military history of the war in the Pacific and Southeast Asia has received considerable attention, persual of any bibliography will emphasise how limited has been the attention given to the war years themselves as opposed to the events in the immediate post-war phase. One answer to this question, for scholars who studied Southeast Asia in the years immediately after the Second World War, is that the period posed such great psychological and political dilemmas that most historians preferred to avoid too close an examination of a painful episode. In a fashion that may be difficult to grasp in the late twentieth century, the populations of countries fighting against Germany and Japan during the Second World War believed with virtually no reservations that their cause

137

was a just one. The doubts expressed about policy in the Korean War and the massive dissent sparked by the war in Vietnam in the 1960s simply had no counterpart in the Second World War. It is necessary to understand this to see why historians should have found it difficult to face the complex facts of the war years; to come to terms with the welcome that some Southeast Asians gave to the Japanese invaders; to deal with the fact that the Japanese interregnum in Southeast Asia provided a vital boost for Southeast Asian nationalist movements.

As memories of the Second World War have faded, so have problems of the kind just noted been lessened. Other problems have, however, remained. The sources that need to be consulted for a detailed history of any part of Southeast Asia during the Second World War are formidable in their volume, in the complexity of the issues they raise and in the linguistic abilities they demand. The result has been a few outstanding studies of the war years with much left unstudied or treated in a superficial fashion. This present chapter must of necessity be superficial too, but it seeks within its limited space to allot due importance to the impact of the 1941−5 period in Southeast Asia.

More important than anything else, the Second World War in Southeast Asia marked a point of no return. Impossible though it may have been for politicians in Europe, such as Winston Churchill and Charles de Gaulle, to accept, the events of the wartime years meant that the old pattern of European colonial dominance could never again be re-established. For the Japanese invasion was not just a military event, or series of events, of notable proportions. It was a political bombshell that shattered some of the most significant presuppositions of the past. The Japanese advance into Southeast Asia gave telling emphasis to the argument that nationalists in the region had been advancing for years—the colonial powers and their representatives in Southeast Asia could be defeated by Asians. And not only defeated. Following their defeat the white-skinned aliens could be toppled from their privileged position in society to become no better off than the coolies who had laboured to maintain the fabric of colonial society in the years of peace. Probably it is impossible to place too much emphasis on the importance of this radical transformation of relationships within the societies of Southeast Asia. Even for those Southeast Asians who had no strong nationalist leanings the fact that the myth of European superiority could be demolished almost overnight was of the greatest importance. The world of Southeast Asia could never be the same again.

16   War in a Malayan Rubber Plantation
Rubber made Malaya a major strategic prize for the Japanese. Rubber
plantations were also the locations for some of the bitterest battles between
the advancing Japanese and the defending British and allied forces. In this
photograph the smoke of battle rises over a Malayan rubber plantation as
the Japanese fought their way south towards Singapore, at a speed that
surprised and shocked the British commanders. *Photograph courtesy of the
Australian War Memorial negative no. 11485*

Even the briefest recital of the principal events of the Japanese
advance stresses the extent to which humiliation upon humiliation
was heaped upon the colonial powers. The Japanese entry into the
countries of French Indochina was followed by the establishment of

an understanding between the French authorities and the Japanese army that was unique for the Southeast Asian region. The French were allowed to retain control of the apparatus of government in return for permitting the Japanese to use French Indochinese territory as a staging, training and supply area. This was never the "victory" claimed by the French Governor-General, Decoux. On the contrary it provided an assurance to the nationalist forces, in Vietnam most particularly, that hopes for independence rested on a firmer base than might have been hoped for only a few years before. While the French flag continued to fly in Vietnam, Laos, and Cambodia, the politically conscious members of the population were well aware that the French administration only functioned at the will of the Japanese.

17   Australian troops preparing to defend the northern approach to Singapore.
By the time the Japanese were approaching the southern tip of Malaya, in Johore, the fate of Singapore was sealed. British defence planning had assumed that an attack on Singapore would come from the open sea, to the south. Instead, the Japanese advanced from the north, across the Johore Straits and bypassing the Causeway linking Johore and Singapore, which is here seen as Australian troops prepared to make their final defence against the rapidly advancing enemy. *Photograph courtesy of the Australian War Memorial negative no. 12449*

The conquest of Malaya and Singapore in 1942 involved an even greater humiliation. Years of planning neglect and a staggering unreadiness on the part of British service chiefs to face up to the reality of Japanese military power led to a debacle of the most staggering kind. The Japanese, it had been confidently asserted in the 1930s, could not become adequate pilots because of an alleged national disposition to weak eyesight. But their pilots not only inflicted the dramatic attack against the American Pacific Fleet in Pearl Harbour. They also, in the British Malaya and Singapore context, sunk the naval ships that might have helped to achieve some readjustment of the balance of forces that pitched jungle-wise Japanese soldiers against ill-trained and badly led British and Commonwealth troops. The Japanese, it was said, could not conquer the Malayan Peninsula since British forces could control the main roads and passage through the jungle would be impossible. More than forty years after the event one can still see the pathetically inadequate pill boxes that were placed beside the north-south roads

18   Death and destruction in Singapore
Well before the Japanese captured Singapore, in February 1942, the largely Chinese civilian population suffered heavy casualties from bombing. In this photograph, two Chinese women react to the cost of the bombing in terms of lives and destruction. Once the Japanese entered Singapore they wreaked a savage retribution on those local Chinese whom they believed were hostile to them. *Photograph courtesy of the Australian War Memorial negative no. 11529/22*

on the eastern coast of peninsular Malaysia in the expectation that the Japanese army could not advance through the jungle. But, of course, this was what the invaders did with skill and efficiency until they had the overcrowded island of Singapore, the population swollen with refugees, the main water supply from Malaya cut off, at their mercy. Singapore fell on 15 February 1942.

After the defeat of the British in Malaya and Singapore it was the turn of the Dutch to face defeat in Indonesia. The Battle of the Java Sea, at the end of February 1942, ensured the capitulation of the Dutch and allied forces in Java and the subsequent surrender of Dutch forces in nearly all of Indonesia by the end of March. In a little more than three months, therefore, Japan was in military control of the countries of French Indochina, the British possessions in Malaya, Singapore, and Borneo, and almost all of the Netherlands East Indies (Indonesia). Thailand retained its independence at the cost of permitting the Japanese the right to move troops through its territory. Unlike the French administration in Indochina, however, the Thai Government could not be said to have held office at the pleasure of the Japanese, no matter how much there was a need to take account of Japanese interests. Only Burma and the Philippines had still not come under something approaching full Japanese military control as March 1942 came to an end.

The end of resistance to the Japanese offensive in these last two countries was not long delayed. Bitter fighting by American and Philippine forces delayed a Japanese victory in the Philippines until the first half of May 1942. And in Burma fighting dragged on into July as British, Indian, and Chinese troops fought to escape, not to hold ground against the advancing Japanese army. The speed of these events, with the greater part of Southeast Asia falling to the Japanese in less than six months of fighting, had never been expected by the colonial powers and had amazed the Japanese themselves who had anticipated more effective resistance. With the old colonial masters removed and their prestige tarnished beyond repair, the people in much of Southeast Asia found that they now had new colonial masters, Asians this time it was true but in other ways occupying just the same sort of position as those they had just defeated. Leaving aside independent Thailand, and the curious state of affairs that prevailed in Vietnam, Cambodia, and Laos, the rest of Southeast Asia saw one alien sovereignty removed to make way for the implantation of another.

In only one of the countries of the region that had witnessed the defeat of a colonial power had there been any effort on the part of nationalists to associate themselves with the Japanese military effort. This was in Burma where the advancing Japanese forces were accompanied by members of the Burma Independence Army (BIA). Numbering barely a thousand members when the Japanese invasion of southern Burma began in January 1942, its numbers grew as the Japanese advance moved steadily onwards. But even at the end of the Burma campaign, when the BIA claimed a membership approaching 30,000, the Japanese gave no sign of alloting the BIA's leaders any real power. In Burma, as elsewhere, Japan saw its interests as supreme and rapidly revealed the hollowness of earlier propaganda couched in terms of an 'Asian Co-Prosperity Sphere' and of 'Asia for the Asians'.

The fact that the Japanese did fill a role that was in many ways not greatly different from that of the colonial powers that it had displaced must not blind us to the differences that existed nor to the extent to which, particularly early in the period of the Japanese interregnum, there was much that the Japanese did and said that was welcomed by Southeast Asians. The Japanese wreaked savage vengeance on thousands of ethnic Chinese in Malaya and Singapore, whom they saw not only as bitter opponents who could not be trusted for the future but also as supporters of the Chinese armies that continued to fight against their brothers-in-arms in China itself. But their treatment of the Malay population was very different as they tried initially to gain the support of this portion of the population of Malaya through careful respect for the Malay sultans and their courts and by placing Malays in positions of prominence, if not power, in the administration that was established to replace the British colonial regime.

In Indonesia the overthrow of the Dutch colonial regime led to the release of the Indonesian nationalists who had languished in colonial prisons, some of them for a decade or more, and this event, as well as the defeat of the former colonial power, led many Indonesians to be well disposed towards the Japanese. Some, such as Sukarno and Hatta, decided to pursue their goal of true Indonesian independence by working with the Japanese. This decision, which involved both the practical judgement that such action was the most effective way to prepare for independence and a readiness to co-operate with those who had defeated the Dutch, was to bedevil relations between the Indonesian nationalists and the Dutch government when the war ended. Instead of recognising that Indonesians could not have been expected to sympathise with the Dutch in their defeat, strong voices in Holland argued at the Second World War's end that men such as Hatta and Sukarno should be regarded as 'collaborators' with the hated Japanese enemy.

There could be no meeting of minds when this post-war clash took place. In part this was so because, with the rarest exceptions, the defeated Dutch simply had no appreciation of the complex and in many ways subtle relationship that developed between the Indonesians and the Japanese during the course of the Second World War. Hailed by many Indonesians as liberators, the Japanese soon came to be seen as another alien power—only this time it was Asians rather than Europeans who ruled. Despite the fact that the Japanese showed very quickly that it was their interests which were paramount, Indonesians during the Japanese occupation were able to involve themselves in a far greater degree of political organisation that had ever been possible under Dutch rule. This was one of the single most important aspects of the Japanese occupation of Indonesia. Nationalist leaders could organise, establish chains of command, and, with the sympathetic acquiescence of some Japanese commanders, advance their nationalist aims through broadcasts in favour of independence.

Japanese military men controlled the various efforts made to develop support for their country's war effort, but for the Indonesians who participated in military training, in Islamic organisations, or in youth groups, the fact of foreign control was far less important than the opportunity to demonstrate their Indonesian identity. The Indonesian national flag, banned from use by the Dutch, could be flown and songs of independence sung. These were symbolic changes, but no less important because of that. The reinforcement of a sense of Indonesian national identity that transcended local, religious, and class interests was an essential accompaniment to such practical matters as the development of an administrative framework and the organisation, both clandestinely and overtly, of a military organisation.

The Japanese occupation provided another important symbolic guide for Indonesians, particularly for Indonesian youth. Throughout much of Indonesia, and most notably in Java, Indonesian cultural values laid great emphasis upon deference and saw ideal behaviour as non-demonstrative and lacking in aggression. Now, the victorious Japanese offered a radically different model to follow, one that involved an admiration for force and accepted that violence could not only be necessary but also desirable. Nothing could have been further apart than the ideals enshrined in Japanese military tradition and those associated with the measured calm of traditional Javanese life. Yet because of this contrast young Indonesians began to question the values of their elders, asking whether it would not have been better in the past to have responded aggressively to Dutch colonialism rather than acquiescing to it and so accepting its

existence. The young Indonesians who found themselves question-
ing the values of their elders did not accept the contrary values of
the Japanese in any total sense. They did, however, see some
aspects of Japanese behaviour that had relevance to their own
position. And in seeing these they came to feel themselves a
separate generation, most particularly separate from those older
men who had acquiesced to Dutch rule in the 1920s and 1930s and
who under the Japanese occupation were prepared to work un-
questioningly with the new rulers.

A readiness to work with the Japanese was a feature of the
wartime years elsewhere in Southeast Asia. This did not mean,
however, that the aims of those who cooperated with the Japanese
were the same from country to country, or from group to group
within each country. The Indonesians who were viewed critically by
their young compatriots were very different from those who worked
with the Japanese as part of a conscious plan to bring about
Indonesia's independence. The Malays and members of the various
Indian communities who worked with the Japanese in what had
been British Malaya did so with much less developed ideas about
the future, at least in terms of the governmental structure that might
succeed the end of Japanese rule. In Burma and the Philippines, in
considerable contrast to the rest of the region, there were not only
members of the local population who were ready to cooperate with
the Japanese. There was, in addition, the opportunity to join that
cooperation to participation in the government of their countries.
This participation always involved the clear dominance of the
Japanese authorities, but it was a participation that was significantly
different from the various levels of cooperation found elsewhere.

The wartime history of Burma and the Philippines was extremely
complex and only the bare outlines can be provided here. In both
countries, in contrast to the policies followed in the rest of the
region, the Japanese encouraged local politicians to become part of
an administrative structure in which, in theory at least, they had a
significant part to play. When the Japanese gained control of Burma
in mid-1942 they found that an end to military hostilities was not
followed by the easy imposition of a new administration. Many
thousands of younger Burmese who had not previously played any
part in the administration of the country under the British now
claimed the right to do so and matched actions to their claim by
seeking to control areas of the country on the strength of their
adherence to nationalist ideals. The results of these haphazard early
attempts at the establishment of a Burmese administration were
very uneven. In some areas the nationalist fervour of the moment
was channelled into confrontation and then bloodshed as Burmans

harried the Indian settlers and members of the various minority groups that form such an important proportion of the Burmese population as a whole. It was in these circumstances that the Japanese established a civilian Burmese administration headed by a well-known older nationalist, Ba Maw, and sought through him to rally the support of the Burmese civil servants who had previously worked with the British.

For a brief period this arrangement seemed to meet the divergent interests of both parties. The Japanese saw the administration headed by Ba Maw as offering the promise of Burmese cooperation in the difficult days of the war that still lay ahead. From the Burmese point of view, in contrast, the arrangement provided the possibility of laying a firm basis for a truly independent Burmese administration once, as was judged likely, Japan emerged as the victor at the end of the war. These Burmese estimations presumed a degree of restraint on the part of the Japanese, a belief that the Japanese would pay due attention to Burmese interests. In this they were wrong and the history of relations between the Japanese and the Burmese from late 1942 until the end of the war in 1945 is of a progressive growth of distrust and the ever-sharper divergence of interests to the point where there was no common thread to hold the two groups together.

What happened in Burma, so far as relations between the Burmese and the Japanese were concerned, was in its essentials the same as what happened in other parts of Southeast Asia. Japanese interests remained paramount and for all the much vaunted discussion of Burmese independence—something that was actually proclaimed in 1943—power remained firmly in the hands of the invading army. Moreover, even in Burma, where the Japanese professed to have deep respect for Buddhism and to be ready to pay all due attention to Burmese interests in more secular matters, the demands of the war soon led to a policy being followed that mocked professions of religious piety and political concern. Japanese interest in Buddhism was readily revealed as motivated by an effort to use the Buddhist church as a vehicle for furthering the war effort. The supposed 'independence' that was accorded Burma did not stop the Japanese authorities from making severe demands upon the Burmese population in terms of the provision of food and other resources and even more disturbingly in terms of coolie labour for their strategic rail and road building projects. The internal results of this situation were apparent in the growing resentment by the Burmese of the Japanese presence and the formation of a clandestine organisation by a group of Burmese who were ready to oppose the Japanese once the fortunes of war started running against them and, at the same time, to work to gain real independence should the British seek to restore the pre-war situation.

The other country to experience the granting of 'independence' while the result of the war in the Pacific and Southeast Asia was still undecided was the Philippines. Just as the Philippines had experienced a very different historical development from the rest of Southeast Asia because of its long period of rule by the Spanish, so in the Second World War once again the history of the Philippines was notably particular. For when the American and Filipino forces were defeated by the Japanese in 1942 a large proportion of the political and economic leadership of the pre-war Commonwealth period decided to cooperate with the conquering Japanese. Because the Philippines had already moved so far towards independence before the war began, the administration that rallied to the Japanese should have been a much more developed and effective body than was the case in Burma. This did not turn out to be what happened. As students of Philippine history have repeatedly observed, the rallying of the elite to the Japanese, whether out of a particular vision of 'patriotism' or because of undisguised self-interest, was not matched by a similar decision on the part of the population at large. The proclamation of Philippine 'independence' in 1943 did nothing to transform the situation. The Philippine politicians who worked with the Japanese never succeeded in seeming other than puppets. At the same time, instances of Japanese brutality against the civilian population and the heavy economic demands made by the conquerors only tended to reinforce a widespread feeling among ordinary, non-elite Filipinos that their interests lay more with their pre-war American rulers than with their supposed fellow Asian 'liberators'. In brief, the wartime experience of the Philippines showed that there as elsewhere Japanese interests were the guiding principle for all important decisions and that talk of mutual interests uniting the Japanese and the population of the lands that had been occupied was little more than cosmetic propaganda. Nonetheless, despite the presence of deep resentment of the Japanese among Filipinos at large and the puppet-like character of those who chose to work with the Japanese, the Philippines was the only country in Southeast Asia in which there was both a significant guerrilla resistance movement that fought against the Japanese throughout the war and such a large group of politicians and administrators who worked with the invaders and then were able to continue their careers once hostilities ended. Collaboration, or cooperation, between the Philippine elite and the Japanese, had been on such a scale that the final practical outcome, which was in effect and after much bitterness to forget about which side an individual politician took during the war, should not be regarded as very surprising. At the same time, the deep underlying divisions caused by the war were to trouble the Philippines for many years.

So far in this rapid review attention has been given almost entirely to those countries in Southeast Asia that were occupied by the Japanese after the defeat of the various colonial powers. In the countries colonised by France, however, Vietnam, Cambodia, and the Laotian states, the French administration continued to function until early 1945, at which point the Japanese seized power. There was some small truth in the argument developed by those Frenchmen who chose to serve in Indochina during the war when they asserted that their actions preserved France's colonial position. In Cambodia and Laos, in the short term at least, the fact that the French continued to administer these territories and to prop up the traditional rulers minimised the growth of nationalist feeling. The force of the argument was always limited, however, since nationalism had not been a notable feature of either Cambodia or Laos before the war and it was to grow only with the rapidly changing political balance of the post-war world. Even more of a qualification to the French position that argued for the 'success' of the arrangement made with the Japanese were the developments that took place in Vietnam, by far the most important part of France's colonial empire in Southeast Asia.

The argument has already been developed in the previous chapter that by the end of the 1930's nationalist resistance to the French in Vietnam had become largely, though not entirely, dominated by the Vietnamese Communists. When war came to Southeast Asia and the French administration struck its dubious bargain with the Japanese the Vietnamese Communists were certainly in no position to make a successful bid for power. Their numbers remained small and the French security services waged an unremitting battle to contain and if possible eliminate the political force that they correctly judged to be the real threat to continuing French rule. As the war advanced, however, the balance of opportunity, though still not power, slowly began to tip in favour of the Vietnamese Communist-Nationalists. To some extent the change came about because of the altered political atmosphere. For all of the speeches by Governor-General Decoux and his subordinates arguing for the unchanging role of France in Indochina, there was a growing awareness that France continued to administer its colonial territories simply at the will of the Japanese. The French retained administrative power, but ultimate political and military power was not in their hands.

Japanese demands for resources and manpower had priority over French policies and made clear the hollowness of claims by the colonial administration that the Japanese presence was the result of mutual agreement.

To the pervasive sense of change was added the slow but nonetheless quite tangible achievements of the Vietnamese Communists. Thwarting the efforts of the Chinese Nationalist forces to aid groups within Vietnam that did not subscribe to Communist aims, the Communists under the leadership of Ho Chi Minh succeeded in developing a political front organisation that was dominated by party members but which recruited to its ranks a broad spectrum of Vietnamese united by the shared aim of gaining independence from the French. The importance of this slow but steady *political* effort cannot be overestimated since the Vietnamese Communists themselves have readily admitted that in terms of *military* power or territory over which they were able to claim any form of administrative control their position, until the dramatic developments of 1945, was very weak. But when the events of 1945 did take place the Vietnamese Communists were quite clearly the most important political group in the country and determined, as the subsequent bitter years of blood were to show, to fight to maintain that position against both internal and external enemies.

For all of Southeast Asia the events of the closing months of the Second World War were of major importance. This was true both for those countries that had experienced a form of Japanese occupation which had provided little opportunity for political participation and for the other countries where the Japanese victories of 1942 had meant the establishment of new administrations in which local politicians played a part. The swift Japanese advance into Southeast Asia had shattered myths of white supremacy and opened the prospect, briefly, to Southeast Asians of participating in something close to true independence. Disillusion set in shortly afterwards as the hollowness of Japanese slogans was revealed and the priority of Japanese interests became apparent. Then as the fortunes of war slowly but steadily turned against the Japanese the peoples of Southeast Asia began to contemplate the increasingly certain probability of a Japanese defeat. Beyond noting the very broadly shared fact that the Japanese interregnum had brought irrevocable change to the region, an account of the outlook before the peoples of the various countries of Southeast Asia at this time must give more attention to the differences than to the common aspects of their experience. For if the end of the war was a dramatic development for the whole of Southeast Asia, the problems and opportunities that it brought with it differed greatly from country to country.

In Thailand, which had aligned itself rather half-heartedly on the Japanese side while the war had run in Japan's favour, the implications of impending Japanese defeat were particularly disturbing. Thai policy at the beginning of the war had taken account of overwhelming Japanese military power and the chance that enlisting on the Japanese side gave of regaining control of areas of Cambodia and Laos, and later of Burma, to which Thai irredentists had long laid claim. This policy had prevented Thailand from suffering the physical destruction of war that was sustained by so many other areas of Southeast Asia. As circumstances changed so did the Thai leadership begin its shift to a position that signalled a clear defection from the Japanese camp, without being of a kind that could provoke a major Japanese reaction. Nevertheless, all of Thailand's traditional capacity for astute diplomacy was required when the war did end and the Allied powers contemplated their policies towards a state that had sided against them. Diplomatic skill and more demanding problems elsewhere in Southeast Asia saved Thailand from any serious humiliation and the country found itself at the end of the war much less affected than any other part of the region. For Thailand the Second World War was important but not the cause for overwhelming change either in its relations with the rest of the world or in terms of the nature of its domestic politics. Such an estimation could scarcely be made about any other country in Southeast Asia.

In two of the other countries of Southeast Asia, Burma and the Philippines, the closing months of the Second World War became a time for preparation for the relatively swift transfer from colonial status to independence. In Burma as British and Indian military forces carried on their successful campaign that led to the defeat of the Japanese army in 1945 the Allied Supreme Commander in the area, Lord Louis Mountbatten, had agreed to cooperate with the leading Burmese nationalists, men dedicated to complete independence for their country. This wartime decision strengthened the subsequent Burmese conviction that the post-war political discussions held with the British were concerned with technicalities for achieving full independence and not about the issue of whether independence should be granted. The path to agreement was not always easy and the policies of the first post-war British government initially seemed a reversal of the approach followed by Mountbatten. In the end, however, and with a minimum of blood-shed, Burma's passage towards independence was assured.

The reconquest of the Philippines took place at a time when the

Japanese were making desperate and largely unsuccessful attempts to rally Filipino support to their losing side and against a background of increasing nervousness on the part of those politicians and administrators who had chosen to work with the Japanese throughout the war. The reconquest also took place with considerable assistance from various guerrilla groups, among which was the Hukbalahap movement, a Communist-led group that had fought with some success against the Japanese in parts of Luzon*. The Huks, as members of this movement were usually known, reflected an important rural tradition in sections of the Philippines, one that questioned the established patterns of patron-client relationships and championed the interests of the poor tenant farmer. Their emergence as a significant force in the latter part of the Japanese occupation period had long-term political consequences since they combined excellent anti-Japanese credentials with a programme for social change that was radically different from the accepted and essentially conservative values of Philippine political life.

As the war drew to a close, however, two other issues dominated political life in the Philippines. First was the need to make rapid progress towards independence, a point on which American and Filipino politicians were essentially of one mind. The other issue that had to be faced was the fact of large-scale collaboration or cooperation with the recent enemy. The commitment that all had to the achievement of independence made it easier to come to terms with the second problem. Some have argued that American politicians and military leaders, most notably General Douglas MacArthur, saw that conservative interests would be best served by disregarding the issue of association with the Japanese and accepting that most of those who had such an association were to be relied on in peacetime to pursue conservative, pro-American policies. Whether such an assessment of MacArthur's thinking is accurate is open to debate, though there would be little grounds for disagreement over the suggestion that the Philippine elite, whatever role its members had chosen to play during the war, was essentially conservative in its political outlook. The elite was also relatively small, closely knit together as the result of intricate political and personal alliances. Assured that independence would be granted, it was able to come to terms with the disagreeable features of the war by looking forward to the possibilities of peace. In doing so, few of its members suspected how difficult those early years of peace were to

* Hukbalahap is a shortened version of the Tagalog words meaning 'People's Army Against the Japanese'.

be when the Hukbalahap, or Huks, went into open rebellion against the government.

While a difficult but still surprisingly smooth transition to independence was being made in the Philippines and in Burma, as the war drew to an end, events of a very different order were taking place in Indonesia and Vietnam. In neither of these countries could the closing months of the Second World War be faced by Indonesians and Vietnamese in the same way as was the case in Burma and the Philippines. For the Dutch as the former rulers of Indonesia and the French as the former rulers of the countries of Indochina were known to be determined to reassert their sovereignty. The result in each country was a bitter war of revolution and independence, one lasting for three years, the other for nine—and some would say for thirty—years.

Well before the final Japanese surrender to the Allies in August 1945, the course of developments leading to an ultimate Japanese defeat had become apparent to Indonesian nationalists. Although various pressures were put upon the occupying Japanese, including some attempt at the use of force, it was only very near to the end of the war that the leading Indonesian nationalists were able to persuade the occupiers that independence should be discussed and proclaimed before the war's end provided an opportunity for the Dutch to return. The moment finally came on 17 August 1945 when Sukarno with Hatta at his side proclaimed Indonesia's independence and so served notice of his countrymen's readiness to fight against any attempt at the reimposition of Dutch rule. The new independent Indonesian state did not have long to wait to prove that it would fight, and fight with surprising effectiveness, against attempts to return to the pre-war colonial state of affairs. Ironically, both in Indonesia and in Vietnam the first armed confrontation in the battle to achieve post-war independence was waged against the British rather than against troops of the former colonial power. Barely two months after Sukarno had declared Indonesia's independence in Jakarta, troops fighting in the new republic's name sought to prevent British forces, acting as the allied representative in this area of Southeast Asia, entering the major port city of Surabaya. The ensuing battle for Surabaya was prolonged and costly to both sides. It led to the British force commanders, who had been ordered to maintain control until the Dutch were able to return, adopting a very cautious approach to further contact with the Indonesians. But more importantly the battle of Surabaya was a signal that the Indonesians were ready and able, even if at heavy cost, to fight for the goal of total independence. The events of the war had made anything less unacceptable.

As the Second World War drew to an end, the situation in Vietnam was possibly more complicated than anywhere else in Southeast Asia. In March 1945, six months before the end of the war, the Japanese forces throughout Indochina overthrew the French administrations that had continued to function throughout the earlier phases of the war and imprisoned French government and military personnel. The Japanese acted as they did in an effort to maintain maximum control over the economically and strategically important Indochinese region as the possibility of defeat became more and more apparent. In Vietnam the Japanese seizure of power was followed shortly after by the proclamation of Vietnamese 'independence' under the leadership of the Vietnamese emperor, Bao Dai. The 'independent' state of Vietnam was, in fact, no more than a device designed to disguise Japanese domination of the country and this was recognised by almost all politically conscious Vietnamese. But with the removal of the French administrators it became possible for the communist-led Viet-Minh forces, both military and political, to accelerate their efforts to gain power. The Japanese remained in military control of the major cities and towns. In both the cities and the countryside, however, the Viet-Minh worked feverishly to develop a political structure that could resist the expected return of the French once the war ended in Japan's defeat. As they worked for the goal of future political power the Viet-Minh were not the only Vietnamese who thought about the opportunities of the post-war situation. What seems undeniable, nevertheless, is that the Communist-led forces were the most able and effective of the various political groupings that jockeyed for power in Vietnam. They had gained a position of pre-eminence in nationalist politics by the end of the 1930s, and they had no intention of losing this position as the war drew to a close. When Japan surrendered, the Viet-Minh were ready, and following a series of events now known as the August Revolution the Viet-Minh leader, Ho Chi Minh, proclaimed the establishment of an independent Vietnamese state on 2 September 1945. For a brief period in the early part of September the success of the Viet-Minh seemed complete. There was opposition from political and religious groups in southern Vietnam and the Viet-Minh's military and political power was spread extremely thin. For all of these problems the possibility seemed to exist that Ho Chi Minh's forces would succeed in establishing an administrative framework that would permit them to convince the French that reconquest was not to be contemplated. The possibility may have been there but, as the months immediately after the war were to show, French policy towards Vietnam was set on a collision course that could only lead, eventually, to war.

Events in the other countries that made up French Indochina, Cambodia and Laos, did not have the high drama that marked the closing stages of the Second World War in Vietnam. Important developments took place, it is true, as Cambodia's king, Norodom Sihanouk, proclaimed an ephemeral independence for his country, and as a limited but important number of Laotians demonstrated their determination to resist the return of France as a colonial power. But in both these countries the strength of the traditional leadership that had, for the most part, linked its fortunes with the French administration before the war, continued to be such that the experience of a brief period without colonial direction was not sufficient to set the stage for a conflict of the sort that developed in Vietnam. Individuals who emerged into prominence at this time

19   Australian POWs in Changi
Those allied soldiers taken prisoner by the Japanese during the war in Southeast Asia suffered terrible deprivation and often appalling brutality. The prisoners of war shown in this photograph were Australian survivors in Changi, the camp in Singapore in which malnutrition reduced healthy men to living skeletons. The fact that the once-proud colonial over-lords could be humbled by the Japanese during their conquest of Southeast Asia was a major factor in making the Second World War period a turning point in modern Southeast Asian history. *Photograph courtesy of the Australian War Memorial negative no. 19199*

were to be important in the post-war history of Cambodia and Laos. For the moment, however, the events of the war seemed less important than the long-established patterns of close association between the traditional ruling classes and the French colonial administration.

High drama was also lacking in the history of Malaya as the war drew to an end. The Japanese occupation of Malaya had differed from the occupation of other countries in Southeast Asia to the extent that no effort was made to promote even the most circumscribed form of 'independence'. Malaya and Singapore were seen as providing resources for the Japanese war effort. But in a society made up of Malays, Chinese, and Indians in which there was little shared interest between the various ethnic groups the Japanese saw

20   MacArthur receiving the Japanese surrender
Japan surrendered on 15 August 1945 to end the Pacific War and its occupation of the countries of Southeast Asia. The Allied Supreme Commander for the Pacific, General Douglas MacArthur, formally accepted the Japanese surrender aboard the USS Missouri in Tokyo Bay on 2 September 1945. The Japanese surrender meant the victory of the colonial powers that had controlled Southeast Asia before the Second World War, but the defeat those powers had suffered in 1942 ensured that the colonial era could never again be reinstituted without challenge. *Photograph courtesy of the Australian War Memorial negative no. 19128*

no point in trying to advance their aims by fostering independence movements. Moreover, unlike some of the other countries of Southeast Asia at the time of the Second World War, Malaya had no significant nationalist movement. One group did emerge during the occupation that waged a limited guerrilla war against the Japanese in the name of the 'Malayan People'. This was a guerrilla force of ethnic Chinese Communists and from 1943 onwards their armed resistance to the Japanese in Malaya was linked with the Allied war effort through the infiltration of a small British military group, Force 136. The significance of these Chinese guerrilla fighters lies more in their later history, when they mounted an insurrection against the post-war government of Malaya, than in their efforts against the Japanese. For the rest, Malaya's war experience was one of relative ease for the Malay population, considerable cruelty and deprivation for the Chinese, and for the Indian minority a chance, particularly for the less prosperous members of that community, to enjoy a sense of improved status as the Japanese elevated them to positions of authority that they had not held before.

In the closing months of the war Malaya was an exception to the rule in almost every way. The Japanese had not promoted an independence movement and there was little local interest in nationalism. No battles were fought to regain Malaya from the Japanese since the war ended before a planned British invasion took place. Despite these and other factors that made the Malayan experience so different from some other sections of Southeast Asia, the impact of the war years was considerable. The world, as one Malayan observer put it, had been turned upside down during the Japanese occupation and there could never be a return to the pre-war pattern of British colonialism, even if there was no resistance to the return of the British themselves once the war had ended. That return, significantly, was not greeted with flag-decked buildings or by cheering crowds.

Earlier in this book the argument was put forward that the eighteenth century was a period that could be regarded as the beginning of an historical watershed that stretched across the nineteenth century and into the twentieth. The period of the Second World War may be regarded as the end of this vast watershed. The events of the war and the changes these brought in the attitudes and outlook of Southeast Asians transformed the region. The war revealed the hollowness of many of the claims made by the colonial powers concerning the 'loyalty' of their colonised subjects and it dramatically and sometimes cruelly showed the weakness of the white rulers when faced by a major military challenge. Whatever words are chosen to describe the changes brought about by the war, the vital point to be grasped was that these changes were fundamental. In political terms the years of war ensured that there could never be a return to the way of life that had seemed so permanent in 1939.

10
Revolution and Revolt: Indonesia, Vietnam, Malaya, and the Philippines

THE emphasis laid on complexity at the beginning of the previous chapter dealing with the Second World War is equally appropriate when attention shifts to the next important phase in Southeast Asia's modern history: the period immediately following the war that ended in August 1945. The experience of each of the countries of Southeast Asia during the first post-war decade was not only complex in itself but also of a character that defies easy regional generalisation. In both Indonesia and Vietnam, for instance, independence from the former colonial power was gained after bitter armed struggle. But the nature of the revolutionary armed struggle in each country and of the politics of those who led it was very different. This point is made apparent when one notes the fact that the Indonesian forces confronting the Dutch had, at one stage, to put down an attempt by their Communist fellow countrymen to seize control of the independence movement. This important event—one that is still clearly remembered by Indonesian army officers as an indication of the utter unreliability of the Communists—contrasts dramatically with the situation in Vietnam, where the struggle for independence from the French was led by the Communists. The points of difference separating the experience of one Southeast Asian country from another in the years immediately after the Second World War can be recorded almost endlessly. Generalizations, if they are to be made, must be at the broadest level, taking account of the fact that each country was facing the problems of achieving independence or of dealing with the reality of independence in its own way. Even Thailand, the country that never experienced colonialism, emerged at the end of the Second World War having to deal with a very different set of problems from those that had been known in the 1920s and 1930s. Because of the importance of each country's individual experience the next two chapters will concentrate on the history of developments on a country by country basis, with only a restricted attempt to dwell on the comparative dimension. The concern of the present chapter will be with two revolutions, those that took place in Indonesia and Vietnam, and with two revolts, the unsuccessful revolt of the Communist insurgents in Malaya in the period known as the Emergency and the revolt, again unsuccessful, of the Communist Hukbalahap (Huks) insurgents in the Philippines.

The Indonesian revolution has repeatedly held the attention of foreign observers. Reasons for this interest are not hard to find. Indonesia is the largest of all the Southeast Asian states, both in terms of national territory and population, and this fact alone has led to wide interest in the country's battle for independence. But more was involved to spark the interest and concern that was given to the Indonesian revolution between 1945 and 1949 when the Dutch finally gave up their attempt to reimpose colonial rule. In part the external interest in developments in Indonesia stemmed from the spectacle that was provided of an economically poor and militarily weak nation seeking to achieve freedom against formidable odds, for though the Dutch were numerically dwarfed by the Indonesians they were able to make use of much more advanced and powerful weapons and equipment. In part, too, many outside observers were aware that the Indonesians, in fighting for their independence from Holland, were pursuing goals that were the same as those for which the Allies had fought against Germany and Japan—the right of a country to maintain its existence against external interference. Although international interest in the events in Indonesia never equalled the later world interest in the Vietnam war, for many, and not least scholars with an interest in Southeast Asia, the Indonesian revolution and war against the Dutch generated an interest and sense of involvement that has continued to the present day.

Dutch administrators returned to Indonesia in early 1946 to find the nationalists were committed to attaining independence, even if there were significant differences of opinion among the various groups that formed the nationalist movement as to just what path should be followed to bring this about. Most importantly, there was disagreement between those, many of them from the younger generation that had already fought against the imposition of British army control in the major cities, who wanted an immediate all-out fight for independence and those who were prepared to pursue their goals through negotiation. The option of negotiation, which appealed to most of the established nationalist leaders, offered the possibility of avoiding bloodshed. Moreover, the initial impression

provided by the returning Dutch was that they accepted the claim of
the Indonesians to independence, so long as due attention was paid
to residual Dutch interests. Fairly quickly, however, indeed well
before the end of 1946, the divergence of views held by the two
parties, Indonesian and Dutch, became sharply apparent.

From the Indonesian point of view negotiation was to be concerned with the implementation of independence. This was in direct
contrast with the Dutch position, which was that negotiation
was to take place so that arrangements might be made to allow
Indonesia to achieve full independence at some unspecified later
date. Having proclaimed Indonesia's independence in August 1945,
the Indonesians were impatient to match reality to the ideal that had
so often been discussed and for which many of their number had
suffered long years of imprisonment and exile. The Dutch, by
contrast, simply could not shake off the attitudes of the colonial
period. Despite vague promises made by the Dutch government
while hostilities against Japan were still in progress, the Dutch
negotiators could not believe that their former colonial subjects
were either ready for complete independence or, in fact, really
wanted it. Their assessments in this regard were not only affected by
an unwillingness to face up to the fact that a Dutch administration
was no longer welcome in Indonesia. In addition, resentment of the
role played by such men as Sukarno, who had been ready during the
war years to work with the Japanese to attain their own nationalist
ends, prevented many Dutchmen from looking at the post-war
situation in a way that took account of reality rather than out-of-
date fantasies dwelling on a Netherlands' vision of the white man's
burden and the supposed wishes of Indonesia's silent masses.

The existence of these two opposing points of view meant that
negotiations, when they were undertaken, had to break down. It
was simply not sufficient that both sides were ready to negotiate
when there was no shared agreement over the essentials of what was
under discussion. The two major agreements concluded between the
Indonesian and Dutch sides during the course of the struggle for
independence—the Linggadjati Agreement of November 1946, the
Renville Agreement (named after the naval vessel on which it was
negotiated) of January 1948—broke down as the result of basic
Dutch unwillingness to think in terms of a truly independent
Indonesia existing in the future. It was never clear, to the Indonesians certainly, that the Dutch were ready to accept the nationalists
as equal partners who would, with the former colonial power, be co-
sponsors of a projected United States of Indonesia. Moreover, the
Indonesian nationalists grew increasingly convinced that the Dutch
advocacy of a federal Indonesian state made up of various semi-

autonomous units was simply another effort to preserve their position. In pursuing this policy the Dutch were taking advantage of the undoubted fact that there was, and still is, some suspicion of Javanese predominance among the inhabitants of other regions of Indonesia—Sumatra, Bali, Sulawesi, and the other eastern outer islands. But however much the Dutch might appeal to the existence of this suspicion and find some response from conservative interests as they did so it became more and more evident that their would-be federal solution was an attempt to maintain Dutch control, or at very least a Dutch presence, through indirect means.

So the Dutch plans were not only bitterly opposed by the active nationalists who, it should always be remembered, were drawn from regions throughout Indonesia; Dutch policy was ultimately unconvincing for the populations of the various regions where the federal states were established. Many factors helped to change minds. The Second World War had already had a major impact in spreading and for many firmly establishing the sense of being an Indonesian as well as being an inhabitant of a particular region with its own particular culture. Equally important in changing and forming opinions were the so-called Dutch 'police actions' of mid-1947 and late 1948.

As negotiations bogged down and both sides concluded that their opponents were acting in bad faith, the Dutch launched what they described as a 'police action' in July 1947. In military terms, for it was a military and not a police campaign that was undertaken, the Dutch achieved some success. They gained control over vital areas of Java and Sumatra and in doing so were able to deny food supplies to the troops of the Indonesian nationalist side. But the price of this 'success' was high, higher indeed than the Dutch had themselves contemplated it would be. This was only one of the many instances in the post-Second World War history of Southeast Asia, and indeed of other colonised regions as well, of the alien colonial power failing to look beyond immediate military considerations to the wider political implications. Although the first Dutch 'police action' gained territory, supplies, and to some extent control over population, it also acted as a major factor in rallying yet further support to the nationalist cause. For those who had doubted the estimations of the nationalist leaders when they had argued that the Dutch were not, in fact, ready to grant real independence, the armed advance of the Dutch forces was a convincing argument. In brief, while the Dutch gained ground between July and August 1947 they also raised the level of support given to the nationalists. The former colonial power did more than this, for the decision to use military force excited the opposition of important sections of the international community. From late 1947 onwards international concern about the developing conflict in Indonesia became ever more important until, in the end, it could be argued that international pressure on Holland played the decisive part in making the Dutch abandon their efforts to postpone the emergence of an independent Indonesia.

International opinion, expressed through the newly created United Nations, was able to bring about an end to the first 'police action' and a return to negotiations. These once again dragged on indecisively from the end of 1947 until late 1948 when, as before, the Dutch opted for an attempted military solution, the second 'police action' that lasted from the middle of December 1948 until early January 1949. The pattern of events during this second military campaign was similar to developments in 1947. The Dutch made military advances but in doing so reinforced the political position of the Indonesian nationalists and undermined the support they received from their allies. And by the end of this second 'police action' there was little significant support among the leaders of the outer islands for any further association with the Dutch. The outcome was yet a further effort at negotiations that did, finally, lead to

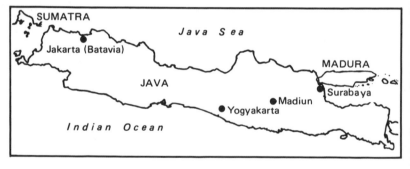

Map 6   Four Key Cities in the Indonesian Revolution
Jakarta (Batavia): The Indonesian nationalists proclaimed their country's independence in this city on 17 August 1945.
Surabaya: The fledgling Indonesian Republican army fought its first major battle in this city in November 1945.
Madiun: Elements of the Indonesian Communist Party based in this central Javanese city attempted to take over leadership of the revolution in September 1948. The attempted coup was crushed by the Indonesian army, which has never forgotten or forgiven this event.
Yogyakarta: This ancient royal city in central Java was the capital of the Indonesian Republic as the revolutionaries fought against the Dutch. In December 1948 the Dutch seized Yogyakarta, but this action only reinforced the nationalists' determination to continue their struggle.

an agreed transfer of sovereignty at the end of 1949. Before surveying that development, however, some account must be taken of developments at the level of internal politics during the Indonesian revolution.

Revolutions are remembered, in general, for their outcomes rather than for the often complex history of developments from their beginnings to their ends. Scholars may be fascinated by the details of politics *within* the history of the French revolution, but in the broader historical sense a non-specialist knows that revolution was important less for the factional fighting between Girodins and Jacobins than for the fundamental political changes that occurred in France in the years following 1789. For the non-specialist looking at the Indonesian revolution, also, the vital point is certainly that independence *was* gained in 1949. But scholars do have some real justification in studying the factional disputes of the French revolutionary period for these were disputes over issues that were unresolved when the revolution was completed. So too were there developments in Indonesian politics during the revolution that were linked to issues that have continued to preoccupy Indonesian politicians until the present day. Two developments are particularly deserving of attention in this regard—the role of the Indonesian Communist Party and the efforts of the extreme Islamic sect, the Darul Islam, to establish an Indonesian Islamic state.

The point has already been made that in Indonesia the Communists were not the leaders of the struggle against the re-establishment of colonial rule, unlike the situation in Vietnam. The Indonesian Communist Party was only one of the many political parties and groups that joined together on the nationalist side, united in their common opposition to the Dutch but seeking to promote their own political programmes at the same time. This concern with their own political interests, as opposed to the interests of the nationalist anti-Dutch movement as a whole, led elements within the Communist Party to attempt a takeover of the revolutionary movement. The attempted coup by the Communists ended in bitter failure. In less than a month, during September 1948, the Communists operating from their central Javanese base in Madiun experienced brief success and then suffered near total eclipse. The best troops in the Indonesian revolutionary army were sent in to Madiun. After their defeat of the Communist forces in that town the army followed up their success by ruthlessly mopping-up the remnants of those who for a brief time had sided and fought with the Communists.

The Madiun Affair, as this event has been known ever since, left shock waves that still agitate the surface of Indonesian politics. Even before the attempted seizure of power there had been many who had argued that the Communists were not committed to the cause of Indonesian nationalism so much as to the triumph of their particular political creed. This had been the view of important figures in the Indonesian army, and events now had proved them correct. The commander of the troops that defeated the Communists in Madiun, Nasution, was to go on to be a major figure in post-independence Indonesian politics and to hold, like so many of his fellow officers, an unshakable belief in the error of ever trusting Indonesian Communists to place nationalism before their own political interests and beliefs. At the same time, as many have observed in earlier analyses of this affair, the fact that the Indonesian revolutionary government and its armed forces were ready to suppress the Communist challenge at Madiun robbed the Dutch of any possibility of making capital from the suggestion that their efforts to maintain a position in Indonesia deserved support as part of a world-wide anti-Communist crusade.

The other notable challenge to the evolving Indonesian political leadership—a challenge that has probably not been given sufficient attention in the past—came from the Darul Islam, an extremist Islamic group that was committed to the ideal of Indonesia as an Islamic state, a concept that had been decisively rejected by all of the leading figures in the nationalist movement. The Darul Islam drew its support from those areas of Indonesia in which adherence to Islam was strongest, regions such as West Java, northern Sumatra, and parts of Indonesian Borneo (Kalimantan). At the time of the second Dutch 'police action' elements of the Darul Islam tried to gain control of territory through armed force. Although this attempt was unsuccessful, Darul Islam continued to oppose the central government until 1962. And as with the Madiun Affair the memory of Darul Islam's actions has remained with Indonesian politicans, both civil and military, ever since. In the face of a general acceptance that a secular (non-religious) nation is what is required in Indonesia there has been and remains a deep suspicion of any efforts by followers of Islam to move from regarding Islam as the most important single religion observed within the state to an advocacy of Islam as the state religion.

The challenge and the defeat of the Communists and the Darul Islam showed that the Indonesian government opposing the Dutch was ready to use harsh measures to maintain its internal position. Of at least equal importance was the way in which Indonesian resistance to the Dutch military, in both the first and second 'police actions', gave the lie to those in the ranks of the former colonial power who had argued that a swift series of campaigns would eliminate the nationalist capacity to fight. Certainly the Indonesian forces had no way of resisting the modern weaponry and equipment of the Dutch. But what they could and did do was to engage in constant guerrilla warface that denied the Dutch control of the population and severely reduced the availability of food or the possibility of exploiting Indonesia's natural resources. The role of the Indonesian army at this time was vital for the continued existence of the revolutionary government and left the army with a very special place within society, one that recognised the army as the guardian of the state with its own special right to play a political role.

The negotiations that followed the end of the second 'police action' took place under substantially different conditions from those that had applied previously. Most importantly the Dutch were under increasing pressure from the United States to make concessions to the Indonesians. In these circumstances the Indonesian side accepted that it too would have to make concessions—the acceptance of a massive debt, including the costs of Dutch military action in Indonesia, and the postponement of a decision on the status of West New Guinea (West Irian). After lengthy discussion the Dutch government finally handed over sovereignty for all areas under its control to the revolutionary government in December 1949. Within a year the semi-independent states that had been propped up by the Dutch throughout the three years of conflict and negotiation were incorporated into the unitary Indonesian state that had always been the nationalists' goal.

Having won independence from the Dutch the nationalists then had to confront Indonesia's many problems. As they did so the euphoria of success dissipated and the fact and variety of these problems became ever more insistently obvious. 'Unity in Diversity', the Indonesian national motto, is an admirable statement of both fact and hope. It is also a reflection of the immense diversity within the Indonesian state that will always pose challenges, some great, some small, to central control and its authority. And the presence of regional and other special interests had by no means been removed because of the revolutionary struggle.

These were problems that were seen as lying ahead in 1949. More important at that time was the fact that independence had been achieved. Success had been the result of many factors and of the work of many millions, some important and many humble. The leadership that held power at the end of the revolution emerged with their previous identity as anti-Dutch nationalists enhanced by their role during the 1945–6 period. Sukarno, in particular, as President of the Indonesian Republic, occupied a position of considerable power and influence. In the same way, if to a lesser degree, others who played a prominent role during the revolution, men such as Hatta, Nasution, the Sultan of Yogyakarta, were assured of prominence in the immediate post-revolutionary years. The revolution had conferred authority on its leaders and it had ensured that the army would be regarded as the protector both of the state and of the revolution's values. These were political benefits that were to last for many years to come. Conversely, the period of the revolution was for the Communists and for the Darul Islam a time that left them weakened and without either immediate or long-term prospect of achieving their goals. While it may be a case of stating the obvious, the events of the Indonesian revolution and the roles played by the various individuals and groups at that time had a clear and direct importance in shaping the nature of Indonesian politics in the decade that followed the departure of the Dutch.

Despite these clear indications of the importance of the Indonesian revolution scholars continue to debate its character. What, they ask, was revolutionary about the developments between 1945 and 1949? The answers different scholars give vary considerably. Most accept that significant social and political changes took place in addition to the fact that independence from the Dutch was achieved. But there are dissenting voices that argue a different point of view and suggest the degree of true revolution was really quite small, that the vested interests which emerged at the end of the revolutionary period were not seriously interested in achieving the major social changes Indonesian society needed. A judgement concerning this question is, in the final analysis, likely to depend on what an observer thinks ought to have happened rather than an attempt to describe what did happen. Quite clearly a very large number of Indonesians believed that their struggle against the Dutch did involve change that went beyond the basic fact of attaining independence and assertion of the importance of the revolution remains widespread thirty years after it took place.

In Indonesia the experience of nearly four years of negotiation and fighting to complete the struggle for independence left all but the remotest part of the former Dutch East Indies (West New Guinea) in the hands of the nationalists. The history of the Vietnamese struggle against the French in Vietnam was very different, with a very different outcome. The difference did not only lie in the fact that the fight against the French was led by the Communists in Vietnam. There was a great difference also in terms of the length of time that the struggle lasted and in the intensity of the military conflict that was joined. Moreover, at the time when the French departed from Vietnam and abandoned their attempt to maintain the posture of a colonial power, in 1954, only half of the territory of

Vietnam was under the control of the Vietnamese forces that had inflicted a stunning defeat on their opponents at the Battle of Dien Bien Phu.

As the prelude to the Second Indochinese War, lasting from the late 1950s until 1975, the Vietnamese war against the French between 1946 and 1954 has remained comparatively little known. The events of the period of American involvement in the 1960s and 1970s have obscured earlier developments. But unless the years between 1946 and 1954 in Vietnam are understood it is impossible to gain a true sense of why the Vietnamese Communists should later have fought for so long to achieve their goals in the years when the French were no longer the enemy.

The Vietnamese August 1945 Revolution and the subsequent proclamation of independence could not prevent the return of the French. In southern Vietnam British troops prepared the way for the eventual re-establishment of the colonial administration. In the northern half of the country Nationalist Chinese forces acted as the Allies' representatives until the French were ready to reassert themselves. These occupying forces, in both the southern and northern sections of Vietnam, prevented the Communist-led Viet-Minh from pursuing its goal of establishing a normal administration. But throughout the country, and in the north in particular, where Communist strength was greatest, the Viet-Minh laboured to reinforce its position politically while the first of a long series of negotiations was undertaken with the French.

Because of the long period of bitter fighting that followed, it is often forgotten that much of 1946 was spent in Franco-Vietnamese negotiations. Here, at least, there was a similarity between developments in Indonesia and Vietnam. In both cases the anti-colonialist forces were prepared to undertake negotiations with the former colonial powers. But in both cases the expectations of the Indonesians and the Vietnamese were so different from those of the Dutch and the French that there could never be any real possibility of a negotiated solution being achieved. Perhaps even more than was the case with the Dutch in relation to Indonesia, the immediate post-Second World War government in France was determined to reassert its control over its former colonial territories in Vietnam, Cambodia and Laos. Since the Viet-Minh was determined to see that the independence that had been proclaimed in 1945 was maintained and with the French still convinced that Vietnam was part of *notre Indochine* (Our Indochina) the only possible outcome was war.

The First Indochinese War began as a series of guerrilla engagements, but by the closing phases of the war it was a conflict fought

at all military levels, from main-force engagements to local skir-
mishes. It was, particularly from the Vietnamese point of view, a
highly political war. Defeating the French was not a goal to be
achieved merely through military means but by the mobilisation of
all resources that could be used to frustrate the enemy's aims. The
Viet-Minh worked to undermine the French position in Vietnam at
every level, setting up a parallel administration alongside that of the
French so that Viet-Minh tax collectors levied taxes not only in
those zones that were under Viet-Minh control, but also clandestinely in those areas that were supposedly the preserve of the
French. More than this, the Viet-Minh view of the war as only one
aspect of a broader political struggle led its leaders to pursue goals
that might not have appeared, at first glance, to have had much
military value but which, in the long run, were vitally important for
overall strategy. Such was the case with the Viet-Minh's efforts to
promote literacy. The eventual benefits of having a literate population that could read its leaders' explanations for the pursuit of a
particular policy meant that such a programme should go forward
despite the presence of war.

The general pattern of the war in Vietnam between 1946 and 1954
can be fairly readily described, provided one accepts that such a
generalisation disguises the details and qualifications that would
emerge in a full-length study. The strength of the Vietnamese forces
fighting against the French was greatest in the northern section of
the country, and it was in this northern region that most of the
major battles of the war were fought. This fact should not be taken
to mean that the First Indochina War was simply a matter involving
the inhabitants of northern Vietnam and the French. Vietnamese
fought against the French throughout the whole of Vietnam, and by
the last years of the war the military maps of the French themselves
showed much of southern Vietnam in the hands of the Viet-Minh.
But whereas the initial guerrilla campaigns by the Viet-Minh in the
north developed into campaigns involving thousands of troops and
major battles, this was not the pattern in the south. There, scattered
units from both sides clashed in frequent guerrilla and small force
actions with 'control' over both territory and population often in
dispute.

A fundamental problem for the French in waging their war to
regain colonial control of Vietnam was that of time. Whereas the
Viet-Minh were prepared to endure the cost of a long war,
accepting that the costs of a prolonged struggle also carried with
them the possibility of more effective pursuit of political goals, the
same point of view could not be held by the French. Their leaders in
Indochina, both military and civil, recognised that endless prolonga-

tion of the war would lead to domestic disillusion in France. Their efforts, therefore, had to be concentrated on bringing the war to a swift end. But this was exactly what Viet-Minh strategy did not permit. The French were able to re-establish themselves in Hanoi and in the Red River delta of northern Vietnam. They could keep many, though not all, of the road and rail links open. And they could ensure that Vietnam's few cities of any size would not fall to sudden assault. Despite this they could not inflict a crippling defeat on their Vietnamese enemy. Between early 1947 and 1950 that enemy fought a classic guerrilla campaign with General Vo Nguyen Giap, the Viet-Minh military leader, demonstrating a clear grasp of the essentials of his forces' capacities. Attacks against the French were mounted when the Viet-Minh had a clear numerical or tactical superiority. The Viet-Minh chose its moments and its locations to attack the French with care to avoid the possibility of swift French reinforcement of its forces or the ready use of air power, a weapon that was never available to the Viet-Minh throughout the duration of the war.

By pursuing such a policy the Viet-Minh not only cost the French vital time, they were also able to develop both their military and political capacities. Here, indeed, is part of the explanation for General Giap's rise to military importance. The man who had taught history as a school-teacher did not simply become a general whose campaigns are studied in military academies all over the world by some sudden act of fate. Rather, Giap's military experience developed in such a fashion that he was able to match the growth of an undoubtedly high degree of talent in military matters to the changing and increasing demands of the strategic situation. Nevertheless, talented as he was, Giap still suffered some significant setbacks in the 1950−1 period as the Viet-Minh more and more sought to operate in large-scale units against the French. The fact of these setbacks is well worth emphasis for it draws attention to the intricacies and costs of the Vietnamese revolution. Successful though this Communist revolution was in the final analysis, any account of the post-Second World War history of Vietnam is misleading if it does not take full account of the difficulties along the way and the high costs that were endured for the results that were achieved.

Such a point is particularly worth remembering in relation to the battle that determined the outcome of the First Indochina War, the Battle of Dien Bien Phu that ended in May 1954. The Viet-Minh's success in this battle played a major part in bringing the Geneva settlement that left the northern half of Vietnam under Communist rule and the status of southern Vietnam a disputed issue that was

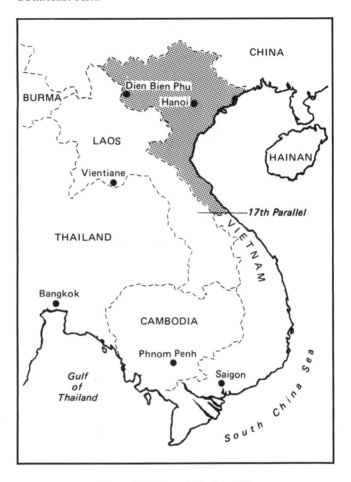

Map 7   Vietnam at the End of the First Indochina War
The French defeat at Dien Bien Phu in May 1954 sealed the end of France's colonial position in Vietnam. Following the Geneva Conference that ended in July 1954, Ho Chi Minh's Viet-Minh gained control of northern Vietnam down to the 17th parallel and an American-backed state was established in the south.

only settled, finally, when the whole of Vietnam passed under the control of the government in Hanoi in 1975. The details of the battle fascinate military historians, not least because of the fundamental errors committed by the French in choosing to seek a major engagement with the Viet-Minh in such a remote location—far removed from French headquarters in Hanoi—and poorly sited in local terms to withstand the siege that developed. Both sides recognised the vital importance of the outcome of the battle, and both displayed remarkable courage and endurance under near intolerable conditions. When the Viet-Minh forces finally overran the French positions their success had cost them dearly, their casualties being far in excess of those sustained by the French. The cost had borne out Mao Tse-tung's insistence that a 'revolution is not a tea party'.

The French defeat at Dien Bien Phu heralded the end of the French effort to maintain a position in Vietnam. Ever since 1946 this effort had been pursued on two levels, the military and the political. The military strategies failed, but the outcome of the political policies followed by the French was, in the short term, ambiguous. Although the French had not been successful in their efforts to promote a truly significant political rival to the Viet-Minh in southern Vietnam, they were able to maintain the framework of an administration that could be built upon once the First Indochina War came to an end and the United States decided to bolster a state in southern Vietnam as part of a worldwide strategy to contain Communism. There is a continuing scholarly and political debate about this period in 1954 when the fighting came to an end in Vietnam but the political issues still remained unsettled. What can be said without contradiction is that once an attempt was undertaken to establish a separate state in southern Vietnam and so to deny to the Communists the victory that they believed entitled them to control over the whole of Vietnam the prospect ahead was for further war.

Revolution in Vietnam in its first anti-French phase entailed by far the highest costs of all the political changes that had taken place in the period immediately after the Second World War in the former colonies of Southeast Asia. But despite these costs, despite the political effort that the Viet-Minh had waged alongside their military battles, the Vietnamese Communists were not initially in a position to risk a frontal collision with the southern anti-Communist state that the United States supported from 1954. Most particularly were the Communists unable to consider such an option since their allies, the Chinese and the Russians, had made clear at the Geneva Conference that the interests of the Vietnamese Communists had to be subordinated to those of the major Communist powers. And these major powers, in 1954, were not prepared to risk a wider conflict in order to ensure that the Vietnamese Communists achieved the success that they believed should be theirs.

In contrast to Indonesia, therefore, the first post-war decade did not settle Vietnam's post-colonial status and leave it unified under a single government. Instead, two states emerged within the territory of Vietnam, each claiming the right to control the whole of that geographic territory. For the Communists in Vietnam the revolution had only half succeeded. There is little doubt that they were confident full success would eventually be theirs. But there is equally little doubt that neither they nor any other observers of Vietnamese politics in the mid-1950s had gauged just how high the final cost of establishing a unified Communist Vietnam would be.

The rest of Southeast Asia had its share of revolt and rebellion in the period immediately following the end of the Second World War, but in no other country were there struggles for independence to match the experience of Indonesia and Vietnam. To a considerable extent this was the case because in no other Southeast Asian country had the former colonial power been so reluctant to give up control as was the case with the Dutch and the French. Some attention will be given in the next chapter to the continuing problems of regional dissent and attempted subversion of the independent states of Southeast Asia. For the moment, however, there is need to consider the two other significant challenges to established authority that did occur following the Second World War—the Huk insurgency in the Philippines and the Communist challenge to the government in Malaya during the Emergency period.

When the Japanese war ended the Philippines rapidly attained full independence and began to face up to the immense physical damage and social dislocation that had been caused by the war. Among those who expected to play a significant part in the post-war process were members of the Huk movement, a Communist-led group that had waged a limited but successful series of guerrilla campaigns against the Japanese in the central and southern sections of the major island of Luzon. Few if any denied that the role of the Huks during the war was admirable. But just as the French Communists, who had played an important part in the Resistance against the Germans, were distrusted by those who had been their wartime allies once peace came, so in the Philippines the largely conservative political elite looked warily at the Huks. This wariness was made even sharper when the Huks successfully contested seven seats in the 1946 elections. For small though these election successes were, the prospect now existed of an outspoken group working within the parliamentary system with aims that ran totally contrary to the generally shared values of the Philippine elite. The Huks, it should be noted, were advocates of a programme of land to the tillers that would have radically altered the established economic structure of the Philippines' primary producing industries, particularly the sugar industry. Fearful of change and doubting their capacity to confront the Huks the other political parties in the Philippine Congress refused to permit the men elected on the Huk ticket to take their seats. This signalled the end to any possibility of an accommodation between conservative and radical interests and the beginning of the Huk rebellion.

In the early phases of their challenge to the government the Huks demonstrated a continuing capacity to rally support among the peasantry as they had done during the war. Within the areas of central and southern Luzon that had been their wartime strongholds the Huks became, in effect, an alternative government. The success that they enjoyed led their leaders to hope that the movement could become a national one, instituting a radical revolution throughout the whole of the Philippines. This estimation failed to take into account the very local factors that had made success possible in central Luzon. In that area of the Philippines, in very considerable contrast to most other sections of the country, the structure of traditional society had already been very weak by the time radical groups first sought to gain power in the 1930s. The Huks had succeeded in this area since there was no real alternative to resist them. When such an alternative did exist, in the form of long-established and entrenched landowning interests, the Huks found it impossible to rally support. Although it was difficult for the Huks to understand why it should be so, the fact that a strong social struc-ture existed linking landowners with tenant farmers and peasants in well-established relationships was more important than the inequal-ities that were part of that social system.

So it was that in early 1950 the Huks reached the height of their success but were not able to move from the plateau of achievement that this success represented. By the end of the same year the Philippine government was on the offensive against the Huks and within a further three years the worst of the insurgency was over. The reasons for this remarkable change are readily recounted, even if there is room for debate concerning the importance that should be accorded to the various factors involved. Of great importance was the government's success in capturing almost the entire Huk polit-buro (political leadership) in a raid carried out in Manila in October 1950. Following information provided by an informer the govern-ment forces were able to seize both personnel and plans in a blow from which the Huks were never able to recover. This success took place at a time when a remarkable Philippine leader, Ramon Magsaysay, was beginning to make his energetic presence felt as Secretary of Defence. Critics of the Philippines and of its relationship with the United States have argued that much of the energy that Magsaysay was able to instill into his forces as they confronted the Huks was the result of American advice and assistance. Such advice and assistance were certainly important, but there seems no reason to diminish the part that Magsaysay played. His energy and personal bravery can scarcely be questioned and the loyalty he won from his troops seems equally to be beyond dispute. Just as importantly, the policies that he announced, even if their implementation was patchy, gave some promise that the government was genuinely concerned with the problems of rural poverty and inequality.

Magsaysay's success in scaling down the Huk threat to the point where control of the insurgent remnants was a police responsibility played a significant part in his election to the presidency of the Philippines in 1953. His sudden accidental death in 1957 came at a time when much of the programme for rural improvement that he advocated still waited to be put into action. But there was no longer any doubt that the Huks were defeated by the time of his death. Remnants of the Huk forces continued to oppose the government and rural insecurity has remained a problem of fluctuating proportions to the present day. But the threat to the unity of the Philippines from the Huks had ended, however much other problems remained to be faced.

The events of the Emergency period in Malaya (the West Malaysia of the later Malaysian Federation) between 1948 and 1960 posed a much longer threat to the government of that country than was ever the case with the Huks, despite the latter's regional success. Having said this, and having noted that the Emergency lasted officially for a twelve-year period, due account should also be taken of the fact of how very different this Communist challenge was from that mounted by the Viet-Minh and discussed earlier in this chapter. In fact, both the defeat of the Huks in the Philippines and the defeat of the Communist insurgents in Malaya have all too often been taken as guides to action that might have been taken in Vietnam once the Second Indochinese War was in progress. Such an erroneous view misses several points that are of vital importance for an understanding of the recent history of Southeast Asia. First, there is the failure to recognise how very particular the Huk insurgency, the period of the Emergency in Malaya, and the Communist-led anti-colonial wars in Vietnam each were. If one fails to take account of the great differences that existed from country to country it is all too easy to disregard the different issues that dominated the thinking of those engaged in the various military and political campaigns that took place. And one is likely to be trapped into thinking that insurgencies occur and can be suppressed according to formula.

Several features of the Malayan Emergency period set it sharply apart from developments in Vietnam and the Philippines. In both of these latter cases the men who fought against the established government, whether it was the French in Vietnam or a government of Filipinos in the Philippines, were members of the dominant population group in each country. The Huks, in the one case, were Filipinos fighting Filipinos. The Viet-Minh, in the other case, were Vietnamese fighting the French, or Vietnamese supported by the French. In the Emergency, in great contrast, the insurgents were overwhelmingly Chinese in ethnic composition in a country in which the Chinese population was itself a minority and in which accept-ance of Malay political dominance was regarded as a matter beyond dispute by all but the smallest group among those who engaged in the country's political life.

Both the Huks, in their period of success, and the Vietnamese throughout their war against the French, could make their appeals for support in terms of their role as nationalists as well as Commu-nists. This was never a convincing possibility for the ethnically Chinese Communist insurgents in Malaya. They claimed to be fighting for the 'Malayan people', and to be leading the struggle against British colonialism. But these claims had to be made against a background in which not only Malay politicians but also Malayan Chinese politicians denounced their activities. What was more, for all of their claims to be fighting for the liberation of the population of Malaya, the insurgents could hardly prevent that population from realising that steady progress was being made towards attaining independence from Britain throughout the Emergency.

Despite the weakness of their propaganda the Communist insur-gents in Malaya gave striking proof of the heavy cost that could be exacted by a determined guerrilla group fighting under geographical conditions that were favourable to them and with the possibility present of gaining the passive support of unprotected civilians. Once the Malayan Communist Party decided to follow an armed strategy its forces faded into the dense jungle that covers so much of the Malayan Peninsula. From there they were able to mount raids against vulnerable targets, isolated police posts, district administra-tive offices, the bungalows of planters and tin mine managers. Judged against the horrifyingly high cost in human lives that marked the war fought in Vietnam, the casualty figures from the Malayan Emergency appear relatively small. But the number of men killed and wounded was not by itself a satisfactory reflection of the impact that the insurgents achieved. That impact was also felt in the threat the insurgents posed to Malaya's economy as it gradually recovered from the dislocation of the Japanese occupation period. And the impact of the insurgents was also significant in terms of the possibility that the granting of independence would be delayed because of insecurity.

The response of the British colonial government to the Emergency recognised the broad range of threats that the insurgency posed. Although the colonial government's initial reactions to the problems of the Emergency involved a degree of uncertainty and even confusion, this was soon replaced by carefully constructed military and political effort. The essentials of the effort involved isolating the insurgents from the rest of the civil population and protecting that population from attack or intimidation by the insurgents. At the same time as these essentially military goals were pursued, the need to work for Malayan independence was never forgotten, a fact reflected in the granting of independence in 1957, less than five years after the most serious period of the Emergency.

Isolating the insurgents from the rest of the population was of particular importance in Malaya because of the existence after the Second World War of a substantial squatter population that lived largely outside normal government control. These squatters were almost all Chinese residents of Malaya who had moved into squatter communities in the course of the economically depressed years of the 1930s or during the Japanese occupation. Their importance to the insurgents once the Emergency began lay in their capacity to furnish both recruits and supplies. The total guerrilla force opposed to the colonial government in Malaya never numbered more than around 9,000, but many of these were recruited from the squatter communities in which there were young people who were readily persuaded that a revolution could transform their lives. Almost as important as the supply of recruits was the capacity of these isolated squatter communities to pass food supplies to the insurgents, since the latter's jungle retreats were mostly unsuited to food production and access to other food sources was vital.

Once the importance of the squatter community was recognised and the magnitude of the problem they posed appreciated, the British colonial government undertook a resettlement scheme that has become known as one of the most distinctive features of the Emergency. Nearly half a million squatters were resettled or relocated in 'new villages' over a space of two years. Once resettled the squatters became the responsibility of the police forces, leaving the military to pursue the guerrillas in the jungles. This was a slow and tedious business, costly more in terms of time and effort than in terms of lives. Even with an overwhelming superiority of personnel

21   Tunku Abdul Rahman
Tunku Abdul Rahman was the 'father' of Malaysia's independence and its country's first prime minister. Born a prince, he became an active politician during the Second World War. During the period of the Malayan Emergency Tunku Abdul Rahman exemplified the commitment of Malay politicians to work with the British to defeat the Communist insurgents while preparing for independence. *Photograph courtesy of* Far Eastern Economic Review

on the government side, the tide did not turn decisively against the Communist guerrillas until 1954. By then, however, there was no doubt that the insurgents would be defeated and that Malaya would gain independence with the capacity to bring the Emergency to a final end. Acting as a minority of a minority, the ethnic Chinese insurgents never succeeded in presenting themselves as bearers of the nationalist banner. Their appeal was strong for a limited group, particularly young Chinese who felt that there was little place for them in existing Malayan society. But for the rest of the Chinese community in Malaya and for the overwhelming bulk of the Malay community, the appeal of Communism launched by guerrillas who were ready to resort to brutal punishment and killings of civilians was limited indeed. The Emergency should not be dismissed as a relatively minor problem because of the way in which, once the initial period of shock and confusion passed, the odds against the insurgents became steadily worse. At the same time, the enormous differences between the problems posed by the insurgency in Malaya and the Second Indochinese War should be firmly recognised. In taking the successful defeat of the Communist guerrillas in Malaya as an indication of what could be achieved in Vietnam later, military planners came close to the hoary old error of comparing a minnow with a whale.

In the four countries of Southeast Asia discussed in this chapter, Indonesia, Malaya, the Philippines, and Vietnam, the years after the Second World War were marked by violence. But as has been repeatedly stressed throughout the chapter the nature of the violence, the issues for which men fought and died, and the results of the conflicts that were joined, differed greatly from country to country. The differences that have been stressed are a forceful reminder of the individual character of the states of Southeast Asia, whatever generalities are noted at other times. The Indonesian nationalist revolution against Dutch attempts to reimpose some form of colonial control reminds us that revolutions need not be mounted only by Communists. The partial success of the Vietnamese Communists by mid-1954 took place in conditions that had no parallel in the rest of Southeast Asia. The unsuccessful Communist revolts in Malaya and the Philippines demonstrated the futility of groups that sought their ends through armed insurrection but which could not, again for different reasons in each case, make their appeal beyond a limited section of the overall population. Revolution and revolt have been a very significant feature of the history of much of Southeast Asia since the Second World War but for different reasons, in different countries, and at different times.

11
Other Paths to Independence

OF the countries considered in the previous chapter two achieved independence through revolutionary means; these were Indonesia and Vietnam. One, Malaysia, prepared for independence while containing and then defeating a major challenge from Communist insurgents. The case of the Philippines was different again since the Huk insurgents were defeated by an independent government. The varied experience of these four countries once again emphasises the diversity of Southeast Asia and an awareness of diversity is reinforced when one reviews the paths followed to independence by the other countries of the region.

The case of Thailand need not detain us long at this stage since it was, as has been noted many times, the only country in Southeast Asia that did not have a history of colonial occupation. As already stated in the chapter dealing with the Second World War, Thailand did for a period have to face the possibility that its association with the losing Japanese side might lead to the victorious Allied forces seeking to impose punishment, either economic or political. This, however, did not take place and Thailand resumed its status as a free nation at the end of the war—freer, in fact, in some ways since it was no longer encumbered with treaties that had once given special privileges to foreigners in Thailand.

We are thus left to consider the cases of Burma and the other two countries that went to make up French Indochina, Cambodia and Laos. In Burma the history of the years following the defeat of the Japanese until the proclamation of independence in 1948 were full of complex and often bitter manoeuvring between the various groups active in Burmese political life. This manoeuvring took place at the same time as frequently acrimonious negotiations between the Burmese and British thrashed out the details of the final steps to independence. The end of the Second World War revealed how factional were Burmese political interests. Some of the factional divisions depended on ideological loyalties, with groups spanning a wide range of positions from conservatism to support for varying interpretations of Marxism. The fact that it was clear the British *were* leaving did little to minimise these divisions. To the contrary, now that independence seemed assured, the various groups felt a greater need to assert their positions. They saw the situation as one in which there might still be advantage to be gained before the British departure introduced a new and unpredictable state of affairs.

Other divisions resulted from the long-established rivalries between the Burmans and the other ethnic groups making up the Burmese population, the Shans, Karens, Chins and Kachins, to mention the most prominent of these minorities. Under British rule special arrangements had been made to govern many of the minority peoples in a fashion separate from the Burman majority. Now that independence was in sight politicians representing sections of the minority peoples strove to ensure that they should continue to enjoy special rights as they had done under the British. To a considerable extent the Burman leadership under General Aung San, the leader of those Burmans who had organised to fight the Japanese in the closing phases of the Second World War, was ready to make concessions to the minorities. Aung San and his colleagues were not ready to permit the establishment of independent states delineated on an ethnic basis, but they were ready to recognise that a sense of ethnic identity and past administrative practice made it necessary for some alternative to treating areas such as the Shan regions in northern and eastern Burma as if they were identical with the Burman-populated Irrawaddy valley.

Because history can only tell us what happened in the past, the question of what *might* have happened in Burma if Aung San had been able to continue at the head of the Burmese Government after independence cannot be answered. What did happen was that the reality of Burmese political factionalism was made tragically clear through the political assassination of Aung San and six of his associates. With Aung San's death in July 1947, Burma lost its most able politician, but progress towards independence was not checked. Aung San's place was taken by U Nu, the man who was to become the first prime minister of independent Burma and the dominant figure in Burmese politics throughout the 1950s. But although progress towards independence was maintained it took place in an atmosphere of increasing disunity and rising violence. When independence was proclaimed in January 1948 it was the prelude to a period of grave instability and finally full-scale rebellion against the central government by several of the political and minority groups who were unready to accept the political structure that independence had brought. The fact that Burma had reached the goal of independence without the costly struggles that had marked developments in Indonesia and Vietnam had not proved to be any guarantee against major and costly disorder once the colonial power withdrew.

Of all the countries that have been studied in Southeast Asia few have received such limited examination of their modern history as Cambodia and Laos. In the case of Cambodia the record of this country's magnificent and distant past has tended to obscure the interest of more modern times. In the case of Laos, the small size of the country in terms of population, numbering perhaps three million in the 1970s, has led to its being treated as little more than a footnote to the dramatic events that have taken place in neighbouring Vietnam since the Second World War. For by comparison with both Cambodia and Laos, indeed, Vietnam's history has been a more demanding and apparently more immediately important subject for study. Because of this relative lack of attention to these two countries there is real difficulty for a casual observer of Southeast Asian affairs to understand why there should have been such momentous changes in such a short span of time since the Second World War. How, both casual and specialist observer alike may well ask, did the apparently sleepy monarchies of Cambodia and Laos become, in the space of less than thirty years, Communist states, with Cambodia undergoing one of the most radical revolutions in modern history? Only now, more than thirty years after Cambodia and Laos gained independence, can we begin to see some of the elements in the period before the attainment of that independence that hinted at the possibility of history following the course that it did.

The contrast between the history of Vietnam and that of the other two components of French Indochina, Cambodia and Laos, could not be sharper. In terms of modern political developments, Vietnam was always in advance of its neighbours in opposing the French colonial presence. The 1920s and 1930s were two decades in Vietnam during which the Vietnamese Communists became a vital if almost constantly persecuted force. The same decades in Cambodia and Laos saw virtually no nationalist, let alone Communist, agitation against the colonial administration. And as has been noted in an earlier chapter the French returned to Cambodia and Laos at the end of the Second World War after encountering a minimum of opposition. Once again the contrast between the tense period in Vietnam in 1946 before the Franco-Viet-Minh War broke out and developments in Cambodia and Laos during the same period is sharp.

Despite this contrast and the apparent comic opera world of royal courts, sacred elephants, ancient temples, and orange-robed monks to be found in both Laos and Cambodia, the Second World War had wrought its changes in these countries too. In Laos an anti-French group had emerged during the years of war with a royal prince of radical persuasion, Souphanouvong, as one of its most prominent members. When the war ended in 1945 Souphanouvong and a small number of companions refused to accept the option that others of their wartime companions embraced. Rather than agree to the return of the French and to waiting for the eventual granting of self-government and finally independence, Souphanouvong and those who shared his views went into the jungle and linked their goal of independence to the struggle that the neighbouring Vietnamese were just beginning.

Much ink has flowed as writers of various views have debated whether or not the Communist movement in Laos possessed an identity separate from the Vietnamese Communists. The best short answer is that it was, and is, a Laotian movement first and foremost but that because of Laos' geographical position and the smallness and weakness of its population the Laotian Communists have always been dependent upon their ideological allies in Vietnam. During the First Indochinese War, in any event, areas of northeastern Laos were vitally important to the strategy of the Vietnamese Communists and the Laotian Communist forces, the Pathet Lao as they called themselves, worked in close conjunction with, and at times under the immediate direction of, the Vietnamese.

French policy in Laos from 1946 onwards aimed at minimising political difficulties while contending with the strategic problems of the Vietnamese and Pathet Lao forces in the northeast. Their search for political calm in the most populated area of Laos along the Mekong River was aided by the general inclination of the Laotian elite, a tiny proportion of the total population of three million, to accept the continuing colonial presence without hesitation. The royal family and the semi-hereditary traditional officials were happy, for the most part, to cooperate in a system that brought them personal rewards for a minimum of effort. Prince Souphanouvong with his political commitment, his knowledge of the West, and his readiness to accept the rigours of life in the jungle seemed very much the exception to the elite Laotian general rule.

The exception represented by Souphanouvong and the other members of the Pathet Lao came to be of vital importance as the First Indochinese War drew to a close. Suffering military defeat at

Dien Bien Phu the French Government that negotiated for with-drawal from Vietnam at the Geneva Conference in 1954 no longer had any interest in maintaining control over the weak Kingdom of Laos, that had been theoretically independent since late 1953. But a problem existed. The French wished to transfer power to those conservative Laotians who had cooperated with them between 1946 and 1954, to the members of the traditional elite. Yet neither the French nor the traditional elite controlled those northern sections of the kingdom in which the Communist Pathet Lao were strongest. A compromise was finally reached. Laos, now fully independent, was to take special account of the Pathet Lao forces and to integrate them, eventually, into the country's army.

Like many compromises determined on paper this provision failed to work in reality. The independence Laos gained in 1953–4 was flawed from the beginning. The conservative groups in the kingdom had little interest in permitting the left-wing Pathet Lao to gain a legal foothold, while the interests of the Pathet Lao most certainly did not lie in acting as the willing subordinates of their political enemies. Just as Laos gained this flawed independence as a side-effect of more important developments in Vietnam, so too was the next major stage in Laotian political history determined by the mounting pressures of the Second Indochinese War.

Unlike Laos, Cambodia did not form a major strategic element in the First Indochinese War. Nor did a clearly defined Cambodian Communist movement emerge between 1946 and 1953, the date when Cambodia was officially declared independent. The important domestic political controversies associated with Cambodia's progress towards independence related, instead, to whether the traditional leadership of the kingdom under the then King Sihanouk would control an independent government or whether power would pass into the hands of men who, while little less conservative, wished the king to act as a constitutional monarch. As for relations with the French, once Sihanouk was able to demonstrate his predominance in domestic affairs the task of persuading the French to grant independence was essentially a matter of time. Just as Laos gained independence in conjunction with developments in Vietnam, so was Cambodia under Sihanouk able to press France for independence at a time when the deteriorating situation in Vietnam in 1953 made resistance to Cambodian demands scarcely worthwhile.

By the time Sihanouk was making his demands he had gained the political ascendancy in Cambodia and in doing so set the stage for more than a decade of independence in which he was the chief political actor. Emerging from a timid and sheltered childhood he

22   Prince Norodom Sihanouk
Prince Norodom Sihanouk of Cambodia has been one of the most
remarkable of Southeast Asia's leaders. Crowned King in 1941, he led his
country to independence in 1953. He abdicated his throne in 1955 and was
overthrown by close associates in 1970. A prisoner of the Khmer Rouge
under Pol Pot, he has been in exile since 1979. *Photograph by David
Jenkins courtesy of* Far Eastern Economic Review

gradually moved from cautious interest to full-scale involvement in
the political affairs of his kingdom. Once he took the decision to
become closely involved in politics, and with the benefit of some
particularly able older advisers, his status as king made him virtually
beyond challenge in the realm of overt politics.

As for clandestine politics before 1953, when Cambodia gained
independence, and 1954 when the First Indochinese War ended,
there was little to suggest that Cambodia would ever become the

site for a full-scale clash between right and left. Whatever has
happened subsequently, the Communist movement was not of
major importance in Cambodia between the end of the Second
World War and the granting of independence in 1953. There were
Vietnamese Communist units that used Cambodia for a base and
there were, undoubtedly, Cambodians who were associated with
these units. Moreover, some at least of the leaders of the new
Communist Kampuchea (the name chosen by the new rulers of
Cambodia after their victory in 1975) were already translating their
beliefs into action by taking to the *maquis* in this period. But to look
back on the years 1946–53 in terms of the clear emergence of a
Communist alternative to Sihanouk would be to commit a major
historical error.

Individual names have been closely linked with the attainment of
independence in various of the countries of Southeast Asia. The
name of Ho Chi Minh is first to mind in relation to Vietnam. Aung
San's name will continue to dominate discussion of Burma's
achievement of independence. When one thinks of independence in
Malaya one thinks of Tunku Abdul Rahman. The matching of name
to country and independence could go on, sometimes with sharp
argument over which name should be chosen. A case can surely be
made, however, for the proposition that in no other Southeast
Asian country was one man so crucially important to and identified
with the gaining of independence as was Sihanouk in Cambodia.
Hesitant to become involved in politics initially and far from always
astute once his involvement began, he came by 1953 to dominate
the scene. This was his triumph. The years that followed, some
would argue, were both his and his country's tragedy.

By the late 1950s almost the whole of Southeast Asia was independent. Thailand had never known formal colonialism. The Philippines had gained independence from the United States at the end of
the Second World War, while Burma's path to independence from
Britain, gained in 1948, always seemed assured if frequently made
difficult by various obstacles along the way. Indonesia's revolution
brought Dutch withdrawal by the end of 1949. And the countries of
French Indochina saw the departure of the colonial authorities in
1954, leaving two rival Vietnamese states, and Laos and Cambodia.

Britain's departure from Malaya was delayed until 1957, in part
because of the lingering problems of the Communist insurgency and
in part, too, because of difficulties associated with finding a political
formula that would reconcile the expectation of the Malay community of political dominance over a population that included a very
large minority of non-Malay (most particularly Chinese) citizens.

With a formula assuring Malay dominance achieved, while involving ethnic Chinese in the open political process, the granting of independence to Malaya left only a residue of British colonial rule in Southeast Asia. Singapore and the territories of Sarawak and North Borneo (now Sabah) were all that remained of Britain's Southeast Asian empire. These, too, were shortly to end their colonial status when, in 1963, the Federation of Malaysia came into being uniting independent Malaya with Singapore, Sarawak, and Sabah.

With the establishment of Malaysia only Brunei remained as a non-independent state—technically a protectorate under Britain, not a colony. Oil-rich, Brunei had been offered the opportunity to join Malaysia, but had declined. The Sultan of Brunei feared that to integrate with Malaysia would lead to the submerging of Brunei's identity and to the loss of a large proportion of his state's revenues, which made it the wealthiest in Southeast Asia. Not until January 1984 did Brunei finally achieve an independent status.

For most, and possibly all of the formerly colonised countries of Southeast Asia the attainment of independence was accompanied by a sense of relief, and in some cases of euphoria. Even in the war-ravaged circumstances of Vietnam, where the Communist administration only gained control over half of the country it had hoped to govern, there was relief that the fighting had ended and an expectation—false, as it proved—that extension of control over the south would not be long delayed. The increasing violence and dissidence that marked the final months leading up to Burma's independence did not make it any less important an occasion. Nor did the fact that the Emergency was still officially in force and the difficulties associated with communal politics in Malaya make *Merdeka* (Independence) seem less desirable in 1957.

Relief and euphoria were natural and readily understood emotions for those who now enjoyed independence. But with that goal achieved the problems as well as the pleasures of independence had to be faced. An attempt to assess those problems and the various ways in which the states of Southeast Asia have confronted them is provided in the next chapter.

12
Independent Southeast Asia

For those who have never known what it was like to live under colonial rule the importance of achieving independence can only be partially understood. Attaining independence, for the peoples of all of the states of Southeast Asia with the recurring exception of Thailand, involved more than a simple change of political control and leadership. These things were important, but if as outsiders we concentrate exclusively on the political changes involved in the attainment of independence we shall fail to appreciate, however imperfectly, the almost magical and certainly spiritual quality that was felt by many Southeast Asians, leaders and their followers alike, when either willingly or otherwise the colonial rulers departed. Independence was seen by Southeast Asians as involving transformation of all kinds, political, economic, and social. But the history of independent Southeast Asia has frequently involved the need to adjust the hopes for change and progress that seemed so readily within reach as the Americans, the British, the Dutch, and the French handed over control of government to their former colonial subjects.

Southeast Asia in the 1980s is not unique in facing major problems, many without clear or easy possibilities for solution. Indeed, the 1960s and the 1970s have made clearer than ever before the error of any Western observer who dares to look at Southeast Asia as a 'problem' area without taking due account of the many and complex difficulties that afflict the so-called developed world. Keeping this fact firmly in mind, the perspective of ten, twenty, and even thirty years of independence for the countries of Southeast Asia—with Thailand's experience revealing a very similar pattern of development despite the lack of a colonial past—does suggest that Southeast Asia is a region that faces major, even intractable problems. In this chapter an attempt will be made to survey those problems that have been of the greatest importance to the governments of independent Southeast Asia. For the three states of Indo-china (Cambodia, Laos, and Vietnam), the wars that have raged over their territory can scarcely be described simply as problems. The history of these three countries between 1955 and 1975 was so special that they are best considered separately from the rest of the region.

Many of the problems that have confronted the leaders of Southeast Asia in the years of independence since the end of the Second World War are similar to those that have been experienced by other countries in what has come to be known as the Third World. In other parts of Asia, in the Middle East, and in Africa, states that once had been colonies emerged into independence, as did the countries of Southeast Asia, with high hopes but frequently limited resources. In almost any field that one chooses to examine the newly independent states faced formidable difficulties. It is easy, moreover, to see why the leaders of the newly independent states should often have felt that the former colonial rulers had failed to tackle major issues that seemed to demand immediate attention from a new, independent leadership. It is important to remember that whatever high-sounding phrases were used to justify the process there is little possibility of disputing the fact that colonial rule was *never* introduced or maintained in the interest of the colonised country or people. This fundamental fact meant colonial regimes had different priorities from the newly independent regimes that followed them. And this fact posed immense difficulties for the new leaders.

A few examples may make the point clearer. Although all of the colonial regimes that ruled in Southeast Asia paid some attention to the need to provide education for at least part of the population that they governed, none, not even the most enlightened, felt it necessary to promote a system of universal education at the primary level on the same basis as that operating in the regime's home country. However one chooses to judge the colonial regimes' policies in education—and different judgements would have to be made for different colonial governments and in different colonised countries—the need to improve educational opportunities was seen as an essential step by all of the newly independent governments of Southeast Asia. At a rather different level, the colonial governments of Southeast Asia were, in general, little concerned to prepare the populations of the countries in the region to play a direct role in the economic life of the community. With the colonies valued for their economic resources, a pattern was widespread in which European or American companies controlled major international commerce, while internal commerce was shared between the colonisers and immigrant Asian communities, usually Chinese or Indian. There were variations on this theme and important exceptions to the general rule. Nonetheless, it is correct to note that the leaders of the newly independent Asian states found all too often that they and their countrymen had only a limited control over their own economies.

The reference that has just been made to the immigrant communities that were such a feature of so much of Southeast Asia under colonial rule points to yet another instance of the assumptions that governed the pre-independent years changing dramatically once independence came. For colonial governments the immigrant communities played a vital role, particularly in commerce and in the provision of labour for plantations and public works. For the independent governments of Southeast Asia the immigrant communities represented something very different, at best a group posing problems of assimilation, at worst a threat to the security and integrity of the state.

The list of problems that confronted the new leaders of independent Southeast Asia and have continued to confront them can only seem lengthy and daunting. Few problems are so widespread as that of essentially unrestrained population growth. For years the problems associated with the growth of Indonesia's population, particularly on the drastically overcrowded island of Java, have overshadowed the implications of rapid population growth elsewhere in Southeast Asia. Only recently, for instance, has there been a broader recognition that the dramatic increase in Thailand's population in the past two decades has begun to strain that country's current agricultural resources. Thailand's problems are still of a different order from those found in Java, where a shortage of arable land even leads to the ground directly alongside railway lines being cultivated. But the old image of Thailand as a country with open frontiers is no longer valid. Population pressure is a significant problem in the Philippines, also, and even in the smallest of the Southeast Asian states, Singapore, effective family planning programmes pursued since the mid-1960s will still not be able to prevent the total population nearly doubling by the end of the century.

Expansion of education, the threats posed by rapid growth of the population, the need to provide adequate health care, all these are social goals that have been proclaimed by the independent governments of Southeast Asia. But such goals are costly and have placed heavy demands on national budgets that have frequently been sharply and adversely affected by changing patterns in the world economic situation and by the difficulties involved in transforming a colonial economy into a national economy. A country such as Indonesia is staggeringly rich in resources that range from oil and copper to rubber and tin. Finding a way of exploiting these resources and developing an economy that can balance the costs of administering and defending a population exceeding 180 million spread over a vast distance from Sumatra to Irian Jaya (West New Guinea) has proved to be a daunting task. And what applies in Indonesia applies elsewhere in the region, if on a smaller scale, as governments have had to establish a set of priorities for economic development, find the personnel able to manage the programmes that have been decided upon, and find the finance to change plans into reality. In pursuit of their development goals the role of foreign aid has, for the non-Communist states of Southeast Asia, been important. Foreign assistance should not, however, be accorded an importance that it does not deserve. In the final analysis success or failure in confronting the problems of Southeast Asia's economic development is a matter that will be decided by the governments and populations of the region rather than by outsiders. This, indeed, has been the philosophy behind the policies that have been followed by the Burmese Government since the early 1960s under which stress is placed upon self-reliance and the limitation of foreign economic activity in the country. The cost in terms of economic growth has been considerable and none of the non-Communist states of the region have sought to follow Burma's example.

Against this background of demanding economic problems and of costly but essential social programmes in the fields of health and education there is another set of problems that faces the independent governments of Southeast Asia that is the most serious of all: the problem of achieving and maintaining national unity. No exaggeration is involved in the observation that without a significant degree of national unity all of the other goals of the independent states are in jeopardy, if they can ever be attained. Working to attain national unity has, for all of the countries of the region, been the prime concern since the gaining of independence.

The problem of achieving and maintaining national unity has existed on two levels in most of Southeast Asia. On the one hand there has been the problem of arriving at an agreed form of national government—a basic issue concerned with such matters as which group or groups in the community should hold power and under what limitations. Then on the other hand there have been the problems associated with the interests of regions and minorities. In this latter case the issue of whether or not a central government's interests should override those of a group or region within the state has been at the heart of extended debate and on occasion armed struggle.

For an outsider the latter type of problem—that connected with the clash of interests between the majority group and the minority, or minorities, in the population, or between a central power and a region—may be easier to comprehend. The extent to which regional and minority interests have not disappeared from Europe are an aid to our understanding. Even as recently as twenty years ago there was a tendency to discount the importance of regional and minority interests within the developed states of Europe. In the 1980s no student of politics could take such a position. In Britain, perhaps the most fundamentally stable of all the Western democracies, the Scottish and Welsh nationalists have shown that the special interests of their regions within a governmentally unified state can no longer be met solely by the central parliament in London. The importance of regional interest has been even more strikingly demonstrated in Spain, following the end of the Franco dictatorship. And in many other areas of Europe the continuing importance of regional interests and the search for a separate identity by the ethnic minorities that are so often closely linked with one geographical area are abundantly apparent.

There should not be very much surprise therefore when we discover that regionalism and the interests of minority groups, who do not see their goals as being the same as those of a central government, are very much a part of contemporary Southeast Asia, and have been major problems for the countries that gained independence since the Second World War. The problems that confront the central government in Burma, for instance, are not really new problems, though there are new elements involved. The fact that there are substantial ethnic minority groups in Burma who wish to live independently, or at least semi-autonomiously rather than be controlled by the central government in Rangoon, is essentially a continuation of a long historical fact of life. The history of Burma for many centuries has had as one of its dominant characteristics the clash between the efforts of the Burmans to impose their control over the non-Burman elements in the population and resistance to these efforts. At best, in the past, the Burmans have succeeded in establishing a tenuous control over the Shans, Kachins, Karens and other minority groups that make up Burma's diverse population. With British colonial rule removed the old tensions between the dominant Burmans and the other ethnic groups within the state re-emerged and continue to pose a problem of real significance forty years after independence.

Regional problems are a continuing feature of the contemporary history of the Philippines. This fact provides another example of the way in which an independent Southeast Asian state has had to face a challenge that has developed from clear historical antecedents but has assumed new and more challenging characteristics in the post-colonial period. Under both Spanish and American colonialism the southern islands of the Philippines were a world apart. In the northern Philippines the impact of the Catholic Spanish rulers was considerable, making the Philippines the only area in Southeast Asia in which Christianity is the dominant religion. To the south, however, a different world existed, and indeed still exists today. For in the southern islands of the Philippines Islam was already established when the Spanish arrived. The Islamic faith sustained the population of large sections of the southern Philippines in their sense of separateness from their northern Catholic countrymen. This sense of separate identity was a cause for some problems, but so long as the government based in Manila, whether Spanish, American, or most recently Filipino did not seek to impose too strict a rule in the south, means could be found to balance the interests of the central government and those of the Islamic southerners.

The independent government of the Philippines has been concerned to impose its authority in the southern Islamic regions and the result has been the long drawn-out struggle that continues there. Put in the simplest terms this is a clash between those at the centre who believe that the integrity of the state requires a strong central government and those in an outer region of the state who do not share the interests, the religion, in a word the identity of those holding power at the centre. Those in the southern Philippines who resist the central government do not feel that they are part of the same complex of interests and shared obligations as those who look to Manila for leadership.

This lack of a sense of shared identity is to be found in other regions of Southeast Asia. The Islamic minority of southern Thailand provides a parallel example to that of the southern Philippines. In years gone by these ethnic Malay followers of Islam, in what is today southern Thailand, lived in a buffer state region. It was a region in which the rulers of Thailand claimed authority but seldom exercised it. Following the territorial adjustments that accompanied the British colonial advance into Malaya a substantial number of ethnic Malays, followers of Islam, found themselves under the control of a Thai state that was increasingly concerned to see an administrative unity prevailing within the kingdom. The numbers involved in the case of the Thai Islamic minority are smaller than is the case in the Philippines, but the nature of the problem they pose

is remarkably similar. From their point of view the Thai Government in Bangkok—ethnically Thai, Buddhist in religion, and
centralist in aims—cannot easily be seen as *their* government. From
the point of view of the rulers in Bangkok, the followers of Islam
within the territories of the state have a right to freedom of religion
but not to any other special privileges. The potentiality for tension
and conflict is obvious.

Even more so is this the case for the Thai Government in its
dealings with the tribal minorities of the northern sections of the
kingdom. Until very recent times the Meo, Karen, Akha and other
hill peoples who live in the north of Thailand had only the most
limited contact with the administrative apparatus of the Thai state.
The hill people lived in remote regions seldom visited by ethnic
Thais, followed their own customs, grew their own specialist crops
including opium, and traded with the lowland regions. In a period
when the government in Bangkok saw no need to demonstrate a
day-to-day control over border regions and when the lack of
population pressure meant that there was little interest on the part
of the lowland Thais in expanding agricultural settlement into the
hill regions such an arrangement was possible. The passage of time
has, however, brought major changes to the situation in Thailand
and so to the relationship between the hill peoples and the Bangkok
government. Thailand over the past twenty years has become
increasingly concerned to establish a clear control in its northern
border regions. As a result there has been an increase in the
government presence and so, for the first time, continuing contact
between the hill peoples and the police, the customs authorities, and
the many other instrumentalities of the state. At the same time the
rapid growth of the Thai population has led to settlement by ethnic
Thais of regions that had once been regarded as the preserve of the
hill peoples. When, to add to these potentially divisive factors, there
has in addition been an effort by supporters of Communism to
direct resentment against the government the complexities and
difficulties of the situation are readily imagined.

For all of the problems posed by its various minority groups,
Thailand's experience since the Second World War has never
matched the threat to the state that occurred in Indonesia in the late
1950s. Very early in this book one of the great differences between
the mainland states of Southeast Asia and those of the maritime
regions was noted. While mainland Southeast Asian states have,
very generally, a dominant population and a varying number of
minorities, the states of maritime Southeast Asia, and most
particularly Indonesia, are composed of a whole series of ethnic
groups, so that no single group is so clearly dominant as is the case,

for instance, with the Thais in Thailand. This contrast needs to be borne in mind when one looks at the threat to national unity that was posed by regional interests in Indonesia in the late 1950s. What was involved was not an attempted rebellion against one dominant ethnic group—the Meo of northern Thailand against the Thais, or the Shans of northern and eastern Burma against the Burmans. Instead, military and political leaders with regional interests in islands away from Java sought to challenge the authority of a central government in Jakarta that was supported by Indonesians of diverse ethnic backgrounds. The rebels were proclaiming through action their belief that regional interests—the interests of those in Sumatra and Sulawesi, particularly—were more important than the national interests embodied in strong central control from Jakarta. Despite clandestine backing from outside forces, the rebels failed and the unitary character of Indonesia was maintained. The rebellion showed, nevertheless, that regional interests were an important feature of Indonesia's society and presented an ever-present risk of division and disunity.

The search for ways to achieve national unity has led to a wide range of political formulas being tried and followed or rejected by the various states of Southeast Asia in their efforts to find a system of government to meet each independent state's individual needs. Given the very different background that the states of Southeast Asia have from the Western world, with different histories and different pressures operating on the governments of the region, the fact that Western models have been little used should not be a matter for great surprise. Western parliamentary systems have evolved over centuries. The history of the twentieth century alone has shown how fragile democratic parliamentary systems can be in many states of Europe. And a universal suffrage is, with the rarest exceptions a twentieth-century phenomenon in the West.

These facts need to be kept firmly in mind when looking at the different choices that have been made by the states of Southeast Asia as to how they should be governed. In three of the non-Communist states of modern Southeast Asia the military has been closely associated with government for lengthy periods. This is true for Burma, Thailand, and Indonesia, while in the Philippines President Marcos's declaration of martial law in the early 1970s depended for its effectiveness on the close support of the military. In each of the cases mentioned the military have seen their role in society as very different from the traditional role assigned to the military in many Western democracies. In those Southeast Asian states where the military has played and plays an important political

23   Ferdinand Marcos
As President of the Philippines between 1965 and 1986, Marcos dominated the political life of his country until he was overthrown in February 1986. *Photograph courtesy of* Far Eastern Economic Review

role this is undertaken with the conviction that the armed forces alone can be trusted to place national before sectional interests.

The army in Indonesia has continued to see itself as the guardian of the revolution that gained independence from the Dutch. During the years of Sukarno's rule, or misrule, the army became more and more disillusioned with the factional fighting of the political parties and more and more concerned with the growth of the Indonesian Communist Party's following. When, in 1965, there was a confused political situation following an attempted *coup d'état* in which the Communist Party was involved the army did not hesitate to assert its power and assume political control. The events of the year that followed the army's assumption of power strikingly illustrate the extent to which politics in modern Southeast Asia can excite passions and violence. While the Indonesian army ensured that it gained a tight control over the administration, tens of thousands of anti-Communists within the population seized the opportunity to strike a devastating blow against their political enemies. No certain figure exists for the numbers of Communists and Communist sympathisers killed at this time. Nor can we exclude the possibility that some, at least, of the killings that took place involved personal as much as political motives. But most foreign observers would regard a figure of 250,000 killed during the political upheaval of 1965–6 as the lowest acceptable estimate. Some estimates would be a great deal higher.

These events in Indonesia underline the extent to which political developments and decisions as to where power should lie and how it should be exercised often have little to do with the parliamentary patterns of the West. For the 'rules' that are accepted in Western countries often do not appear to Southeast Asians as valid for their own situation. The ballot box may indeed be used, and parliamentary forms adhered to, but usually in a system that allows the party or group that holds power to ensure that it retains that power. In Thailand, for instance, the military remain a vital feature of contemporary political life despite the increasing importance of a party system linked to a growing range of interest groups. The Malay politicians who have dominated the politics of Malaysia since independence have had no intention of altering the system that allows members of the Chinese minority within the country to participate in politics — and indeed to hold high office — but not to play the role of equal partner. And in the most recently independent state in Southeast Asia. Brunei, the ruler, and members of the royal family, exercise autocratic power without any indication of an intention to introduce a participatory form of government.

So long as the challenges that the established governments of Southeast Asia face include extra-parliamentary action such as insurgency, as well as opposition of a legal character, then so long should an outside observer expect that these governments in their search for ways to achieve their goals will pursue the means that seem best suited in their judgement rather than in accord with any model from the West.

One of the most important challenges that has confronted the various governments of Southeast Asia since the end of the Second World War has come from the political left, from Communism. Given the instability of the Southeast Asian region as a whole and the immense problems of social inequality that have existed and still exist, the fact that there should have been a radical left-wing challenge to governments that have often been conservative in character is to be expected. But because of the immense importance of the Vietnam war it is, perhaps, too easy to assume that Communism and those who have embraced its philosophy have been an equal force throughout Southeast Asia as a whole. Although it is true that there have been efforts to advance the cause of Communism in all of the states of modern Southeast Asia, only in Vietnam, Cambodia, and Laos have Communist governments come to power.

No single chapter in a general introduction to the history of Southeast Asia, let alone a section of a chapter, can do justice to the almost endless series of issues raised by any discussion of Communism in Vietnam. For Cambodia and Laos, by contrast, another problem arises. For Cambodia, in particular, we are still groping towards an understanding of the deeper history of developments over the past twenty-five years. Gaps in our knowledge of the history of the Communist movement in Cambodia, both before and after independence was gained in 1953, are only slowly being filled and it still must be the case that explanations as to why a shockingly radical Communist movement finally gained power in 1975 remain incomplete and even superficial. What we do know for each of the three countries of Indochina is that their historical experience from the middle 1950s onwards has been singularly different from that of the other countries of Southeast Asia. In brief, the fact that Communist governments have come to power in Cambodia, Laos, and Vietnam tells us little about the nature of left-wing politics elsewhere in the region, whether in terms of the past or of assessments for the future.

The ultimate success of the Vietnamese Communists in establishing a government over the whole of Vietnam reflects a long history of struggle and effective organisation. Of all the groups that sought to play a political role during French colonial times and to oppose colonial rule only the Communists were able both to survive severe French repression and to show that they had a coherent programme relevant to the facts of Vietnam's colonial situation. To make these observations does not involve an endorsement of the goals the Vietnamese Communists pursued. But history, as has been observed before in this book, is about what happened, not about what *might* have happened. In Vietnam the Communists, through a combination of outstanding leadership, political skill that sometimes included ruthless suppression of their Vietnamese rivals, and adherence to a political programme that offered clear, if not always successful, answers to problems posed by French colonialism, became the dominant political group in Vietnam by the end of the Second World War. The experience of the First Indochina War only served to reinforce that position. The subsequent American attempt to develop a rival Vietnamese government in southern Vietnam after 1954 failed to take account of the fact that however much an outside power could provide great quantities of material aid, and ultimately massive military assistance, no political movement existed in the Vietnam of the 1950s, 1960s, and 1970s that could challenge the Communists in the political field.

It is true, of course, that the Vietnamese Communists won their final battle through military means, but those military means would never have been successful if there had not been political cohesion in northern Vietnam. As for the southern region of the country in which war raged for so many years, argument can be joined as to how successful the Communists were in maintaining a political grip on the population. There is little room for debate, however, about the fact that none of the many governments in Saigon between 1954 and 1975 was able to demonstrate a capacity for associating the mass of the population with the goals they pursued. In contrast to the national goals pursued by the Communists, non-Communist politics in southern Vietnam were marked by squabbles between special interest groups, and by an incapacity to forge a sense of national purpose such as was achieved by the Communists. This sense of national purpose did not vanish with the end of the war. But peace brought a new set of problems to the Communist leaders of the country. The advent of peace also revealed the extent to which a country and a leadership so long geared for war lacked the managerial skills their new situation required. The costs of the long and bitter separation of southern from northern Vietnam brought their own special problems, shown most starkly and tragically in the flood of refugees seeking to escape from a society in which they felt there was no place for them. Vietnamese Communist leaders have repeatedly said that they value independence above all else, and this they did, indeed, gain in 1975. In the years that have followed it has sometimes seemed that there has been little else beyond independence that the Hanoi leadership has been able to offer its people as the policies that leadership has pursued have led to a regime of severe austerity.

The final success of the Communists in Vietnam came only after thirty years of war and more than forty years of political action. No comparable experience is to be found anywhere else in the history of modern Southeast Asia. Events in Laos after the Second World War did, it is true, have a certain parallel inasmuch as the Communist-led Pathet Lao forces were engaged in a political and military struggle that began with the end of the Second World War and continued until the Communist victory in Vietnam ensured that there would be a Communist victory in Laos also. To make this observation is not to dismiss the importance of the Laotian element in the developments that took place in Laos. But it would be foolish not to take note of the extent to which the military manoeuvring that took place in Laos was closely linked to developments in Vietnam. For here indeed was an important example of historical continuity. Laos has traditionally occupied a role as a buffer state region between the two powerful states of Vietnam and Thailand. In seeking to ensure the victory of the Laotian Communist forces the Vietnamese were also pursuing what had long been historical policy, that of ensuring that no other hostile state could play a significant role in Laos, and in particular in those regions of Laos that border Vietnam.

But if the accession to power of a Communist government in Laos may be seen as to some extent a footnote to developments in Vietnam, the same cannot be said with any accuracy of Cambodia. How then does one explain the dramatic change involved in Cambodia's history from the middle 1950s, when a king still ruled over the country, to the installation of a radical revolutionary government in the middle 1970s? At the outset it is wise to acknowledge that tremendous gaps remain in our knowledge of what happened in Cambodia in the 1960s when Prince Norodom Sihanouk appeared to dominate political life but when, it is now clear, there was a slowly developing group of men and women who were preparing themselves to fight for a Communist revolution once conditions made such a fight possible. Our knowledge of developments after Prince Sihanouk was overthrown in a right-wing *coup* in 1970 is even more incomplete. We do know enough, however, to sketch a rough outline of the most important developments.

It appeared to many outside observers of Prince Sihanouk's rule over Cambodia during the 1950s and 1960s that he had been re-markably successful in finding a governmental formula that guaranteed control of domestic politics and achievement of his foreign policy aims. Much of this success now appears to have been an illusion. Internally Sihanouk provided no place in his state for those who disagreed with his policies. For those who had embraced left-wing politics this increasingly meant that there were only two alternatives. Either one could remain silent or one could fade into the countryside and join the small but growing band of those who were waiting for a time when changed circumstances might make it possible to attempt a seizure of power. As it happened, it was the politicians of the right who finally turned Sihanouk out of office in

1970 and in doing so set the stage for one of the bitterest struggles by a left-wing group to gain power in all of recent Southeast Asian history.

The *coup* by men of the right was followed by Cambodia's involvement in the Vietnam war as the United States sought to buy time for the withdrawal of its troops from that latter country. With the American invasion of Cambodia in 1970 there was a Vietnamese response so that the new government in Phnom Penh found it was having to face the challenge of Vietnamese Communist forces as well as the left-wing Cambodians who now emerged to fight for their goal of controlling the country. By the end of 1972 the role of the Vietnamese Communists in fighting against the right-wing government in Phnom Penh was limited to supply and training assistance for the so-called *Khmer rouge*, or Red Khmer (Cambodians). The Cambodian civil war settled into a bloody pattern in which the government in Phnom Penh with massive American assistance— including bombing strikes of unparallelled intensity—faced a much smaller but remarkably dedicated left-wing enemy. If numbers and massive military and economic assistance could win wars, then the regime in Phnom Penh should have won. Its army vastly out-numbered the men of the left, who probably never had more than 60,000 troops fighting in their cause. But the outcome of wars depends on other things as well. The Cambodian left-wing forces were able to sustain their efforts in the face of tremendous odds—just how is still not really clear. The right-wing forces under Phnom Penh's leadership, on the contrary, lacked effective direction and a general conviction of the worth of what they were doing.

As the war continued so did it become clear that widespread brutality was the norm and not the exception. Perhaps the left-wing forces saw the use of harshly violent tactics against civilians as well as soldiers as the necessary weapon of the numerically weak. Possibly too their use of violence was not only to match the violence of the Phnom Penh forces but also a response to the ferocity of the bombing by United States aircraft. Whatever the reasons, the level of political violence and of atrocities against both combatants and civilians that marked the actions of both sides accelerated as the war continued. It seems clear that the leaders of the left-wing forces were reinforced by the experience of these desperate times in their conviction that once the war ended there could be no place for half measures. Cambodia was to be transformed completely, and at whatever cost in human lives and suffering.

Total transformation of society was, indeed, what the new radical government in Phnom Penh worked for after it gained power in April 1975. Led by Pol Pot, the government of Democratic

24   Exhumed skulls, Cambodia
Mass graves throughout Cambodia are a ghastly legacy of the Pol Pot
period of misrule over Cambodia. Following the Vietnamese invasion of
Cambodia in late 1978, many of these graves have been exhumed and the
skulls of Pol Pot's victims have been grouped by the graves as a reminder of
the hundreds of thousands who died by execution between 1975 and 1979.
The skulls and bones in this photograph were at a grave close to Phnom
Penh that was being exhumed in late 1981.

**27   Cambodian refugees awaiting food distribution on the Thai-Cambodian
border**
The Vietnamese invasion of Cambodia in late 1978 overthrew the Pol Pot
regime and was followed by a refugee exodus to the Thai-Cambodian
border. More than two hundred thousand refugees grouped along the
border, dependent on international aid for their survival. The refugees in
this photograph were waiting for rice distribution in Nong Chan camp in
1980.

25 Cambodian resistance fighter
In the aftermath of the Vietnamese invasion of Cambodia that began in late
1978, a variety of Cambodian resistance groups established themselves
along the Thai-Cambodian border. The largest of these resistance groups
were the remnants of Pol Pot's army, but others were loyal to Prince
Sihanouk and to other non-Communist leaders. The resistance fighter
pictured here was a member of the Khmer People's National Liberation
Front. He wears amulets and a Hindu god, Ganesha, about his neck as
charms against death.

Kampuchea pursued a series of policies that had as their justification the need to remove the corrupting influences of foreign and
capitalist societies and the goal of making Cambodia agriculturally
self-sufficient. The means by which these goals were to be achieved
only slowly became known to the outside world as Cambodia after
the Khmer Rouge victory was largely sealed off from foreign
visitors. It gradually became clear, however, that Pol Pot and his
associates were prepared to use shocking means in pursuit of their
ends. The mass forced evacuation of Phnom Penh in circumstances
that involved great cruelty and suffering was only the start of a
pattern of governmentally sponsored actions that were marked by
brutality and a disregard for human life. Herded into vast agricultural cooperatives, the bulk of the Cambodian population was
forced to work under inhuman conditions, risking sudden punishment including execution for even minor infraction of the harsh
rules that now governed their behaviour.

Much research remains to be done on the period when Pol Pot's
regime governed Cambodia. There do seem to have been some
variations between the degrees of brutality shown from one
administrative region to another within the country. And it may
never be satisfactorily possible to determine whether or not some,
or indeed many, of the executions that took place in Cambodia were
the result of government directive or the result of individual
decisions in a society that placed absolute loyalty to the state above
all other moral standards. Whatever may have been the case, the
cost in human lives was staggering. It will never be clear exactly how
many Cambodians were executed during the years of Pol Pot's rule.
Nor will it be possible to determine with any absolute certainty the
loss of life that took place between 1975 and 1979 as the result of
the terrible conditions under which the Cambodian population was
forced to live. Few informed observers would, however, suggest that
less than a million Cambodians died as a result of the policies that
were followed by the government of Democratic Kampuchea. Of
that one million perhaps as many as five hundred thousand were
executed.

How long Pol Pot and his associates might have continued their
bloody rule of Cambodia is another of the many alternatives to what
did happen that have been raised in this book. The disturbing
possibility is that the rule of Pol Pot's government might have
continued its horrific course for some considerable time. The
reality is that the decision Pol Pot and his colleagues took to
challenge Vietnam brought an eventual Vietnamese decision, in late
1978, to invade Cambodia and to place their Cambodian proteges in
government in Phnom Penh. The Vietnamese invasion was a tragic

26   Vietnamese conscripts training in Kampong Chhnang
The Vietnamese invasion of Cambodia ended the Pol Pot tyranny but left
Cambodia an occupied country. Having won their war against the southern
Vietnamese regime backed by the United States, the Vietnamese
Communists faced a new enemy in Cambodia after their invasion as
Cambodian resistance forces, both Communist and non-Communist,
established bases along the Thai-Cambodian boundary. Many of the
Vietnamese troops in Cambodia were southern conscripts, such as these
new recruits seen drilling in Kampong Chhnang in late 1981.

deliverance for Cambodia that led to the Indochinese region becoming ever more sharply embroiled in the Sino-Soviet dispute, a
fact underlined by China's punitive invasion of Vietnam in February
1979 and the Soviet Union's subsequent close support for its Indochinese clients.

Once the course of recent Cambodian history has been charted
the questions remain. How did a somnolent kingdom, even if it did
contain much more social inequality than was widely recognised,
become the arena for such a bitter struggle? Would the course of
events have been different if the United States Government of the
time had not acted to ensure Cambodia's total involvement in the
Second Indochinese War? Was the bitterness of the years of combat
responsible for the new Cambodian leadership's absolute determination to introduce its radical programme regardless of cost? The fact
that these questions have to be posed and for the moment cannot be
answered with any certainty is clear testimony to the existence of
areas of knowledge in the history of modern Southeast Asia that

remain quite outside our grasp. If nothing else, what we do know about Cambodia's recent history sets it apart from the rest of the region. The way in which Communism came to Cambodia has little to tell us of the possible success or failure of the advocates of Communism elsewhere.

One direct consequence of the Communist victories throughout the three countries of Indochina was the strengthening of the shared interests of the Association of Southeast Asian Nations (ASEAN), and the effective division between the ASEAN states of Indonesia, Malaysia, the Philippines, Singapore and Thailand, joined in 1984 by Brunei, and Communist Vietnam, Cambodia and Laos. ASEAN was formed in 1967, with the essential purpose of promoting economic cooperation among its member states. It was not until 1976 that ASEAN held its first summit meeting of leaders, by which stage the Communist victories in Indochina lent a new impetus to ASEAN leaders' desire to develop a more coordinated political response to the changing strategic situation in Southeast Asia. Vietnam's invasion of Cambodia, beginning in late 1978, further solidified ASEAN's interest in a coordinated political approach to what was seen as a shared interest in dealing with a common problem: the emergence of a Vietnamese-dominated Indochina. Burma, alone of the countries of Southeast Asia, continued its established policy of eschewing alliances with any power group in the region.

The nearer we come to the present day, the more complex Southeast Asia's history becomes, or at any rate appears to become. The difficulties of working with too many facts seem at least equal to the difficulties associated with trying to work with too little information. Certainly consideration of independent Southeast Asia suggests that whatever broad similarities one may find throughout the region, such as the problem of assuring national unity, the details of developments in the individual countries of the region often differ greatly. The greater a student's concern with more recent times the more difficult it becomes to engage in generalities as the particular issues and developments demand attention. The need for recognising the general features of modern Southeast Asia does, nevertheless, remain. In a region where the countries of Southeast Asia share many common features of the historical past so too is there a need to see that the broad patterns of their recent experience are often very similar whatever differences may be seen in the details of that experience.

For all of the countries of Southeast Asia the modern period has been a time, whether consciously or not, for attempting to strike a balance between the demands of the present and the values of the past. This, a sceptical observer might comment, is true of other, indeed all, regions of the world. There is a difference, however, since in Southeast Asia's case the road to the present for the countries of the region, with one partial exception, has not always been travelled at a Southeast Asian pace. The pace of many developments in Southeast Asia during much of the nineteenth century and for the first half of the twentieth century was largely influenced and sometimes almost totally controlled by alien forces. This is not an argument in favour of the view that Southeast Asians are an unimportant part of their own history. Quite to the contrary, it is simply a recognition of the fact that the impact of European and American colonialism was of immense importance in some areas of life. But now that the era of colonial control has ended, Southeast Asians are free to make their own decisions and to determine how much they should rely on their own values and the lessons they draw from their own history. As the various governments of the countries of Southeast Asia seek to deal with the problems of the present we as outsiders studying the region perhaps can do no better than to ask, and attempt to answer, a final question: What have been the essentials of Southeast Asia's modern history?

13
Southeast Asia's Modern History

THROUGHOUT the preceding chapters there has been great emphasis on the importance of change in the history of Southeast Asia, particularly on the changes that have taken place in the period since the eighteenth century, the last century when the traditional Southeast Asian world was largely unaffected by external influences. Attention has been given to the political developments that involved most of Southeast Asia passing under alien colonial control and to the subsequent differing ways in which the various countries in the region achieved independence. Economic developments have been surveyed to show how Southeast Asia was increasingly drawn into the international economic system and the extent to which there was large-scale economic transformation in the domestic economies of each country. And some attention—perhaps too little—has been given to the social changes that have taken place in association with political and economic change.

So is modern Southeast Asian history, and most notably the history of the twentieth century, essentially a record of major change, some coming rapidly, some slowly? Or are we allowing ourselves to be hypnotised by one aspect of the region's history so that we fasten our eyes upon the obvious fact of change and fail to see the less obvious fact of continuity? The argument over the relative importance of continuity and change is an old one, and not limited to the history of Southeast Asia. It is probably also an argument that can never have a final conclusion. Consider some of the problems. The sort of answer that will be given to the question of whether continuity or change is dominant will vary greatly according to which region of Southeast Asia is being discussed. Of necessity the areas and the peoples discussed in this book have been, for the most part, the better-known examples. So there has been reference to the Javanese and Java, rather than to the Sumbanese, the people living on Sumba, one of the 'outer' islands of eastern Indonesia. It has been the lowland Vietnamese and the Thais rather than the hill-dwelling Rhade of southern Vietnam or the Yao of Nan province in northern Thailand, that have caught the greater part of our attention. Among these better-known peoples of Southeast Asia and in the better-known regions that they inhabit the degree of change has been greatest. These peoples and regions have, after all, had the longest contact with the change-inducing ideas and forces of both their own and the non-Southeast Asian world. A city-dwelling office worker in a Kuala Lumpur travel agency, for instance, is clearly more likely to have adopted a way of life that involves a significant departure from traditional Malay patterns of behaviour than will be the case for a village-dwelling rice cultivator in some distant, up-river region of the northern Malaysian state of Kelantan.

But if this contrast between the impact of change in the cities and continuity in the more remote regions of the countryside of Southeast Asia is obvious, it can also be misleading. To return to our imaginary office worker, whether he or she is in Kuala Lumpur, Bangkok, Manila, or a host of other cities that have grown so rapidly throughout Southeast Asia, how much of this person's life has really changed as the result of adopting an apparently modern style of life? The answer, despite the taste for modern dress, for modern music, may be a great deal less than it seems upon first impressions. Behind the appearance of modernity and great change in the bustling, crowded cities of Southeast Asia, where the impact of the West nowadays seems so strong, there is another side to life that is seldom glimpsed by the casual visitor. It is a side to life that is made apparent when one suddenly hears a Balinese *gamelan* orchestra beating out a staccato rhythm in a back street of Jakarta, the players having come to the capital from Bali in search of jobs. If one shuts one's eyes one is momentarily transported from a dusty, painfully crowded suburb in Indonesia's capital to a temple courtyard in Bali, where the members of a rajah's orchestra are decked in rich fabrics to play their gongs and xylophones as they accompany one of the dramatic episodes from the Balinese rendering of the Indian epic, the Ramayana.

In Bangkok a different experience can offer the same insight. Away from the plush hotels that cater for wealthy foreigners and Thais alike are the more modest places of entertainment for the less privileged. Go to one of these restaurants and find that apart from the modern electronics of the microphones and loudspeakers— usually booming forth at ear-splitting level—the entertainment that is provided still smacks of the traditional world of the country. The Thais from the agriculturally poor northeastern regions of the kingdom who have migrated to the capital in such numbers meet to drink their ice-cold beer and savour fiery curries, to join in the singing or dance traditional circular dances as if they were in a bucolic provincial centre or perhaps at a celebration in their home village. Apart from the constant background sound of Bangkok's traffic the scene that a visitor witnesses has little to do with the superficially dominant modern world.

The further a visitor travels away from the urban centres the more superficial the impact of the modern world becomes. The presence of motorcycles, of electricity, of telephones in scattered numbers and of omnipresent transistor radios are signs of change. But remarkable continuity remains in the strength of village festivals and entertainments. Even more importantly, throughout much of contemporary Southeast Asia continuity is represented in the disposition of power and influence at the sub-national level. Here is an instance of continuity that belies so much of the change associated with such superficial matters as dress styles and musical tastes. While there are great variations from region to region, and while too the circumstances in the Communist states of the region are clearly different, the power and influence of traditional leaders at the district and village level remains notably strong.

In any broader discussion of power and politics, however, the debate about continuity and change becomes extremely complex. While it is true that traditional patterns of power have survived remarkably strongly at the local or district level, the picture is not nearly so clear when one considers developments at the national level. To what extent, for instance, is it true to say that the forms of government that have been chosen by the various states of Southeast Asia reflect more or less continuity with the past? Almost everywhere one looks there will be some continuity to set against some change, and disagreements as to the relative importance of each. Even in the case of Cambodia (Kampuchea), surely the most clear-cut case of an effort being made to remove all traces of the past, the bloody conflict between that country and Vietnam brought forth policy statements that seemed to directly echo earlier regimes. Possibly, then, and despite the superficial attractions of an attempt to balance change against continuity, it is best to abandon an attempt to gain an overview of Southeast Asia's modern history in these terms and to turn, instead, to other methods of analysis.

One such approach is to consider the nature of government in Southeast Asia. If we look at the various governments in the region, the continuity versus change issue might be endlessly debated both in terms of form and leadership. But here, surely, what should preoccupy us is the tremendous transformation in the nature of government over the period that has been examined in this book. In the eighteenth century the major states of Southeast Asia were ruled by kings, and the lesser states by men who took a variety of titles. These rulers and their courts embodied tradition. Contrast this situation with that existing in the late twentieth century. Only in Thailand and Brunei does an hereditary monarch remain the chief of state. A king is the chief of state of Malaysia, but his is an elective office with no real power. Even more importantly, the disappearance of the traditional rulers has been accompanied by the end of a system of government that linked administration to the ruler's court. The nineteenth and twentieth centuries saw instead the slow establishment of administrative systems largely based on Western models that not only represented a sharp break with the past but brought in addition the increasing involvement of the state in the day-to-day affairs of the people.

In this regard the temptation to which many historians succumb of engaging in the continuity versus change debate has often diverted attention from thinking about such matters as administration in favour of discussing whether Prince Sihanouk should have been regarded as a 'god-king' or President Sukarno as an example of a traditional Javanese leader. The point is not that there are no worthwhile insights to be gained from a discussion of the elements of tradition that certainly were associated with both Sihanouk and Sukarno and their styles of leadership. Rather, what is worthy of attention is that no matter how modern or how traditional the leader of an individual Southeast Asian state may be that leader functions as part of an administrative system infinitely different in form from the governmental systems of traditional times. Certainly a Sukarno or a Sihanouk can come close to crippling the capacity of an administration to play its supposed role. Nevertheless, and however inefficient some of the bureaucracies of Southeast Asia may be for a variety of reasons, the governments of the region work through administrative systems that are the product of dramatic innovation over the past one hundred years. And here it is not just the change but the nature of that change which is important.

The presence of these administrative systems goes some way towards explaining why increasingly it appears that leadership is either in the hands of politicians who fit into a general Westernised intellectual mould, or who are served by such men acting as close advisers. This is a generalisation that, more than most, requires amplification and qualification. One of the first that should be made is that leadership of the most important Communist state in Southeast Asia should not be excluded from the general comment. Vietnam's leaders must be regarded as having had a rather special exposure to Western influence, but Marxist thought still must be reckoned, in part at the very least, a Western product and Vietnam's socialist planning owes much to modern, and in some cases Western ideas. It scarcely needs emphasis that importance must also be given to Vietnamese traditional influences and to models from China. A more important qualification is that the situation cited as a generalisation has varied greatly from country to country and from period to period. At any one time since the Second World War and the achievement of independence by the countries of Southeast Asia the style and character of leadership has varied greatly. But what one is discussing is a broad trend. Although leaders whose style may hark back to the past will undoubtedly remain important in Southeast Asia for many years, the ever-increasing complexities of economic and political life in the last two decades of the twentieth century seem likely to confirm the pattern that has developed through the century.

Perhaps there is place for yet one further qualification. The pattern that has been identified as a general trend seems least likely to continue should a time of severe crisis arise in one or other of the states of Southeast Asia. It is still difficult to be sure about many of the internal developments in Cambodia after 1975, but it might be argued that the massive crisis that country experienced during the terrible war that raged from 1970 until 1975 provides one of the essential keys to understanding the rejection of the Western-influenced models of administration that occurred while the Pol Pot regime was in power. Elsewhere, however, whatever the variations and qualifications it is the West (the Soviet Union included in this case) that has provided the models. Even in the very special case of Burma, where for nearly twenty years there has been a determined effort to find a Burmese route to socialism, the leadership and the bureaucracy have not by any means totally turned their backs on basic Western models of how an administration should be constructed. In brief, the twentieth century has seen the rise to prominence and influence of the technocrat in Southeast Asia as well as elsewhere in the non-Western world. At times these 'new men' dominate the political system and on other occasions they work in uneasy balance with traditional leaders. But only in very special circumstances can they be ignored.

And the 'new men' are not merely 'new' in terms of training. It is certainly the case that throughout Southeast Asia the men who have risen to power in the post-war period have frequently been members of the traditional existing elite. But this has not been the case exclusively and slowly but surely men from non-elite backgrounds have come to play prominent parts in the government of even the most traditionally oriented Southeast Asian societies. To some extent what has taken place involves the replacement of one form of elite (the traditional) by another (the elite of merit). The fact that it is possible to make this observation should not diminish the great importance of the change. Changed political conditions and improved educational opportunities do not guarantee the success of talent in modern Southeast Asia, but the barriers are significantly lower than once was the case. Most particularly is this true in Singapore, where the long-serving prime minister, Lee Kuan Yew, has made intellectual ability the key qualification for advancement in the administration of his state.

28 Lee Kuan Yew
Lee Kuan Yew has dominated Singapore's politics since 1959. A brilliant British-trained lawyer, he has presided over Singapore's extraordinary transformation from a colonial entrepôt into a thriving modern city.
Photograph by S.T. Tan courtesy of Far Eastern Economic Review

The great administrative changes that have taken place in Southeast Asia over the past century, with the resultant rise to positions of power of men who are either themselves cast in a Western intellectual mould or are advised by men who have absorbed ideas from the West, should not divert our attention from other changes of no less importance that can easily, because of the demanding interest of the present, be overlooked. Although the point has been made at various times through this book, it may be easy to forget that several of the modern Southeast Asian states only achieved their present territorial existence in very recent times. To recapitulate: Laos was a cluster of principalities and even smaller petty states when the French imposed colonial control at the end of the nineteenth century; the Federation of Malaysia is made up of sultanates that had no shared unity a century ago, and of territories in Borneo that owed disputed loyalty to at least two sultanates as well as areas that lay quite outside the control of the maritime Islamic sultans' world; the Indonesia of today was forged from the colonial empire of the Dutch East Indies, which itself only achieved overall control over the islands it claimed to govern at the end of the nineteenth century; and the Philippines, although regarded as a single entity by the Spaniards when they were the colonial power, could not have been said to have become an administrative unity under one central government before the period of American rule, and perhaps not even then.

In short, one distinctive feature of modern Southeast Asia's history has been the extent to which over the past one hundred years the old loose boundaries and administrative arrangements have become tighter, confirming the existence of old states and defining the territorial existence of new states. Indonesia, Malaysia, and Laos are quite clearly modern creations, whatever long historical traditions may be discerned to show that these modern states had important precursors. Southeast Asia's modern history, in both colonial times and otherwise, has confirmed the boundaries of Burma, Thailand, Cambodia, and Vietnam, and given emphasis to the existence of the Philippines as a governmental entity. Singapore, as a striking special example, is both a creation of the nineteenth and twentieth centuries and a state that has emerged to occupy its present unique position where no comparable state previously existed, unless one sees in Singapore a lineal descendant of the ancient state of Srivijaya.

The emergence of new states in Southeast Asia or the 'solidification' of old states, particularly on the mainland, has set the scene, again following the changes brought by the past one hundred or two hundred years, for the contemporary political process that varies so greatly from country to country. If we look at the West the generalisation can probably be made that the essence of modern politics is the continuing debate over class and economics. Class may be defined by different factors in different Western countries, but by and large the central issues of Western domestic politics relate to how national wealth shall be distributed and what policies shall be followed to ensure the future creation of further wealth that will benefit both the state and individuals.

It is far from clear that this debate is the central issue for many of the politicians of Southeast Asia, nor that a common central thread links the politics of all the countries in the region, other than that most fundamental of considerations, the desire to gain or retain power. Although economic issues cannot be ignored by any of the states of the region there are clearly many instances in which economic considerations are, at very least, secondary to other concerns. The case of Burma is a striking example of this situation. The search for a 'Burmese road to socialism' was proclaimed as the chief concern of the state, but the old concerns of ethnic rivalry have been as important, if not more important a component in contemporary Burmese political life. A very real concern for economic development is without doubt a feature of Malaysian political life, but the constant need to be preoccupied with the facts of Malaysia's multi-ethnic society means that politics and political discussion in that country have a very special, ethnically oriented character. The problems associated with ethnic minorities that lack a sense of identity with the central government have already been noted several times in relation to Thailand and the Philippines.

Ethnic or communal politics therefore inject a very special element into the character of modern Southeast Asia. At an earlier stage in this book the observation was made that the West was not free from ethnic tensions that had, at least until fairly recent times, been too often ignored. When this point is made, however, the tensions and problems associated with ethnic minorities or the impact of communal politics in the West are scarcely comparable with the importance that attaches to these same features in contemporary Southeast Asia. The great changes that have been such a feature of Southeast Asia's history over the past one hundred or two hundred years have not, for much of the region, been of an order to move politics to the point where there is a common set of assumptions about the interests of the state nor of the general right of all to participate in the discussion and determination of those interests.

Is this situation likely to change? Some commentators would argue that change, if it is to come, will depend as much on economic considerations as on more narrowly political factors. One reason for taking this position is the fact that Southeast Asia still remains so dependent on foreign capital so that, the argument runs, it will only be when Southeast Asian governments control their own economic destinies that it will be possible to achieve both greater economic equality and a more egalitarian political process. This is to put the argument in excessively simple terms, but even its more sophisticated versions are far from fully convincing. The role of external capital in Southeast Asia has been vital over the period surveyed in this book and the vast transformations that have taken place since the eighteenth century owe much to that foreign input. Here, in the economic field, has been an affirmation of a feature that has been so much part of the history of Southeast Asia, not just during the past two hundred years but since the very earliest times. In a variety of ways Southeast Asia's essential character has made it a receiver of ideas, of external government, and of capital. Indonesia's vast riches might, in an ideal world, be exploited by Indonesians without the need for foreign capital, but in a less than ideal world that prospect has little possibility for success. The flow of Western capital into Southeast Asia that has been so much a feature of the region's history since the end of the nineteenth century has certainly left a heavy reliance on external forces. For those countries of the region that do not have Communist governments a continuing reliance on external capital seems certain for the foreseeable future. And this reliance may be tempered in Vietnam by the existence of its socialist economy but it has not by any means been removed. If the West no longer exerts colonial control in Southeast Asia the power of Western, and nowadays increasingly Japanese capital, remains a vital feature of the region's modern history.

Economic development, or the lack of it; the difficulties associated with ethnic or communal politics; the transformation of administrative systems and the emergence of a new type of leader or administrator; all these are features of the course that Southeast Asian history has followed over the past two centuries. But there is another feature, or set of features, in Southeast Asia's history that must not be ignored. This is the turbulent presence of revolt and rebellion, and on occasion of revolution that has demonstrated at a whole range of levels the resentments and dissatisfactions of groups ranging from ethnic minorities to forces reflecting national interests, as was the case with the anti-colonial revolutions that followed the Second World War.

The fact that there has been such a long record of revolt, rebellion, and revolution in Southeast Asia focuses attention once again on the extent to which governments in the region, before, during, and after the colonial period, have had difficulty in providing leadership that has been either acceptable or meaningful for all of the population within their borders. For the outside observer there is little difficulty in understanding at least part of the motivation that led to men taking up arms to fight against colonial governments. And with only a little more difficulty one may sense the frustrations involved in ethnic or regional minorities' feeling that, on occasion, their lack of identity with the central authorities has left them no alternative to armed dissidence. Most outsiders will, however, have real difficulty in understanding the forces that have operated to bring into being a long record of peasant protests and rebellions, particularly since the odds have generally seemed so heavily weighted against the success of such movements. In a concluding summary chapter there is no room for an attempt to analyse the always complex factors that have lain behind such manifestations of peasant politics. Rather the point to be absorbed is that discontent at the peasant level has frequently been of such a deep and desperate nature that men and women have seen no alternative to revolt. And this fact alerts us to the continuing great divide that separates the 'haves' of Southeast Asia from the 'have-nots'.

For the gloomy possibility, indeed probability, is that in many parts of Southeast Asia one of the most important features of the region's history since the nineteen twenties has been the progressive impoverishment of the rural community. Few areas of Southeast Asia match the problems of agricultural poverty associated with central and eastern Java, where to speak of the life of a peasant being balanced on a knife-edge between having a bare sufficiency of food and an insufficiency leading to famine and starvation may be to present too rosy a picture of reality. But impoverishment of a less dramatic sort is a feature of many other regions, and will grow as a problem so long as population increases continue to outstrip resources. The history of modern Southeast Asia has been, for many of the inhabitants of the region, a record of bitter disappointment rather than of promise.

The history of Southeast Asia during the nineteenth and twentieth centuries has involved change and transformation of a momentous form, very different from the changes that accompanied the industrial revolution in the Western world but for the region itself no less significant. At the same time the changes and transformations that have been sketched throughout this book have left the countries of Southeast Asia still facing problems that are, in their essential character, of a separate order from those facing the states of the developed world. To take the issue of rapid population growth alone: no European country will have to contend, as will the Philippines, with a population increase that will double the number of inhabitants of the country by the end of the twentieth century.

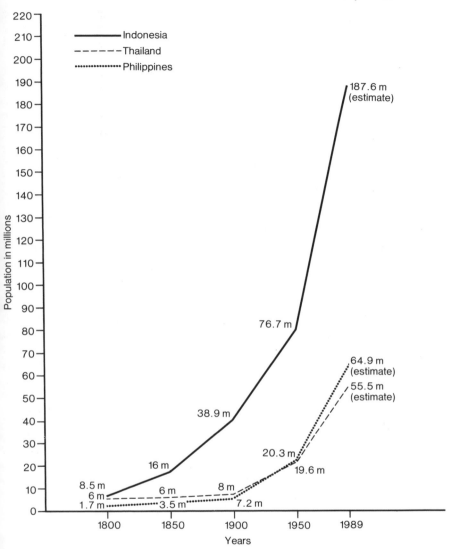

Graph 2   Population Growth in Indonesia, the Philippines and Thailand 1800-1987

Population growth in Southeast Asia has been dramatic during the 20th century. Even with government-supported efforts to limit population growth in Indonesia, it is estimated that country's population will exceed 220 million early in the 21st century.

Nor do the countries of Europe, or the developed world generally, have to contend with the problems associated with ethnic minorities and their special interests on anything like the same scale as is found in some of the countries of Southeast Asia.

Physical resources, or the lack of them, will also be an increasing problem in wide areas of Southeast Asia in the 1990s. Deforestation, for instance, has had a dramatic effect in both mainland and maritime Southeast Asia. Nowhere has this been more striking than in the Philippines. There, the 30 million hectares of hardwood forests that existed in 1946 had been reduced to 1 million hectares in 1987. In Vietnam, the cost to the environment as a result of the Second Indochina War was the destruction of 2.2 million hectares of forest and farmland. Even more forest has been destroyed since 1975 when the war ended: in the course of post-war reconstruction, Vietnam has been using up about 200,000 hectares of forest each year.

Because of the course that Southeast Asia's history has followed over the past two centuries the region will remain subject to great stresses and beset by the overriding problem in each state of achieving or maintaining national unity. A sense of identification between those who govern and those who are governed will remain an elusive goal for some states of the region, so that the problem of substantial internal dissidence is unlikely to vanish from the future Southeast Asian scene. That future scene will be remarkably different from the Southeast Asia of one hundred years ago, let alone from the 'classical' world when the great monuments of Angkor, Pagan, and Borobodur were built. Just as importantly, Southeast Asia in the future will continue to retain its own distinctive character, or more correctly the character of the individual states that make up the region as a whole. For if there is one feature of Southeast Asia's history about which there can be general agreement it is that change and transformation have not turned the countries of Southeast Asia into some pale copy of any other part of the world. The countries of Southeast Asia retain their individual identities, the products of a rich and complex history. It is a history that has only recently begun to be explored in depth so that scholars, students and specialists alike still have the prospect before them of new insights and greater understanding. Whatever the history of Southeast Asia may be in the future the study of its past involves an intellectual journey through a world full of interest and fascination. It is a world that deserves to be better known.

14
Discovering Southeast Asia Through Art and Literature

IN any effort to understand Southeast Asia's past, an awareness of the region's rich artistic heritage helps add cultural flesh to history's analytic bones. Similarly, a sampling of fictional writing, by both Southeast Asian and Western writers, can provide a sense of time and place that is sometimes lacking from conventional history. With these considerations in mind, this chapter presents, in a very cursory fashion, a review of some important aspects of Southeast Asian art history. It also offers a selective survey of fictional writing on Southeast Asia that may help readers to gain a deeper sense of some of the human aspects of the region's history.

Southeast Asia's Art

Surprising though it may seem today, many of the first Europeans to come in contact with Southeast Asia's grandest 'classical' architectural monuments either ignored them or denigrated them for presumed offences against European values. During the eighteenth century, for example, Dutch merchants regularly journeyed from Batavia (Jakarta) to the central Javanese courts at Yogyakarta and Surakarta (Solo). In doing so they passed close to the mighty monuments of the Borobodur and Prambanan. Yet no mention of these striking temples was made in their records. Trade was the merchants' preoccupation and the exotic aesthetics of Javanese art did not bear on their commercial concerns. In the case of these central Javanese monuments, it was left to Thomas Stamford Raffles to commission the first modern survey of the Borobodur during his years as lieutenant-governor of Java between 1811 and 1816. As noted in an earlier chapter, Father Bouillevaux, the first European visitor to Angkor for some hundreds of years, was grudging in the account he provided of the temple complex. With all of the sense of superiority of a mid-nineteenth century man and priest, he declared that attempts by Angkorian artists to render the human form were 'grotesque'.

But although virtually unknown or unappreciated until the latter half of the nineteenth century, Southeast Asian art in its many forms is now recognised both for its aesthetic worth and as evidence that helps historians to chart the political, cultural and technological characteristics of earlier societies. As interest and appreciation have developed over the years, the range of art receiving attention by scholars and collectors has grown greatly. While early research, particularly by some outstanding scholar–administrators in Indochina and Indonesia, concentrated on monuments and sculpture, today a much wider range of objects receives attention. Most particularly, the past two decades have witnessed a greatly increased interest in ceramics and textiles.

Monumental Art

By their very size, the great temple complexes of Angkor in Cambodia, Pagan in Burma, and the Borobodur monument in central Java have been a focus for scholarly and tourist interest throughout the twentieth century. But impressive and culturally important as they are, these monuments are only the best-known of a wealth of individual temples and complexes scattered throghout the major settled areas of Southeast Asia and built before the impact of the European advance. In eastern Java, for instance, there are important temple remains near Malang and Blitar. Difficult of access today, there is a major temple dating from Angkorian times, Wat Phu, set on a feature overlooking the Mekong River in southern Laos. Along the coast of central modern Vietnam, Cham temples recall a vanished kingdom that was able in its heyday to challenge the power of the Khmer kings at Angkor. In Thailand there are major temple remains from Angkorian times, but there are, too, the important early Thai city and temple complexes at Ayuthia, Sukhothai and Si Satchinalai, as well as lesser known complexes such as the northern site of Chiang Saen.

These monumental remains excite interest for many reasons. Even to those with little knowledge of the history of Southeast Asia or the symbolism embodied in the monuments, the physical presence and the extent of the temple complexes at Angkor (9th to 15th centuries) and Pagan (9th to 13th centuries) command respect. In the case of Angkor, dozens of temples are scattered over an area of about two hundred square miles. Among them is Angkor Wat, the largest religious monument in the world. Despite its great size, Angkor Wat, as already noted earlier in this book, was constructed in the amazingly short time of thirty-five years. The number of temples at Pagan almost staggers the imagination. Thousands of temples constructed from brick dot the vast central Burmese plain. A different impression is provided by the Borobodur near the central Javanese city of Yogyakarta. This massive stupa towers over the modern visitor as he or she approaches it just as it would have towered over the Buddhist pilgrims who came to the monument following its completion around 800 A.D. Circumambulating the stupa and 'reading' the Buddhist birth stories from

29 Discovering an Angkorian period temple
After some initial reservations about the artistic importance of the temple
ruins in Cambodia, French officials and archaeologists played a major role in
revealing these monuments to the world. In this engraving, French officials
supervise the clearing of jungle around the Prea Khan temple at Kompong
Svay, an Angkorian period site in Kompong Thom province, in 1873. *From*
Le Cambodge, *by Louis Delaporte, 1880.*

30 An Angkorian bas-relief from the Bayon
The bas-reliefs decorating the late-13th century Bayon temple at Angkor are
remarkable for combining narrative depictions of recent historical events with
scenes from everyday life. In this illustration the central part of the carving
shows Cham war canoes on their way to attack Angkor while below are
Cambodians watching a cock fight, playing dice and blowing on a flute.

the low reliefs carved on the terraces, the pilgrims slowly ascended to the
top of the monument, where surrounded by partially hidden Buddha images
they could gaze at distant sacred mountains. To repeat this experience in
modern times gives a visitor some sense, at least, of the power this
monument would have exerted over its devotees a thousand years ago.

Whether large or small, the pre-modern monumental remains scattered
throughout Southeast Asia share certain common characteristics, as well
as being individually marked by the time and place of their construction.
Often sited in locations that had links with the local religions that pre-dated
the arrival of Indian cultural influence, the monuments we can still see
today were inspired by Hinduism and Buddhism, sometimes singly,
sometimes as a syncretic combination. But inspired by Indian religions,
and drawing on architectural and artistic styles from India, the monuments
that were erected in Southeast Asia were never mere copies of the temples
and shrines to be found on the sub-continent. Whatever the similarities
in the way in which temples were sited or the basic form of the architectural
lay-out with symbolic renditions of the Hindu and Buddhist universes,

even an unskilled observer immediately recognises that the temples of Angkor, or Prambanan in central Java, are different from those found in, say, an Indian site such as Orissa. Just as clearly, the temple styles of one country of Southeast Asia are different from those of another.

Here, of course, is where the interests of the cultural historian intersect with those of the scholar more concerned with political issues. Thailand's history, for instance, is not only recorded in chronicles. Just as importantly, its transformation from a region on the periphery of the Cambodian empire to an independent state was reflected in its development of architectural styles that held echoes of earlier Cambodian models but which were distinctively Thai in character.

One of the most striking features of the monuments of pre-modern Southeast Asia is the richness of their decoration. Much of the decoration has suffered the ravages of time, war and vandalism. This is particularly true of those monuments, such as some temples at Sukhothai in Thailand, that were decorated in stucco, and those at Pagan decorated externally with stucco and internally with paintings. Elsewhere, and notably in the case of the temples at Angkor, low and high relief carving still adorns the walls, pillars and lintels of temples with a sharpness little affected by the passing of centuries. The range of subjects treated in pictorial reliefs and

31 Wat Sri Sawai, Sukhothai
Lying within the walls of the Thai city complex of Sukhothai, Wat Sri Sawai dates from the 14th century and shows clearly the evolution of the Thai *prang* or tower from the earlier Cambodian style found at Angkor (see illustration 2, Angkor Wat). The development of a Thai architectural style accompanied the achievement of independence from Cambodian political control.

the inventiveness of the decorators is breathtaking. At Angkor the low reliefs depict scenes from the Hindu epics, historical events such as the clashes between the Cambodian and Cham armies, and 'snapshots' of everyday life. At Angkor Wat alone, the low reliefs along the walls of the first storey gallery would cover more than a mile. The energy and organisation that would have been necessary for work of this kind at Angkor, or on the walls of the Borobodur in Java, underline the vital part played by religion in the societies of pre-modern Southeast Asia. For these great temples to have been built, decorated and then maintained required a major concentration of resources, in a fashion similar to the effort required to construct and maintain the great monastic foundations of medieval Europe. Although not entirely satisfactory as an analogy, the image of Southeast Asia's temples having an importance within their societies similar to that of Europe's great cathedrals and monasteries emphasises their centrality to the times in which they were built.

Sculpture

Attention has just been given to the low and high relief carving as a feature of the decoration, that was so important a part of the monuments of pre-modern Southeast Asia. Just as important an aspect of Southeast Asia's artistic heritage are the free-standing sculptures in stone, bronze and wood that have increasingly been recognised as enshrining aesthetic qualities equal to those of any other culture.

The range of Southeast Asian sculpture is enormous, whether categorised in terms of chronology, subject matter, or the materials used. In pre-Angkorian Cambodia sculpture in stone has been found dating back to the sixth century A.D.. Although sculpture in stone continued to have a widespread presence throughout large areas of Southeast Asia, casting in bronze, which has even earlier antecedents, grew to be more important, particularly in the years following the decline of the great early kingdoms both on the mainland and in Sumatra and Java. Wood was also used as a sculptural medium, with some of the most notable examples coming from Burma.

As with the temple complexes of pre-modern Southeast Asia, sculpture drew its inspiration and iconography from Indian religions—Hinduism and Buddhism—and then transformed Indian models into local and national Southeast Asian artistic statements. Nor was it only from India that Southeast Asian image makers drew inspiration. Not just in Vietnam, where Chinese influence on art was extremely strong, but also in Burma, there is artistic evidence that Chinese models influenced Burmese sculptors.

Although sculpture in bronze is found throughout Southeast Asia, the richest tradition, in terms of numbers of images and, in the opinion of many observers, in aesthetic terms also, is found in the Buddha images of Burma and Thailand. To make this assertion is not to dismiss the monumental bronzes of Angkorian Cambodia or the small but beautifully sculpted statuettes of Java. But in Burma and Thailand unknown artists working within a rigid canon of iconography were able over the centuries to produce a range of images that are outstanding in their aesthetic quality. The most impressive of them blend a sense of authority with the quality of serenity. The images of the Sukhothai period (13–15th centuries) are

32 Arakanese Crowned Buddha
A fine example of a Crowned Buddha image from Arakan (western Burma), in bronze with traces of gold leaf gilding. Dating from the late 17th century and in the 'calling the earth to witness' posture, this image shows elements of Chinese influence in its ornamentation. (Height 28cm.)

particularly notable in this regard, but images from other centres also deserve attention. Buddha images from Arakan in the west of Burma are, at their finest, notably successful both as interpretations of Buddhist iconographic requirements and as universally appealing works of art. Indeed, it is the universality of these images' aesthetic qualities that has led to their being such an object of interest in recent years. Even without more than the slimmest understanding of Buddhism, a non-Southeast Asian observer can react to the artistic achievement of the anonymous craftsmen who cast these images centuries ago.

Buddhism and Hinduism are not the only religions to have held sway in Southeast Asia. Uniquely, in the Philippines, Christianity became entrenched in the northern and central islands of that archipelagic country. Since it was the Spaniards who brought Christianity to the Philippines, Spanish forms of worship and Spanish religious art dominated the expansion of the church through the islands. A notable example of the sub-branch of Iberian art that took root in the Philippines were the *santos* or saints figures carved in wood and ivory, that adorned the altars of churches and religious foundations and the private shrines of worshippers. At their finest, these *santos* with their fluid carving match the best examples of religious art in the Iberian peninsula.

Ceramics

No other category of Southeast Asian art has enjoyed such a growth in interest over the past two decades as has the study of the region's ceramics. For many years the existence of a range of Southeast Asian ceramics was known to specialists, but fine Chinese ceramics, particularly porcelain, dominated the interests of both scholars and collectors. From the 1960s onwards, and more particularly from the 1970s, there has been a change in attitude resulting from a realisation that ceramics from a range of Southeast Asian sources are both worthy of aesthetic approval and of vital importance in tracing the course of the region's history.

Many factors contributed to the growing interest in Southeast Asian ceramics. Of considerable importance was the discovery in the mid-1960s of a major archaeological site at Ban Chiang, in northeast Thailand, in which ceramics and bronzes dating back to 3,600 B.C. revealed the presence of an indigenous Southeast Asian culture of an earlier date than had previously been known to exist. While scholars began to assess the implications of the articles found at Ban Chiang, others became aware of a mass of ceramics from much later periods that had suddenly become available for purchase in Southeast Asia and which were not Chinese in origin. Excavated from sites in Indonesia, the Philippines and Thailand, were ceramic items of enormous variety that had been produced in Cambodia, Vietnam, Burma and Thailand. The appearance on the market of these ceramics acted as a spur to research that has not only left us with a much richer understanding of the range of ceramics produced in Southeast Asia, but also with a better knowledge of the course of historical developments in particular regions. Analysis of kilns found in central Thailand, for instance, has raised the possibility that Thai states may have emerged at an earlier date than has previously been supposed. In sum, the finds and research of the past three decades have underlined the fact that, in addition to the widespread circulation of Chinese export ceramics through much of Southeast Asia in pre-modern times, there were also important production centres of local ceramics in mainland Southeast Asia over the same period. It is now clear that the products of these centres also circulated widely through the region.

33 Cambodian Ceramic Bottle
This late 12th–early 13th century Cambodian bottle is typical of stoneware produced during this period. It is finished in a dark brown glaze. (Height 29cm.)

The types of Southeast Asian ceramic objects dating from pre-modern times that have been found through the region are extremely diverse. In terms of size, the objects can range from tiny jarlets produced in Vietnam, Cambodia and Thailand, to large stoneware jars standing upwards of a metre tall that were produced in Burma and are known under the generic title of Martaban jars. The forms in which ceramics were produced were equally varied, with jars, bowls, vases and plates being the most common varieties. But there were other distinctive items; among Cambodian ceramics zoomorphic items (covered jars and water dispensers in the shape of animals and birds, for instance) were relatively common. From the kilns of central Thailand around Sawankalok came ceramic votive figures to ensure female fertility and ceramic elephants that recall the part played by these animals in various episodes in the life of the Buddha.

The processes used in the manufacture of Southeast Asian ceramics have an interest that goes beyond efforts to understand the degree of technical expertise that was required to produce particular results. Scholars are seeking to establish where this expertise came from and to what extent particular technical skills were developed locally or imported from other areas. Although it seems likely that Chinese potters played a part in the

34 Vietnamese Ceramic Dish
Dating from the late 15th–early 16th centuries, this dish is decorated in blue/black underglaze with a central peony design. (Diameter 26cm.)

initial establishment of some, if not all of the Southeast Asian production centres of the classical period, it is equally clear that local potters were quickly able to adopt and adapt whatever techniques were imported. The interplay between local and imported skills may have been quite complex. In Thailand, for instance, some scholars believe it may have been Vietnamese potters who first carried their skills to the sites that became important for the production of distinctive celadons. These Vietnamese in their turn almost certainly would have learnt some of their skills from China.

Even where there is no doubt about the origin of particular forms of design and ceramic technique, the ability of Southeast Asian craftsmen to produce distinctively national objects stands out quite clearly. Vietnam's long association with China ensured that there was strong Chinese influence on the development of Vietnamese ceramics. In particular, the period of Chinese reoccupation during the Ming dynasty, between 1407 and 1421 A.D., led to the production of blue and white wares that in their early forms had direct echoes of contemporary Chinese objects. Later, although Chinese influences could still be identified in the products of Vietnamese potters' kilns, the local craftsmen injected their own local personality into the forms and the decoration on their ceramic works. Most strikingly, the Vietnamese decorators adopted styles that were freer and less stereotyped than those dominant in China.

Textiles and Other Craft Objects

The increased scholarly attention given to ceramics reflects a general broadening of interest in the culture of Southeast Asia that has extended the definition of 'art' to include items previously relegated to a presumed lesser category of 'crafts'. Few would now discuss ceramics in terms of 'crafts'. Similarly, growing interest in Southeast Asian textiles has, at the very least, moved these items into a category in which they are treated as part of the region's general artistic heritage, if not as part of Southeast Asia's 'high art', characterised by sculpture and monumental remains.

Without question the best known of Southeast Asia's textiles are the batiks of Indonesia, cloth decorated by a process of repeated dyeing controlled by the application of wax to the fabric. In contemporary terms, particularly with the growth of tourism, batiks are widely known in the world outside Indonesia. But the batik cloths bought by tourists are usually of the cheaper mass produced kind, in which the painstaking work of applying the design by hand has been abandoned in favour of printing by blocks or even by machine. While there are still batik makers who work in the traditional fashion, the slow and precise work required to produce batik in this manner means that their product risks becoming increasingly rare.

Seen together, there is no comparison between batik produced in the

35 Javanese Silk Batik
Detail from a silk *slendang* (shoulder shawl) showing a phoenix in dark blue dye, highlighted in gold leaf. Batiks of this kind were manufactured in north Java and were very popular in Bali. The cloth illustrated is approximately 50 years old.

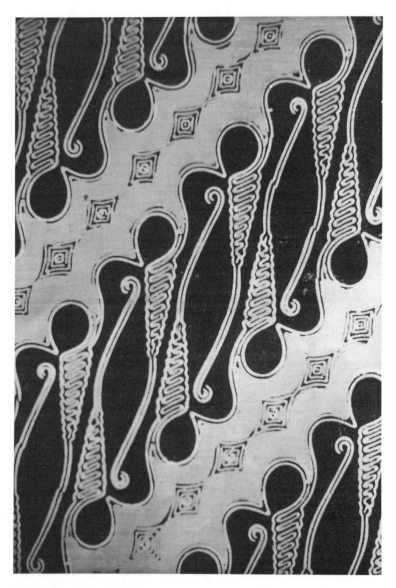

36 Javanese Cotton Batik
Detail from a Javanese batik decorated in the traditional 'broken sword'
pattern. The batik is coloured dark blue against a grey background rather
than the traditional brown of central Java, suggesting a possible north Java
origin. The cloth illustrated dates from the early post-Second World War
period.

traditional manner and that printed by modern means. The traditional methods allow an infinitely greater variety of designs to be applied to the cloth, many of them full of symbolism for the Indonesian inhabitants of Java, where the bulk of batik cloth has always been produced. Certain designs and favoured combinations of colours are associated with geographical localities. Both Yogyakarta and Surakarta (Solo) in central Java are known for batiks that are dark in colour and restrained in design, characteristics that echo the norms of public behaviour associated with their traditional courts. Batiks from Ceribon and Pekalongan on the north coast of Java, by contrast, are much more colourful, almost certainly as a reflection of the strong Chinese influence that has long been present in that region.

In other parts of Southeast Asia woven textiles were traditionally the predominant cloth craft. The variety of these woven cloths was and is great, ranging from the silks of Burma, Thailand and Cambodia, to the fibre cloths of the Dyaks of Borneo and the hill peoples of northern Luzon in the Philippines. In their variety, textiles alert us to a general feature of Southeast Asian material culture. Despite the broad underlying similarities that scholars of various disciplines perceive throughout the region, regional and national characteristics have been and still remain a feature of Southeast Asia's artistic heritage. This observation is true whether one is discussing wood carving or the metal work associated with weaponry. In this latter category the *kris* of Indonesia and Malaysia with their intricately worked serpentine blades are distinctively different from the straight-bladed swords of the mainland kingdoms.

Change is just as much a feature of contemporary Southeast Asia as of any other region of the world, so that the rich artistic and craft traditions that may have been so much a part of the region's history are in many cases slowly being eroded. The period of monumental building came to an end centuries ago, though it has left an echo in the temples of Bali, where an immensely rich artistic and cultural tradition has survived with a vigour unmatched anywhere else in the region. Traditional textiles have continued as a major feature of contemporary life despite the inroads of mass produced substitutes. And ceramic production has received a new lease of life, particularly in Thailand. The work of silversmiths has never been lost from northern Thailand and has been revived in the east coast states of modern Malaysia. But whatever the changes that have taken place and those still to come, Southeast Asia's artistic heritage is rich and varied, a testimony to past greatness and continuing cultural energy.

Southeast Asia in Fiction: A Gallimaufry

The body of fictional writing on Southeast Asia, particularly during the period of modern history treated in this book, is enormous in size. In the late 1920s, for instance, a French writer estimated that over the preceding eighty years his compatriots had published nearly one thousand novels on Indochinese subjects. Taking into account only those novels and shorter fictional writings that deal with Southeast Asia since the mid-nineteenth century, a student would face an impossible task in seeking to review even those items available in the English language alone. And much of the effort would be misplaced, for a very large number of the novels written with Southeast Asian settings have deservedly been forgotten as offering neither literary nor historical interest.

Yet if the daunting undertaking of reviewing the whole body of fictional writing can be properly put aside, there is reward to be gained from a selective examination of some of the most readily available, most influential, and most evocative novels and short stories that take Southeast Asia as their setting. Suggesting some of the books and stories that students of Southeast Asia might read is what is attempted in this, the book's final section. The selection is personal and heterogeneous, a gallimaufry. Moreover, the bulk of the novels examined were written by Europeans and about Europeans in Southeast Asia. The number of readable novels by Southeast Asians that are available in English is sadly limited.

The Novel as a Political Statement

The use of the novel to make a political statement about Southeast Asia has not been restricted to more recent times, when in relation to the Vietnam War many of the fictional works taking that conflict as their subject have been written with a clear position in favour of or against the war. What is without doubt the most famous Dutch novel with Indonesia as its setting, *Max Havelaar*, was written with the deliberate aim of changing the way in which the Netherlands Indies were administered.

First published in 1859, the novel's author was Eduard Douwes Dekker (pseudonym Multatuli), a Dutchman who had served in Indonesia for eighteen years. During that time he had grown disillusioned with the character of colonial rule, which he saw as corrupting of the Dutch and disregarding of the interests of the Indonesians. Largely autobiographical, the book remains a powerful indictment of the colonial system. Although there is debate about the extent of the novel's influence in the decades that followed its publication, most commentators credit Dekker's novel with having touched the conscience of many of the officials who came to Indonesia in the latter part of the nineteenth century and who believed that more 'liberal' policies should be followed by the colonial power. For some this attitude reflected a genuine shift towards the idea that colonial administrations had a responsibility to improve the lives of those whom they administered. For others the need for change was seen as a necessary practical response to the risks that would follow from a failure to change the abuses described in *Max Havelaar*. Whatever their motivations, these officials were reacting to the spectre of colonial revolt that Dekker raised when he asked 'Must not the bent spring eventually recoil? Must not the long-suppressed discontent—suppressed so that the Government can deny its existence!—finally turn to rage, desperation, madness?'

A much more complex novel about colonial Indonesia is Louis Couperus's *The Hidden Force*, first published in 1900. As in *Max Havelaar*, the hero of Couperus's novel is a colonial official. But unlike the principal character of Dekker's novel, Couperus's protagonist, Van Oudijek, is less a questioner of the colonial system than a victim of its innate inequities and of the gulf that separated the Dutch rulers from their Indonesian subjects. Although not conceived as a polemic, *The Hidden Force* carries a strong political message and may be profitably read alongside *Max Havelaar*.

Two other novels deserve mention in this brief review of writing which was both conceived with political intent and succeeded in that aim. The outstanding figure of the Philippine nationalist movement against the Spaniards was José Rizal. A man of extraordinarily wide-ranging talents, Rizal was the author of two polemical novels that helped shape the course of the aborted Philippine revolution against Spanish rule at the end of the nineteenth century. *Noli me tangere* (first published in 1886 and published in English as *The Social Cancer*, 1912) and *El filibusterismo* (first published in 1891 and published in English as *The Reign of Greed* in 1912) were devastating critiques of the colonial system in the Philippines, and in particular of the part played by the Catholic friars as the instruments of Spanish policy. While lacking the readable quality of *Max Havelaar* and the *Hidden Force*, Rizal's works should be noted for the passion embodied in them and the impact they had in their own day.

Exoticism and the Romance of Southeast Asia

Southeast Asia has stirred the imagination of many Western writers through its exoticism, its physical and cultural character that was so different from the West. This exoticism or 'romance' is a recurring feature of fictional writing taking Southeast Asia as its setting and is reflected in the four novels and one collection of short stories briefly noted here.

Few novelists have attempted to write of Southeast Asia in the early historical period, and fewer still have succeeded in that endeavour. One of those few was Maurice Collis, who in his novel *She Was A Queen* writes of Burma in the thirteenth century. Based loosely on a court chronicle, the novel tells the story of Queen Saw, a woman of powerful character who lived through one of the most turbulent periods in Burmese history. Collis was certainly not one of the greats of English fictional writing, though his better-known popular histories repay attention, but in *She Was A Queen* he provides a convincing sense of the folly and decadence of an inbred oriental court facing challenges to which it was not equal. As a portrayal of intrigue, treachery and the clash of two cultures, Burmese and Chinese, this novel offers a rare insight into a Southeast Asian world centuries before it was touched by the European interlopers.

Another writer who sought to portray the world of pre-colonial Southeast Asia was Sir Hugh Clifford, one of the notable examples of those scholar–administrators who worked in Malaya in the early years of the British expansion into that country. Clifford was a prolific writer, a fact that is the more remarkable when it is remembered that writing was for him a part-time activity. His output was uneven, but in his collection of short stories, *The Further Side of Silence*, he provides a telling insight— however much marked by the prejudices of his own time—into the character of traditional Malay society in the late nineteenth century. Clifford's stories in this collection were, he claimed, based on personal experience, and there is no reason to doubt this. His accounts of pre-colonial Malaya have the ring of truth to them, even though that truth was recorded with a clear and non-literary goal in mind. For Clifford makes no secret of the fact that his aim in writing is to celebrate the way in which, under British colonialism, the Malays emerged 'from the dark shadow in which their days were passed, into the delight of a personal freedom such as white men prize above most mundane things'.

Clifford corresponded with the great Anglo-Polish writer Joseph Conrad to discuss his writing and it is to one of Conrad's most notable works that we now turn. If Collis's novel is interesting and Clifford's short stories contain a mix of historical and cultural interest, Conrad's *Lord Jim* is one of the towering novels of the twentieth century. In a work concerned with the flawed character of a merchant marine officer who becomes a power in the imaginary Malay or Indonesian sultanate of Patusan, Conrad modelled his protagonist on James Brooke of Sarawak. The resemblance is superficial, and Jim of the title dies tragically, even futilely, rather than founding a dynasty. But in his masterly fashion Conrad captures the sense of what one man could do in a world that was still open to adventurers. At the same time, and drawing on his own experience of Southeast Asia in the late nineteenth century, Conrad offers wonderful literary portraits of the men who were to be found in the trading ports and settlements of the region.

The exotic is even more powerfully a feature of André Malraux's novel *The Royal Way* (originally published in French as *La Voie royale*). Partly based on Malraux's own attempt to steal statuary from the Angkorian temple of Banteay Srei in the 1920s, *The Royal Way* combines criticism of the oppressive political system of French Indochina with a powerful adventure story. Searching for antiquities in the still-unknown interior of Indochina, the protagonist Claude, and his older companion Perken, move steadily deeper into a fictionalised area somewhere to the north of the real ruins of Angkor. In this distant region, where aspects of Thailand, Laos and Cambodia combine, the adventurers become entangled in a revolt of hill people against lowlanders. The book closes with Perken dying and Claude's fate unclear. Dense, evocative, and revealing of its author as well as the time about which he wrote, *The Royal Way* is a minor classic.

Finally, in this brief listing of books marked by their authors' interest in the 'romance' of Southeast Asia, mention should be made of Vicki Baum's *A Tale From Bali*. Published in 1937, Baum wrote her story after a visit to Bali when she, like so many others, became enchanted with the island and its people's rich cultural life. The tale she tells is of life in the courts and villages of Bali just before the Dutch took control of the island and of the tragedy of the unequal contest between the Balinese and the Dutch invaders in 1906. Anthropologists may quibble over the accuracy of Baum's portrayal of Balinese life, but she has given non-specialist readers a lively story that is soundly based on historical fact.

Colonial Society in the Inter-War Period

European colonial life forms the basis of the largest body of Western fictional writing on Southeast Asia. Much is unflattering to the individuals portrayed and the world within which they moved. Foremost among those who wrote with their pens dipped in acid was Somerset Maugham. Although Maugham spent only a limited time in the region in the 1920s, he wrote both on the basis of his own experience and with an eye alert for past and present scandal. Probably the most famous of Maugham's short stories with Southeast Asian settings are 'The Letter' and 'The Yellow Streak'. The first was devised from an actual and famous marital scandal and murder in Malaya. The second drew on Maugham's own experience in a boating accident in Sarawak. In these, and in other stories, Maugham captures the flavour of the times, so well that he was regarded as an unwelcome vistitor in Singapore and Malaya years after he published his stories.

George Orwell (Eric Blair) was no less a critical observer of Southeast Asian colonial life. With a much longer experience of living in the region, he wrote an outstanding short novel based on his work as a British colonial official in Burma. This novel, *Burmese Days*, and two of his essays drawing directly on his own duties in Burma, 'Shooting an Elephant' and 'The Hanging', probably have no match in terms of twentieth century writing in English for capturing the boredom of colonial life and the inseparable divide between ruler and ruled.

A much later novel, *The Singapore Grip*, is notable for a similar ironic examination of colonial life just before and during the fall of Singapore. Written by a highly accomplished novelist, J. G. Farrell, this is an entertaining and complex book which, in addition, is characterised by the author's meticulous attention to historical accuracy.

Plantation Life

Novels taking life on the rubber plantations of Southeast Asia as their subject form an interesting sub-group within the broader category of books dealing with the colonial period. Two pre-Second World War novels and one that spans the period before and after that war offer a clear, if rather depressing, insight into the closed and monotonous world of the great rubber plantations that were developed in Sumatra and Malaya. Madelon Székely-Lulofs and her husband Laszlo Székely both wrote powerful novels that focussed on the inequities of the plantation system, in which the white managers could ill-treat their Indonesian workers with impunity. Both wrote from personal experience in Sumatra, and *Tropic Fever*, by Laszlo Székely, and *Rubber*, by Székely-Lulofs, played a part in arousing Dutch public opinion against the abuses they described.

The interest attaching to these two books does not just lie in their account of the arrogant and sometimes cruel behaviour of the European colonisers towards their indigenous workers. In both *Rubber* and *Tropic Fever* the boredom and the hardships of plantation life are vividly evoked. Writing about a later period, Pierre Boulle, best known for his novel of the Second World War in Southeast Asia, *The Bridge Over the River Kwai,* also dwells on the boredom of plantation life in his *Sacrilege in Malaya*. Boulle, too, wrote on the basis of personal experience, having worked on a French-owned plantation on Malaya for ten years. With a sharp satiric eye he mocks the way in which the senior managers enslave themselves to a rigid set of rules that govern every element of their lives and those of the workers they employ. A keen observer of colonial life, Boulle is particularly successful in depicting the divided world of pre-war Malaya in which an individual's race so often determined occupation; there were European managers, Tamil rubber tappers, Chinese merchants and storekeepers, and Malay aristocrats or small holders.

That not all was grim or open to mockery for those associated with the rubber industry is made clear in another, justly-famous autobiographical novel about plantation life. Henri Fauconnier's *The Soul of Malaya* is based on the author's experiences in the 1920s. Fauconnier is not uncritical of the colonial life he observed, but the more optimistic picture he provides needs to be put against the almost unrelieved gloom of *Rubber* and *Tropic Fever*.

The Second World War

Perhaps a little surprisingly, the Second World War in Southeast Asia did not generate a notable body of fictional writing. Possibly the reason for this situation lies in the fact that the war did result in the publication of many outstanding non-fictional accounts of events. Spenser Chapman's

The Jungle is Neutral, for instance, which recounts the exploits of the British-led guerrilla group, Force 136, is as exciting as any fictional portrayal of the war could hope to be.

As with the overwhelming bulk of the novels that have been cited so far, the fictional literature of the Second World War tells the story of the Europeans in the region, rather than providing an account of the war as it was seen by the indigenous people of Southeast Asia. Among the most powerful of the novels to emerge from the wartime years was James Clavell's *King Rat*. Based on Clavell's own experience of life as a prisoner in Changi jail in Singapore, *King Rat* provides a chilling picture of men struggling to come to terms with sometimes brutal imprisonment. Now better known for his later historical epics, Clavell's first novel still repays reading for its success in portraying men under stress, their weakness and their courage.

Two novels inspired by the Burma campaign deserve mention. Often described as the 'forgotten war', the Burma campaign was marked by a bitter British withdrawal and then, under General Slim, a dogged return that finally brought the defeat of the Japanese. Some of the perils of the Burma campaign are effectively captured in two novels, one by a famous author, the other by a man whose name is scarcely remembered today. The famous writer H.E. Bates tells the story of three Englishmen struggling to survive in the Burmese dry zone following the crash of the aircraft in which they had been flying. Like almost all of Bates's writing, *The Purple Plain* is a professionally crafted book, convincing in its detail. A similar sense of the accuracy of detail emerges in Sidney Butterworth's *Three Rivers to Glory*. This novel is a fictional account of the fighting that took place in western Burma, where troops of the West Africa Frontier Force were pitched against not only the Japanese but also elements of the Indian National Army, Indian troops who fought on the side of the Japanese in the hope of gaining independence from Britain. Yet, in a manner that reinforces the comment made earlier, these two novels about the war in Burma are probably correctly seen as less impressive than a non-fictional account of the same period. Written by a man who was to have a very successful career as a novelist, *The road past Mandalay*, by John Masters, is one of the finest pieces of writing to have come out of the war in Southeast Asia.

One further novel should be mentioned in a review of writing inspired by the Second World War, for its high literary quality. Widely acclaimed for his fiction set in India, Paul Scott also numbers among his novels a book set in Malaya at the end of the war. *The Chinese Love Pavilion* is one of Scott's less known books, but it possesses the same high literary quality that marks his other novels.

The Post-War World

If there is a relative drought of quality novels dealing with the Second World

War in Southeast Asia, the post-war years by comparison brought forth a flood of titles, many both readable and effective in their capacity to provide a sense of time and place. To list and discuss even a small proportion of the novels set in the post-war period would be a major exercise. What follows is a very selective account of some of the more interesting books that deal with the years after 1945.

As noted in earlier chapters of this book, the years after the Second World War were marked by turmoil. This is reflected in some of the best novels of the period, of which Graham Green's *The Quiet American* must rank among the finest. Set in Vietnam around 1952, *The Quiet American* is in part a political statement—the French were always fated to lose *their* Indochina War, and so was any other Western power that sought to shape the course of Asian history. It captures wonderfully the tone of life in the expatriate community in Vietnam. A reader is able to sense the tension of daily life in Saigon, where a visit to a bar or a cafe meant being exposed to the risk of a grenade attack. The book has two marvellous set-piece descriptions in Greene's account of the Roman Catholic bishopric of Phat Diem under siege and the visit by the novel's narrator, Fowler, to the Cao Dai temple at Tay Ninh. Spare, cynical and realistic, *The Quiet American* repays many readings.

Of a quite different literary quality, but nonetheless effective in capturing the atmosphere of the First Indochina War from the point of view of the French soldier, is Jean Lartéguy's *The Centurions*. This novel records the bitter disillusionment of the French officer corps as they fought the 'dirty war' only, in their judgment, to be betrayed by their political leaders in France. As a fictional account of the factors that played such a part in bringing about the French army's revolt in Algeria—the subject of Lartéguy's later novel, *The Praetorians*—*The Centurions* deserves mention in any review of fiction dealing with the First Indochina War.

Another novel that takes post-war conflict as its central theme is Han Suyin's ... *and the Rain my Drink*. Set in the Malayan Emergency, this novel makes no pretence to being a balanced account of the issues involved in that struggle. Yet although the author writes as a partisan for the ethnic Chinese point of view, including those Malayan Chinese who went into the jungle as guerrillas to fight against the colonial government, her portrayal of other races in Malaya does not lack sympathy. Han Suyin's passion for the plight of the ethnic Chinese underdog gives her readers an insight into why it was that the Emergency took place, lasted so long and had such a profound effect in shaping opinions in independent Malaysia.

Turmoil of a different kind provides the background for the novels of the Indonesian writer Mochtar Lubis and the Australian Christopher Koch. In one of the more important novels by a Southeast Asian writer to be translated into English, Mochtar Lubis offers a pessimistic view of

Indonesian society in his *Twilight in Djakarta*. Set in the 1950s, Lubis offers a highly critical view of the Sukarno era. Corruption is portrayed as endemic; hopelessness and poverty are the lot of the masses. Most of those who appear in the novel are flawed in character—few attract the reader's sympathy. Yet despite the didactic tone of much of Lubis's writing, *Twilight in Djakarta* is a forceful account in an elegant translation of a city in political and social decay. How the Sukarno era came to an end forms the central theme of Christopher Koch's novel *The Year of Living Dangerously*. Written from the viewpoint of an outsider, Koch's novel provides a fictional counterpoint to the world so vividly evoked by Lubis. Another novel to take the closing stages of Sukarno's rule over Indonesia as its setting is Blanche d'Alpuget's *Monkeys in the Dark*. Like Koch, d'Alpuget is concerned to present the personal dilemmas of an expatriate confronting a climactic period in Indonesian politics. (This theme of non-Southeast Asians beset by personal problems in an exotic locale recurs in d'Alpuget's later, and perhaps more accomplished, *Turtle Beach*, which is set principally in Malaysia.)

Another Southeast Asian writer whose theme is the inequities of the society in which he lives is the Filipino novelist Francis ('Frankie') José. In his novel *Mass* he presents a convincing portrait of a young man's flirtation with the communist movement. As he struggles to come to terms with the need for political choice, the novel's protagonist reflects on the nature of Philippines society, the corruption it breeds and the apparent impossibility of achieving change without resorting to violence.

An outsider's look at the same society is found in Robert Drewe's *A cry in the jungle bar*. Written with an irony that at times borders on satire, Drewe's account of an Australian aid expert's experiences in the Philippines has a serious purpose, in particular the difficulty even the best intentioned foreigners have in penetrating another society.

In introducing this review of fictional writing on Southeast Asia, the present writer stressed the personal nature of the selection being made. For each item cited another commentator might well choose to offer an alternative. And as one draws nearer to the present day the greater will be the differences of judgment as to which books should be included and which should not. The task of selection is made the more difficult by the still growing number of fictional acounts of the Second Indochina War that are being published.

At the risk of being criticised for making too limited a selection from the growing canon of fiction based in Vietnam during the 'American period', the final citations in this section are of two fine and very different novels, Tim O'Brien's *Going After Cacciato* and John M. Del Vecchio's

The 13th Valley. Del Vecchio's novel is brutally realistic, the war seen from the foot soldier's perspective and based on the bitter fighting that took place in the valleys running up to the central highlands of southern Vietnam in 1970. O'Brien's book by contrast mixes reality with fantasy. It is a complex novel that commands the reader's attention from its simple opening sentence, 'It was a bad time'.

Fiction can only ever be one route into an understanding of Southeast Asia, and for the most part a route limited by the bulk of the authors' perspective being that of a non-Southeast Asian outsider. Yet, with an area of study both as diverse and in many regions and disciplines still awaiting thorough exploration as Southeast Asia is, to ignore any route to knowledge and understanding would be a mistake. Whatever their limitations, the books and stories reviewed here can form one more piece in each person's mosaic of the immensely diverse study that is the history of Southeast Asia.

Notes

The brief review of fictional writing on Southeast Asia contained in the preceding chapter touches upon only some of the best known of the books and stories that take the region as their geographical setting. A more detailed examination of the body of fiction on a country by country and region by region basis will shortly be available in a new symposium edited by Robin W. Winks and James Rush *Asia in Western Fiction* due for publication in 1990.

The following is a compilation of the works cited in this chapter. Where possible the publication date provided is that of the first edition.

Fiction

Bates, H.E., *The Purple Plain*, 1948
Baum, V., *A Tale From Bali*, 1937
Boulle, P., *The Bridge Over the River Kwai*, 1954
—— *Sacrilege in Malaya*, 1959
Butterworth, S., *Three Rivers to Glory*, 1957
Clavell, J., *King Rat*, 1963
Clifford, H., *The Further Side of Silence*, 1916
Collis, M., *She Was A Queen*, 1937
Conrad, J., *Lord Jim*, 1900
Couperus, *The Hidden Force*, first published in Dutch in 1900
d'Alpuget, B., *Monkeys in the Dark*, 1980
—— *Turtle Beach*, 1981

Del Vecchio, J.M., *The 13th Valley*, 1982
Drewe, R., *A cry in the jungle bar*, 1979
Farrell, J.G., *The Singapore Grip*, 1978
Fauconnier, H., *The Soul of Malaya*, 1931
Greene, G., *The Quiet American*, 1955
Han Suyin, ... *and the Rain my Drink*, 1956
José, F., *Mass*, 1979
Koch, C.J., *The Year of Living Dangerously*, 1978
Lartéguy, J., *The Centurions*, 1961
—— *The Praetorians*, 1963
Lubis, M., *Twilight in Djakarta*, 1964
Malraux, A., *The Royal Way*, 1935
Multatuli (pseud. E.D. Dekker), *Max Havelaar*, first published in Dutch
    1859.
Maugham, S., *Collected Short Stories*, 1977—84
O'Brien, T., *Going After Cacciato*, 1978
Orwell, G. (pseud. E. Blair), *Burmese Days*, 1934
—— *Shooting an elephant and other essays*, 1950
Rizal, J., *Noli me tangere*, 1886
—— *El filibusterismo*, 1891
Scott, P., *The Chinese Love Pavilion*, 1960
Székely, L., *Tropic Fever*, 1937
Székely-Lulofs, M., *Rubber*, 1931

Non-Fiction

Masters, J., *The Road past Mandalay*, 1961
Spenser Chapman, F., *The Jungle is Neutral*, 1949

Suggested Readings

The following suggested readings should, like the rest of this book, be regarded only as an *introduction* to the ever-increasing literature that deals with Southeast Asian history. Much of the important writing related to Southeast Asian history that has appeared since the Second World War has been published in the form of articles and anyone wanting to go deeper into the subject will need to consult a wide range of journals as well as the many books that are available. The following listing does not include material published in languages other than English, though readers should be aware of the very large body of material that exists in Dutch (for Indonesia in particular) and French (for the Indochinese region). Moreover, there is a substantial amount of writing dealing with the history of Southeast Asia in the languages of the region.

For readers wishing to pursue their interest in Southeast Asia at a deeper level there is now a wide range of bibliographic aids available. For the period covered by the present book the best bibliographic guidance is that provided in the extended 'Bibliography' of D.J. Steinberg, ed., *In Search of Southeast Asia: A Modern History*, New York, 1971, reprinted, Honolulu, 1985. A revised edition of this book, published in 1987, includes bibliographic guidance to material published up to 1985.

Bibliographies and Guides

Hay, S.N., and M.H. Chase, *Southeast Asian History: A Bibliographic Guide*, New York, 1962. Now dated, but still useful.

Herbert, P. and A.C. Milner, eds., *South-East Asia Languages and Literature: A Select Guide*, Whiting Bay, Arran, 1989.

Steinberg, D.J., ed., *In Search of Southeast Asia: A Modern History*, New York, 1971, reprinted, Honolulu, 1985, revised edition, New York, 1987.

Tregonning, K.G., *Southeast Asia: A Critical Bibliography*, Tucson, Ariz., 1969.

General Works

History and Historiography

Bastin, J. and H.J. Benda, *A History of Modern Southeast Asia*, Englewood Cliffs, N.J., 1967. A stimulating book by two well-known historians.

Bellwood, P., *Man's Conquest of the Pacific: The Prehistory of Southeast Asia and Oceania*, New York, 1979.

Embree, A.T. *et al*, *Encyclopedia of Asian History*, 4 vols, New York, 1988.

Hall, D.G.E., *A History of South East Asia*, 4th Edition, London, 1981. This massive study remains the most important single history of the region.

—— ed., *Historians of South-East Asia*, London, 1962. A series of essays that provide a commentary on the 'state of the art' in the early 1960s.

Jeffrey, R. ed., *Asia: The Winning of Independence*, London, 1981.

Pluvier, J.M., *Southeast Asia from Colonialism to Independence*, Kuala Lumpur, 1974. A detailed history of the end of the colonial period.

Reid, A. and D. Marr, eds., *Perceptions of the Past in Southeast Asia*, Hong Kong, 1979. A recent review of Southeast Asian historical writing with particular attention to Indonesia.

Scott, J.C., *The Moral Economy of the Peasant: Rebellion and Subsistence in Southeast Asia*, New Haven, Conn., 1976. An outstanding recent study of an important aspect of Southeast Asia's history.

Soedjatmoko, *et al.*, eds., *An Introduction to Indonesian Historiography*, Ithaca, N.Y., 1965.

Steinberg, D.J. ed., *In Search of Southeast Asia: A Modern History*. Already noted for its excellent bibliography, this is a sophisticated interpretive history.

Tarling, N., *A Concise History of Southeast Asia*, New York, 1966.

Williams, L.A., *Southeast Asia: A History*, New York, 1976.

Wolters, O.W., *History, Culture, and Religion in Southeast Asian Perspectives*, Singapore, 1982.

Geography

Dobby, E.G.H., *Southeast Asia*, 11th edition, London, 1973.

Fisher, C.A., *South-East: A Social, Economic, and Political Geography*, 2nd edition, London, 1966. The major text covering the whole region.

Hill, R.D., *Rice in Malaya: A Study in Historical Geography*, Kuala Lumpur, 1977.

Hill, R.D., ed., *A Systematic Geography of South-East Asia*, Kuala Lumpur, 1978. A recent introduction to the subject.

McGee, T.G., *The Southeast Asian City: A Social Geography of the Primate Cities of Southeast Asia*, London, 1967.

Ulack, R. and G. Pauer, *Atlas of Southeast Asia*, New York, 1988.

Ethnology

Kunstadter, P. ed., *Southeast Asian Tribes, Minorities, and Nations*, 2 vols, Princeton, N.J., 1967.

Lebar, F., G. Hickey, and J. Musgrave, *Ethnic Groups of Mainland Southeast Asia*, New Haven, Conn., 1964.

Lebar, F., *Ethnic Groups of Insular Southeast Asia*, 2 vols, New Haven, Conn., 1972 and 1975.

Society and Economy

Booth, A., O'Malley, W.J. and A. Weidemann, eds, *Essays in Indonesian Economic History*, New Haven, Conn., 1987.

Burling, R., *Hill Farms and Paddy Fields*, Englewood Cliffs, N.J., 1965. A useful introduction to the mainland peasant world.

Cushman, J. and Wang Gungwu, eds, *Changing Identities of the Southeast Asian Chinese since World War II*, Hong Kong, 1988.

DuBois, C., *Social Forces in Southeast Asia*, Cambridge, Mass., 1959. A classic study of continuing importance.

Guy, J.S., *Oriental Trade Ceramics in South-East Asia, Ninth to Sixteenth Centuries*, Singapore, 1986.

Hickey, G.C., *Sons of the Mountains: Ethnohistory of the Vietnamese Central Highlands to 1954*, New Haven, Conn., 1982. *Free in the Forest: Ethnohistory of the Vietnamese Central Highlands 1954–1976*, New Haven, Conn., 1982.

Kahlenburg, M.H., et al., *Textile Traditions of Indonesia*, Los Angeles, 1977.

Keyes, C.F., *The Golden Peninsula: Culture and Adaptation in Mainland Southeast Asia*, New York, 1977.

Owen, N.G. ed., *Death and Disease in Southeast Asia: Explorations in Social, Medical and Demographic History*, Singapore, 1987.

Purcell, V., *The Chinese in South-East Asia*, revised edition, London, 1965.

Ramseyer, U., *The Art and Culture of Bali*, Oxford, 1977.

Reid, A.J.S., ed., *Slavery, Bondage and Dependency*, St Lucia, Brisbane, 1983.

Sandhu, K.S., *Indians in Malaya: Immigration and Settlement, 1786–1857*, Cambridge, 1969.

Wang Gungwu, *Community and Nation: essays on Southeast Asia and the Chinese*, Sydney, 1981.

Art

Achjadi, Jo, *Seni Kriya: The Crafts of Indonesia*, Singapore, 1988.

Brown, R., *The Ceramics of South-East Asia: Their Dating and Identification*, Kuala Lumpur, 1977, second edition, Singapore, 1988.

Groslier, B.P., *The Art of Indochina: including Thailand, Vietnam, Laos, and Cambodia*, New York, 1962.

Pisit Charoenwongsa and M.C. Subhadradis Diskul, *Thailand*, Geneva, 1978.

Rawson, P., *The Art of Southeast Asia: Cambodia, Vietnam, Thailand, Laos, Burma, Java, Bali*, London, 1967.

Shaw, J.C., *Introducing Thai Ceramics, also Burmese and Khmer*, Chiangmai, 1987.

Sheppard, M., *Living Crafts of Malaysia*, Singapore, 1978.

Wagner, F.A., *The Art of Indonesia*, New York, 1959.

Journals

Journal of Asian Studies, Ann Arbor, Mich.

Journal of Southeast Asian Studies, Singapore.

Modern Asian Studies, Cambridge.

Pacific Affairs, Vancouver.

In addition to the above journals, which are essentially academic in character, an observer of contemporary Southeast Asia will find excellent coverage of major political and economic developments in the weekly editions of:

Far Eastern Economic Review, Hong Kong

Early Southeast Asian History

Coedès, G., *The Making of Southeast Asia*, Berkeley, Cal., 1966.
——, *Angkor, An Introduction*, London, 1967.
——, *The Indianized States of Southeast Asia*, Honolulu, 1968. These are three translations of the works of one of the most distinguished of all French historians of early Southeast Asia.
Hall, K.R., *Maritime Trade and State Development in Early Southeast Asia*, Honolulu, 1984.
Higham, C., *The Archaeology of Mainland Southeast Asia*, Cambridge, 1989.
Marr, D.G. and A.C. Milner, eds., *Southeast Asia in the 9th to 14th Centuries*, Singapore and Canberra, 1986.
Taylor, K.W., *The Birth of Vietnam*, Barkely, Cal., 1983.
Wheatley, P., *The Golden Khersonese: Studies in the Historical Geography of the Malay Peninsula Before A.D. 1500*, Kuala Lumpur, 1966.
Wolters, O.W., *Early Indonesian Commerce: A Study of the Origins of Srivijaya*, Ithaca, N.Y., 1967. An outstanding survey of the rise of the Srivijayan empire.
——, *The Fall of Srivijaya in Malay History*, London, 1970.

The Traditional World

Andaya, B.W., *Perak: The Abode of Grace: A Study of an Eighteenth Century Malay State*, Kuala Lumpur, 1979.
Andaya, L.Y., *The Kingdom of Johor, 1641–1728*, Kuala Lumpur, 1975.
Gullick, J.M., *Indigenous Political Systems of Western Malaya*, London, 1958.
Heine-Geldern, R. von. *Conceptions of State and Kingship in Southeast Asia*, Ithaca, N.Y., 1956.
Lieberman, V.B., *Burmese Administrative Cycles: Anarchy and Conquest, Fifteen Eighty to Seventeen Sixty*, Princeton, New Jersey, 1984.
Milner, A.C., *Kerajaan: Malay Political Culture on the Eve of Colonial Rule*, Tucson, Arizona, 1982.
Reid, A., *Southeast Asia in the Age of Commerce 1450–1680: The Lands Below the Winds*, New Haven, Conn., 1988.
Shrieke, B.J.O., *Indonesian Sociological Studies*, Part Two, The Hague, 1957.
Taylor, R.H., *The State in Burma*, Honolulu, 1988.
Woodside, A.B., *Vietnam and the Chinese Model*, Cambridge, Mass., 1971.

The Colonial Advance

Boxer, C.R., *The Dutch Seaborne Empire 1600–1800*, New York, 1965.
Chandran, J., *The Contest for Siam, 1889–1902: A Study in Diplomatic Rivalry*, Kuala Lumpur, 1977.
Cowan, C.D., *Nineteenth-century Malaya: The Origins of British Political Control*, London, 1965.
Osborne, M.E., *The French Presence in Cochinchina and Cambodia: Rule and Response (1859–1905)*, Ithaca, N.Y., 1969.
Phelan, J.L., *The Hispanization of the Philippines: Spanish Aims and Filipino Responses, 1565–1700*, Madison, 1959.

Ricklefs, M.C., *Jogjakarta under Sultan Mangkubumi, 1749–1792: A History of the Division of Java*, London, 1974.
Roberts, S.H., *The History of French Colonial Policy, 1870–1925*, reprinted edition, London 1966.
Woodman, D., *The Making of Burma*, London, 1962.

Modern Southeast Asian History–To the Second World War

Brunei

Turnbull, C.M., *A Short History of Malaya, Singapore and Brunei*, Melbourne, 1980.

Burma

Adas, M., *The Burma Delta: Economic Development and Social Change on an Asian Rice Frontier, 1852–1941*, Madison, 1974.
Cady, J.F., *A History of Modern Burma*, Ithaca, N.Y., 1958.
Hall, D.G.E., *Burma*, London, 1960.
Maung Htin Aung, *A History of Burma*, New York, 1968.
Sarkisyanz, E., *Buddhist Backgrounds of the Burmese Revolution*, The Hague, 1965.
Taylor, R.H., *The State in Burma*.

Cambodia

Until recently there has been no satisfactory general history of Cambodia. A new book by David Chandler has changed that situation. The other two items listed are useful in relation to the French colonial period.

Chandler, D.P., *A History of Cambodia*, Boulder, Colorado, 1983.
Osborne, M.E., *The French Presence in Cochinchina and Cambodia: Rule and Response (1859–1905)*.
Reddi, V.M., *A History of the Cambodian Independence Movement: 1863–1955*, Tirupati, 1970.

Indonesia

Abeyasekere, S., *Jakarta: A History*, Melbourne, 1987.
Day, C., *The Policy and Administration of the Dutch in Java*, reprinted edition, Kuala Lumpur, 1966.
Furnivall, J.S., *Netherlands India: A Study of Plural Economy*, reprinted edition, Cambridge, 1967.
Geertz, C., *Agricultural Involution*, Berkeley, Cal., 1963.
Ingleson, J., *The Road to Exile: The Indonesian Nationalist Movement 1927–1934*, Singapore, 1979.
Legge, J.D., *Indonesia*, 2nd edition, Sydney, 1977.
Ricklefs, M.C., *A History of Modern Indonesia*, London, 1981.
Taylor, J.G. *The Social World of Batavia: European and Eurasian in Dutch Asia*, Madison, Wisconsin, 1984.
Wertheim, W.F., *Indonesian Society in Transition*, revised edition, The Hague, 1959.
Zainu'ddin, A., *A Short History of Indonesia*, North Melbourne, 1968.

Laos

There is no satisfactory general history of Laos available in English.

Malaysia

Allen, C. ed., *Tales from the South China Seas*, London, 1983.
Andaya, B.W. and L.Y., *A History of Malaysia*, London, 1982.
Butcher, J.G., *The British in Malaya, 1880–1914: The Social History of a European Community in Colonial South-East Asia*, Kuala Lumpur, 1979.
Emerson, R., *Malaysia: A Study in Direct and Indirect Rule*, reprinted edition, Kuala Lumpur, 1964.
Gullick, J.M., *Malaysia*, New York, 1969.
Roff, W.R., *The Origins of Malay Nationalism*, New Haven, Conn., 1967.
Stenson, M., *Class, Race and Colonialism in West Malaysia: The Indian Case*, Vancouver, 1980.
Turnbull, C.M., *The Straits Settlements 1826–67: Indian Presidency to Crown Colony*, London, 1972.
——, *A Short History of Malaya, Singapore and Brunei*.
Winstedt, R.O., *A History of Malaya*, revised edition, Singapore 1962.

The Philippines

Corpuz, O.D., *The Philippines*, Englewood Cliffs, N.J., 1965.
Cushner, N.P., *Spain in the Philippines: From Conquest to Revolution*, Quezon City, 1970.
Friend, T., *Between Two Empires: The Ordeal of the Philippines, 1929–1946*, New Haven, Conn., 1965.
McCoy, A. and E. de Jesus, eds., *Philippine Social History: Global Trade and Local Transformations*, Sydney, 1981.
Zaide, G.F., *Philippine Political and Cultural History*, 2 vols., revised edition, Manila, 1957.

Singapore

Lee Poh Ping, *Chinese Society in Nineteenth Century Singapore*, Kuala Lumpur, 1978.
Turnbull, C.M., *A History of Singapore, 1819–1975*, Kuala Lumpur, 1977.

Thailand

Bunnag, T., *The Provincial Administration of Siam, 1892–1915*, Kuala Lumpur, 1977.
Prince Chula Chakrabongse, *Lords of Life: The Paternal Monarchy of Bangkok, 1782–1932*, New York, 1960.
Vella, W., *The Impact of the West on Government in Thailand*, Berkeley, Cal., 1955.
Wyatt, D.K., *Thailand: A Short History*, New Haven, Conn., 1984.

Vietnam

Despite the great interest generated by the war in Vietnam no satisfactory general history has yet been published in English for this country.
Buttinger, J., *A Dragon Embattled: A History of Colonial and Post-Colonial Vietnam*, 2 vols, New York, 1967.
Duiker, W.J., *The Rise of Nationalism in Vietnam, 1900–1941*, Ithaca, N.Y., 1976.

Huynh Kim Khanh, *Vietnamese Communism, 1925–1945*, Ithaca, N.Y., 1982.
Marr, D., *Vietnamese Anticolonialism, 1885–1925*, Berkeley, Cal., 1971.
——, *Vietnamese Tradition on Trial, 1920–1945*, Berkeley, Cal., 1981.
Nguyen Van Long, *Before the Revolution: The Vietnamese Peasants under the French*, Cambridge, Mass., 1973.
Osborne, M.E., *The French Presence in Cochinchina and Cambodia: Rule and Response (1859–1905)*.
Smith, R.B., *Vietnam and the West*, London, 1968.
Truong Buu Lam, *Patterns of Vietnamese Response to foreign Intervention, 1858–1900*, New Haven, Conn., 1967.
Woodside, A.B., *Vietnam and the Chinese Model*.
——, *Community and Revolution in Modern Vietnam*, Boston, 1976.

The Second World War

General

Collier, B., *The War in the Far East 1941–1945: A Military History*, New York, 1969.
Elsbree, W.H., *Japan's Role in Southeast Asian Nationalist Movements*, Cambridge, Mass., 1953.
Friend, T., *The Blue-Eyed Enemy: Japan Against the West in Java and Luzon, 1942–1945*, Princeton, 1988.
Jones, F.C., *Japan's New Order in East Asia, 1937–1945*, London, 1974.
Lebra, J.C., *Japan's Greater East Asia Co-Prosperity Sphere in World War II: Selected Readings and Documents*, New York, 1974.
——, *Japanese-trained Armies in Southeast Asia*, New York, 1977.
McCoy, A.W. ed., *Southeast Asia Under Japanese Occupation*, New Haven, Conn., 1980.
Silverstein, J., ed., *Southeast Asia in World War II*, New Haven, Conn., 1966.

Burma

Ba Maw, *Breakthrough in Burma: Memoirs of a Revolution*, New Haven, Conn., 1968.
Trager, F.N., *Burma: From Kingdom to Republic*, New York, 1966.

Cambodia

Herz, M., *Short History of Cambodia*, New York, 1958. This book is often unreliable and has a marked bias. Despite these faults it has useful insights into the 1940s in Cambodia.

Indonesia

Anderson, B.R.O'G., *Java in a Time of Revolution; Occupation and Resistance, 1944–1946*, Ithaca, N.Y., 1972.
Benda, H.J., *The Cresent and the Rising Sun: Indonesian Islam under the Japanese Occupation*, The Hague, 1955.
Kahin, G.McT., *Nationalism and Revolution in Indonesia*, Ithaca, N.Y., 1952 and subsequent editions.

Laos

Kemp, P., *Alms for Oblivion*, London, 1961.

Malaysia and Singapore

Caffrey, K., *Out in the Midday Sun: Singapore 1941–1945*, London, 1974.
Chin Kee Onn, *Malaya Upside Down*, Singapore, 1946.
Spenser Chapman, F., *The Jungle is Neutral*, London, 1949.

The Philippines

Agoncillo, T.A., *The Fateful Years: Japan's Adventure in the Philippines, 1941–1945*, 2 vols, Manila, 1965.
Friend, T., *Between Two Empires: The Ordeal of the Philippines, 1929–1946.*
Steinberg, D.J., *Philippines Collaboration in World War II*, Ann Arbor, Mich., 1967.

Thailand

Once again this is a period that has not been treated in any notable single study so that the period is best considered on the basis of accounts provided in general histories.

Vietnam

Hammer, E.J., *The Struggle for Indochina*, Stanford, Cal., 1955.
McAlister, J.T., *Vietnam: The Origins of Revolution*, New York, 1968.

The Post-War World

The period following the Second World War with its record of successful bids for independence, of revolts, rebellions, and revolutions, of successes and failures, has prompted a truly massive amount of writing and publication. Any attempt to provide a comprehensive list of suggested readings for this turbulent and exciting period would go far beyond the purposes of this present book. The following suggested readings aim at providing a basic introduction to the region in general and to the post-war history of the individual countries of Southeast Asia. The selections probably reflect the author's own view that a stimulating and controversial book is as valuable as those judged to be safe and solid. Since the post-war period is not the principal preoccupation of this book the listings are deliberately not extensive.

General

Bloodworth, D., *An Eye for the Dragon: Southeast Asia Observed, 1954–1970*, London 1970.
Broinowski, A. ed., *Understanding ASEAN*, London, 1982.

FitzGerald, C.P., *China and Southeast Asia Since 1945*, Camberwell, Vic., 1973.

Kahin, G.McT., *Governments and Politics of Southeast Asia*, 2nd edition, Ithaca, N.Y. 1964.

Leifer, M., *The Foreign Relations of the New States*, Camberwell, Vic, 1974.

Osborne, M., *Region of Revolt: Focus on Southeast Asia*, Harmondsworth, 1971.

Shaplen, R., *Time Out of Hand: Revolution and Reaction in Southeast Asia*, New York, 1969.

Somers Heidhues, M.F., *Southeast Asia's Chinese Minorities*, Camberwell, Vic., 1974.

Tilman, R.O., ed., *Man, State, and Society in Contemporary Southeast Asia*, New York, 1969.

Burma

Maung Maung, U., *Burma and General Ne Win*, New York, 1968.

Silverstein, J., *Burma: The Politics of Stagnation*, Ithaca, N.Y., 1978.

Tinker, H., *The Union of Burma: A Study of the First Years of Independence*, 4th edition, London, 1967.

Cambodia

Chandler, D.P. and B. Kiernan, eds., *Revolution and its Aftermath in Kampuchea: Eight Essays*, New Haven, Conn., 1983.

Kiernan, B., *How Pol Pot Came to Power*, London, 1985.

Leifer, M., *Cambodia: The Search for Survival*, New York, 1967.

Norodom Sihanouk, Prince, *My War with the CIA*, New York, 1973.

Osborne, M., *Politics and Power in Cambodia: The Sihanouk Years*, Camberwell, Vic., 1973.

——, *Before Kampuchea: Preludes to Tragedy*, Sydney, London, Boston, 1979.

Smith, R.M., *Cambodia's Foreign Policy*, New York, 1965.

Indonesia

Dahm, B., *The History of Indonesia in the Twentieth Century*, New York, 1970.

Hughes, J., *Indonesian Upheaval*, New York, 1967.

Kahin, A.R. ed., *Regional Dynamics of the Indonesian Revolution: Unity from Diversity*, Honolulu, 1985.

Kahin, G.McT., *Nationalism and Revolution in Indonesia*.

Legge, J.D., *Sukarno: A Political Biography*, London, 1972.

McVey, R., ed., *Indonesia*, New Haven, Conn., 1963.

Reid, A.J.S., *The Indonesian National Revolution, 1945–1950*, Camberwell, Vic., 1974.

Robison, R. *et al* eds., *Southeast Asia in the 1980s*, Sydney, 1987.

Laos

Adams, N.S., and A.W. McCoy, *Laos: War and Revolution*, New York, 1970.

Halpern, J., *Government, Politics and Social Structure in Laos*, New Haven, Conn., 1964.

Stuart-Fox, M., ed., *Contemporary Laos*, St Lucia, Brisbane, 1982.
Toye, H., *Laos: Buffer State or Battleground?*, London, 1968.

Malaysia

Bedlington, S.S., *Malaysia and Singapore: The Building of New States*, Ithaca, N.Y., 1978.
Clutterbuck, R.L., *The Long, Long War*, New York, 1966.
Means, G.P., *Malaysian Politics*, New York, 1970.
Milne, R.S., *Government and Politics in Malaysia*, Boston, 1967.
Ratnam, K.J., *Communalism and the Political Process in Malaya*, London, 1965.
Vorys, Karl von, *Democracy Without Consensus: Communalism and Political Stability in Malaysia*, Kuala Lumpur, 1976.

The Philippines

Corpuz, O.D., *The Philippines*.
Grossholtz, J., *Politics in the Philippines*, Boston, 1964.

Thailand

Darling, F., *Thailand and the United States*, Washington, 1965.
Girling, J.L.S., *Thailand: Society and Politics*, Ithaca, N.Y., 1981.
Wilson, D.A., *Politics in Thailand*, Ithaca, N.Y., 1962.
——, *The United States and the Future of Thailand*, New York, 1970.

Singapore

Chan Heng Chee, *The Dynamics of One Party Dominance: The PAP at the Grass Roots*, Singapore, 1976.
George, T.J.S., *Lee Kuan Yew's Singapore*, London, 1973.
Josey, A., *Lee Kuan Yew*, revised edition, Singapore, 1971.
Minchin, J., *No Man is an Island*, Sydney, 1986.
Turnbull, C.M., *A History of Singapore, 1819–1975*.

Vietnam

Duncanson, D., *Government and Revolution in Vietnam*, London, 1968.
Fall, B., *The Two Viet-Nams: A Political and Military Analysis*, revised edition, New York, 1967.
FitzGerald, F., *Fire in the Lake: The Vietnamese and the Americans in Vietnam*, Boston, 1972.
Kahin, G.McT., *Intervention: How America Became Involved in Vietnam*, New York, 1986.
Karnow, S., *Vietnam: A History*, New York, 1983.
Lacouture, J., *Ho Chi Minh*, New York, 1968.
Lewy, G., *America in Vietnam*, New York, 1978.
McAlister, J. and P. Mus, *The Vietnamese and Their Revolution*, New York, 1970.
Maclear, M., *Vietnam: The Ten Thousand Day War*, London, 1981.
Porter, G., *A Peace Denied: The United States and the Paris Agreement*, Bloomington, Indiana, 1975.
Race, J. *War Comes to Long An: Revolutionary Conflict in a Vietnamese*

Province, Berkeley, Cal., 1972.

Shaplen, R., *Bitter Victory*, New York, 1986.

Warner, D., *The Last Confucian*, New York, 1963.
Vo Nguyen Giap, *People's War People's Army*, New York, 1962.
Woodside, A.B., *Community and Revolution in Modern Vietnam*.

Time Chart of Modern Southeast Asian History

The simplified time chart indicates the growth of external (colonial) control over Southeast Asia, starting from the beginning of the nineteenth century when, with the exception of Indonesia and the Philippines, and with the minor British settlement of Penang, the bulk of the region was still under traditional rule. Examined as a whole the time chart emphasises how relatively recent was European expansion in Southeast Asia. It also gives emphasis to the way in which the Second World War represented a sharp break with the past and played a vital part in setting the scene for the achievement of independence by the countries of Southeast Asia.

One cautionary point is necessary. The shading on the time chart represents the expansion of colonial control so that for Vietnam, for instance, the shading indicates the existence of French control over all of the country from the mid 1880's. As has been made clear in the text, there was continuing resistance to French rule after the 1880's. Moreover, it should be further recognised that the degree of impact of colonial control in, say, Malaya, was much greater as at 1939 than in 1919 even though British control extended over the whole country before this latter date. In brief, what the time chart depicts is the broad fact of colonial rule rather than the details of resistance and rebellion and the degree of impact of external rule.

A different hatching is used to indicate continuing external rule after the Second World War since in each case where such rule continued external control was either disputed by movements demanding independence (Cambodia, Indonesia, Laos, Vietnam) or the colonial power had given some form of undertaking to grant independence (Burma, Malaysia, Singapore). Even Brunei's long-delayed accession to independence took place against a background in which Britain had made clear its intention to give up its role as a protecting power.

BRUNEI

1841 Brunei loses control of Sarawak to James Brooke

1877 Brunei cedes Sabah to the North Borneo Co.

1888 Brunei becomes a British Protectorate

1906 Britain appoints a Resident to administer Brunei

Once exercising power over much of coastal Borneo and the Sulu Archipelago, Brunei was a declining power in the early 19th century

Brunei decides not to join Malaysia in 1963

Brunei gains independence in 1984

BURMA

Burma governed by the Konbaung Dynasty since 1752

1824-26 First Burma War

1852-53 Second Burma War

1885 Third Burma War

Burma governed as a British colony until Second World War

1948 Burma gains independence

CAMBODIA

Cambodia by the end of the 18th century a weak state paying tribute to Thailand and Vietnam

1864 Cambodia comes under French colonial control

Cambodia governed as a French "Protectorate" until Second World War

1953 Cambodia gains independence

INDONESIA

By the end of the 18th century Dutch control extended over Java and the principal port centres in much of the archipelago

Throughout the 19th century Dutch control slowly extended over the archipelago with the greatest territorial advances taking place in the period 1890-1910.

Indonesia (Netherlands Indies) governed as a Dutch colony until the Second World War

1949 Indonesia gains independence after conflict with Dutch from 1946 to 1949

LAOS

No single Laotian state existed at the end of the 18th century. A series of principalities and petty states existed as vassals of stronger neighbours

1893 France established control over almost all of the territory of modern Laos

Laos governed as a French "Protectorate" until the Second World War

1953 Laos gains independence

MALAYSIA

At the end of the 18th century the only parts of modern Malaysia under foreign control were Penang and Malacca

1824 control of Malacca passes from Holland to Britain

From the early 1870's onwards Britain gains colonial control of the Malay states

Modern peninsular Malaysia governed under British colonial control

1957 Malaysia gained independence as the Federation of Malaya

Second World War and Japanese Interregnum

| 1800 | 1820 | 1840 | 1860 | 1880 | 1900 | 1910 | 1920 | 1930 | 1940 | 1950 | 1960 | 1980 |

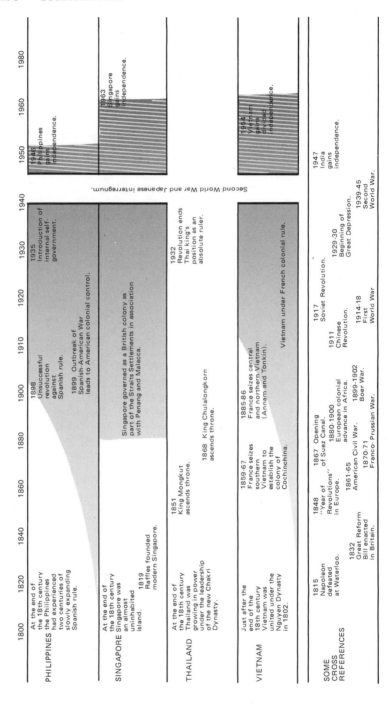

Index